Underwater with the Nikonos & Nikon Systems

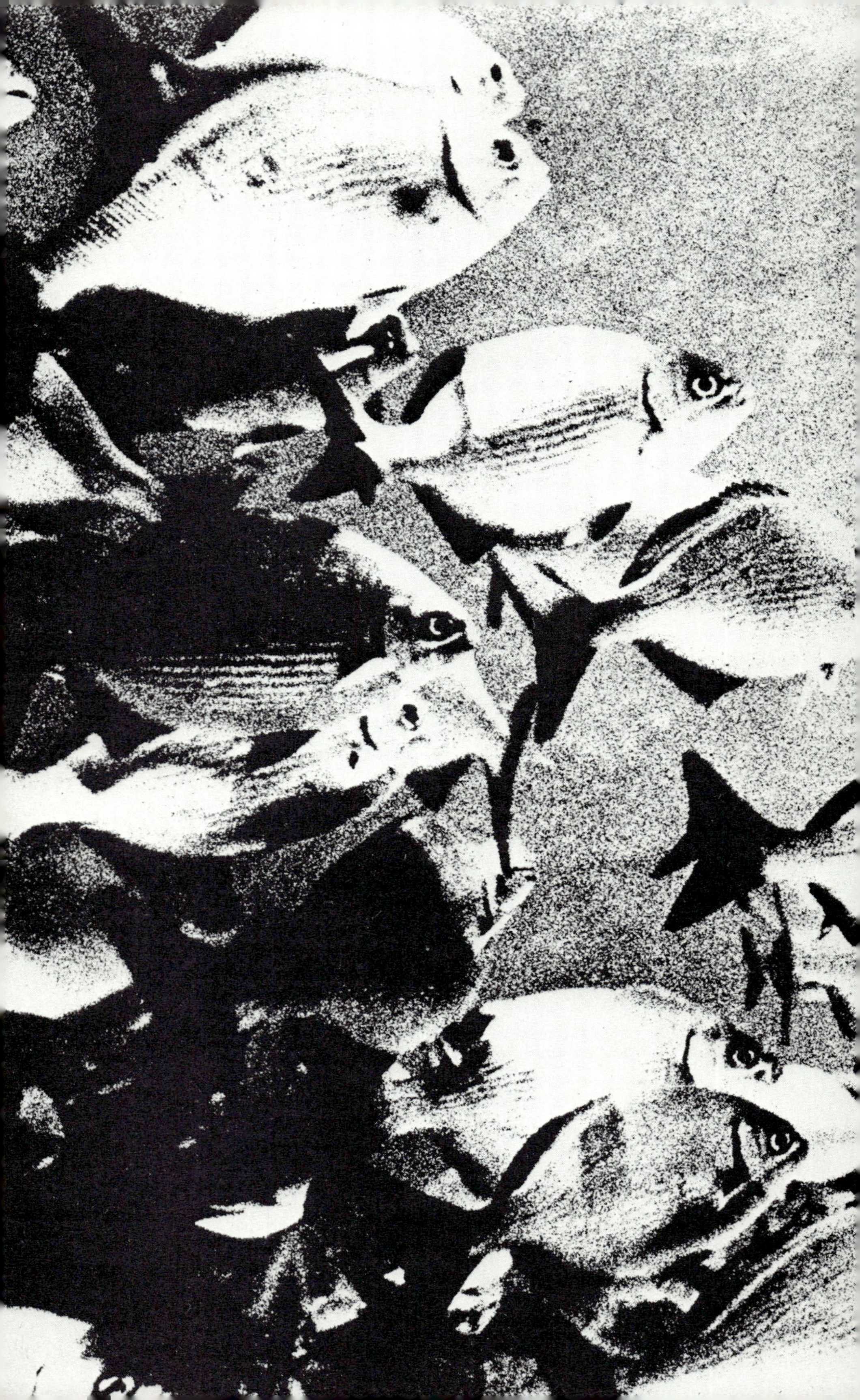

Underwater with the Nikonos & Nikon Systems

Herb Taylor

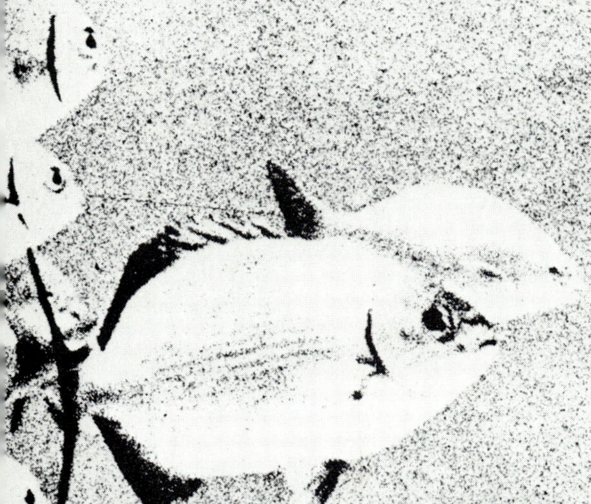

AMPHOTO
American Photographic Book Publishing Co., Inc.
Garden City, New York

Photo Credits

All the underwater photos in this book were taken by the author except the following: pg. 49 and 51, Ron Church; pg. 63, Cathy Taylor. All the equipment pictures were supplied by the various manufacturers or taken by the author, except the photo of the Calypso on pg. 8, which was thoughtfully provided by John Pemberton.

Second Printing 1978
Third Printing 1979

Library of Congress Catalog Card No. 76-16462

ISBN 0-8174-2401-6

Manufactured in the United States of America.

ACKNOWLEDGEMENTS

This book could not have been written without the help of a great many people. First and foremost I must thank Seymour Uslan of Amphoto and Joseph Abbott of Ehrenreich Photo-Optical Industries. Without their help and encouragement this book would never have been started—let alone finished.

At Amphoto I am also indebted to the editorial staff: Shirley Keller, Judy Kiviat, and Gail Schieber. In the art department, special thanks to Richard Liu, who helped with book design and picture selection, Steve Bloom, who did the line drawings, and Lorraine Hargrave, who was also helpful. Herb Cowan and Cora Marquez, in the production department, got the book into print. Meryl Koukly typed the manuscript.

At Ehrenreich Photo-Optical Industries I am also grateful to: Richard LoPinto for his assistance and support; Hideo Fukuchi for reading my manuscript and providing me with suggestions and technical assistance; and Randy Utell for his help.

For the photos and information provided by the manufacturers of the auxiliary equipment mentioned in the book, I am most grateful. Their names and addresses are listed in Appendix B.

Dan Capalbo was helpful with equipment information and he made pool time available for me for film and equipment testing. John Schuch, of Cougar Sports, was helpful too with auxiliary equipment information.

Many of the underwater photos in this book were taken in the waters off Bonaire, in the Netherland Antilles. Special thanks to E.B. Berlinrut and Virginia Casey, of the Bonaire Tourist Office in New York City, for arranging the trip to do that photography. For cooperation while on Bonaire, many thanks to Don Stewart and Bruce Bowker of Aquaventure. Thanks too to Tony Derby and Niki Tromp. For helping me learn about the audience for which I was writing this book, thanks to all the divers I met on Bonaire, especially Marty Dunn, George Buetow, Satinder Singh, Ed Fioravante, and Vi Richardson. This is a good place to thank Morey Ruza for introducing me to E.B. Berlinrut.

Thanks to all my diving friends who've posed, carried cameras, and helped in many other ways.

Finally, thanks to Cathy Taylor for giving up one summer, and a lot more, for this book.

HERB TAYLOR
BROOKLYN, N. Y.

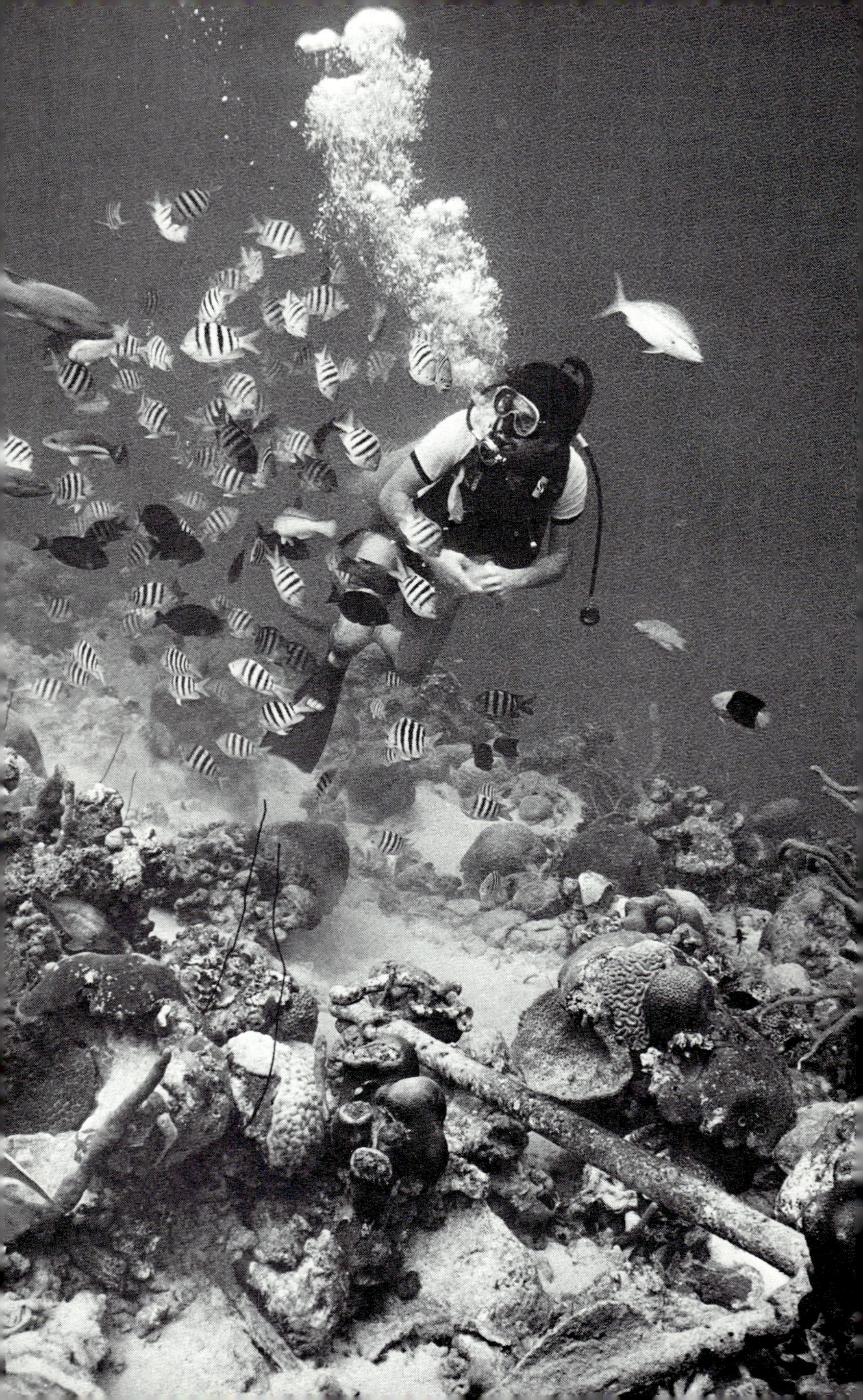

CONTENTS

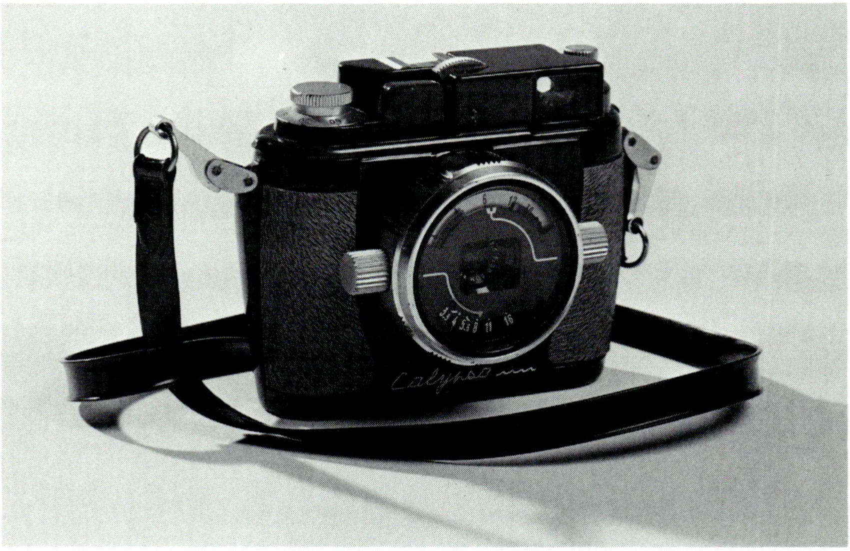

Invented and developed by Jean de Wouters, the Calypso-phot was the forerunner to the Nikonos System.

Introduction

In the winter of 1951–52, aboard a research vessel in the Red Sea, two men talked and dreamed about a camera that didn't exist. The two men were Jacque-Yves Cousteau and Jean de Wouters. The camera, eventually developed by De Wouters over the next eight years, was to revolutionize the world of underwater photography.

De Wouters, Belgian aeronautical engineer, worked singlehandedly on the camera that was to be called the Calypso-phot. Appropriately named after a sea spirit because it was at home in water as well as on land, the camera could be taken into the sea without a housing of any kind. The camera itself was completely sealed against dust, rain, snow, and dirt, and it could withstand the pressure of being deep underwater.

The first cameras were made in France in 1959 by Spirotechnique and were equipped with Som Berthiot Flor 35mm *f*/3.5 lenses. Realizing the potential of a camera with such capabilities, Nippon Kogaku K.K. of Tokyo (Nikon, Inc., in the U.S.) shortly thereafter acquired the license to manufacture and distribute the Calypso worldwide. In Europe, the camera came to be known as the Calypso/Nikkor. To the rest of the world, it became the Nikonos (pronounced Nick′ a - nos, Nye - cone′ us, or Nye′ cun - os—all correct).

Immediately after their introduction in 1963, the first Nikonos cameras were in the hands of photojournalists, sport and commercial divers, and photographers eager to expand their horizons. *National Geographic, Life,* and other magazines began to use regularly pictures taken with the Nikonos, and the general public became more aware of a world it hadn't seen much of before—the underwater world.

In 1968, the Nikonos became the Nikonos II, most all the changes requiring the redesignation being internal. During the years that followed, the camera evolved into a professional system with incredible capabilities. Nippon Kogaku added lenses and a close-up outfit, and independent manufacturers began in earnest to provide auxiliary equipment for the system. Lenses, underwater electronic flash units, extension tubes, close-up lenses, plus brackets, arms, and handles to hold the equipment together were made available to divers around the world.

In 1975, after seven years without a design change, the Nikonos II underwent a complete revamping in response to owner suggestions and years of research and testing. The basic design of the camera remained the same, but the camera had a completely new look, and internally, many new improvements were made. The best thing about the changes made was that almost all the equipment developed around the earlier Nikonos cameras could still be used with the Nikonos III.

For clarity and convenience in the pages that follow, the term "Nikonos" will apply to the whole family of cameras, since most often the information being discussed will apply to all three versions of the camera. When necessary to distinguish between models, the original Nikonos will be referred to as such, or as the "Nikonos I." Of course, the Nikonos II and III will be referred to as such when necessary. At times, the Nikonos I and II will be referred to as "the earlier models."

Also for clarity, only the U.S. Customary System of measurement will be used in the text, except where metric usage is widely understood, as in lens focal length measurement. Metric equivalents can be derived by using the information given in Appendix A.

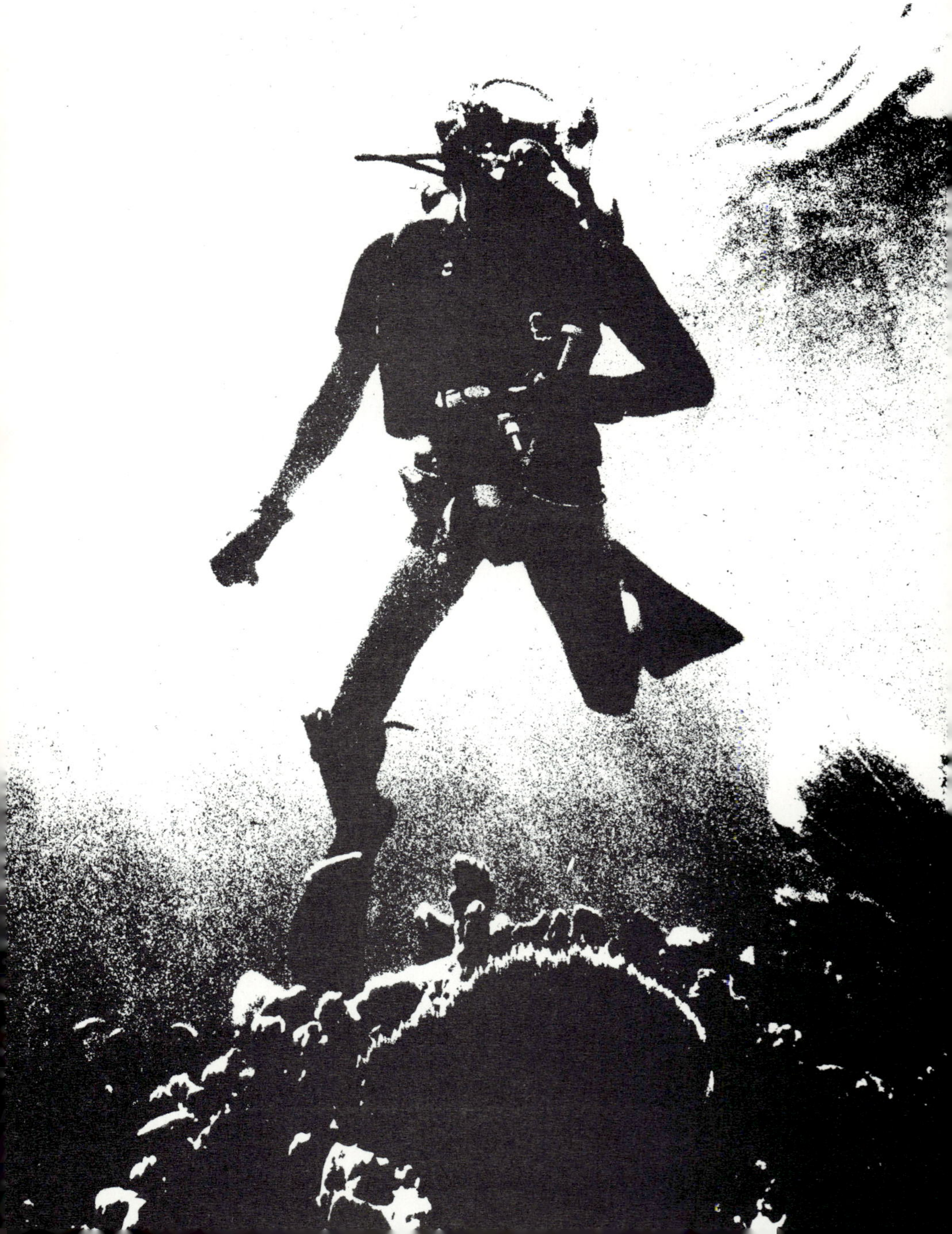

1

The Camera

CAMERA DESIGN

The Nikonos owes its unique capabilities to its special construction. The camera consists of three main sections that interlock to form a completely waterproof and pressureproof unit. The manufacturer states that assembled, the Nikonos camera is capable of withstanding pressure up to 86 psi., the pressure found 160 ft. underwater. In practice, though, the camera has been taken to much greater depths. U.S. Navy divers, commercial divers, and photojournalists on assignment have all used Nikonos cameras well below 200 ft.

O-ring gaskets seal all the joints of the Nikonos and ensure the watertightness of the camera. These synthetic rubber rings actually improve their sealing capacity as they are subjected to increasing pressure. With periodic lubrication, the life of the o-rings will be increased and their sealing ability guaranteed. Proper lubrication also facilitates the assembly and disassembly of the camera's three principal parts: the lens, the outer body, and the inner body.

The Principal Parts

The lens. The camera is locked together by the lens. It is the first component removed when the camera is disassembled, and the last one put in place when the camera is reassembled. All Nikonos lenses have a special spring-loaded mount that keeps them in the proper position for correct focusing despite the effects of increasing and decreasing pressure underwater. An o-ring around the lens barrel seals the lens securely in the outer body's bayonet mount.

The outer body. This outer shell, made of a die-cast aluminum alloy, acts as a housing for the separate inner workings of the camera. The outer body is covered with a polyethylene carbonate that protects it against the corrosive effects of salt water. The outside surface of this component is heavily textured to provide a non-slip surface that ensures a good grip even with wet hands or gloves.

The inner body. This component is the heart of the camera. It contains the actual working mechanisms of the camera and the viewfinder. This section fits into the outer shell and is sealed in position by the o-ring that encircles its top.

MODELS COMPARED

The Nikonos I and Nikonos II

The Nikonos I and Nikonos II are similar in outward appearance, yet they can be distinguished from one another easily. The rewind knob on the model II has a crank to facilitate film rewinding; the model I does not. The shutter-speed dial on the model II includes an "R" setting; the model I does not. The film pressure plate on the Nikonos II is hinged along its top edge to ease the loading of film; on the Nikonos I, the film pressure plate is stationary.

In addition to these visible differences, many internal improvements made the mechanical workings of the model II more reliable than the model I.

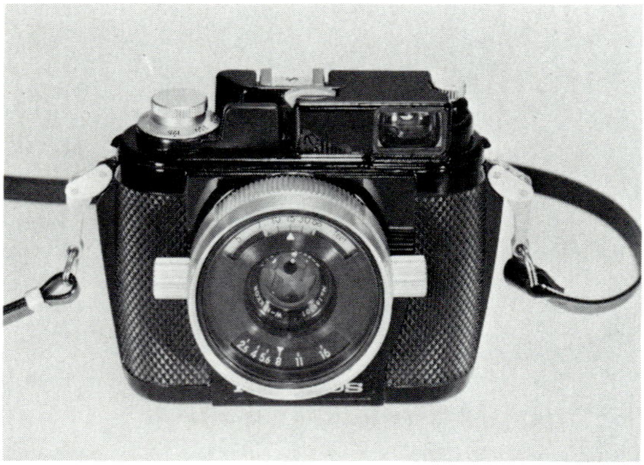

The original Nikonos. Manufactured from 1963 to 1968.

The Nikonos II. Manufactured from 1968 to 1975.

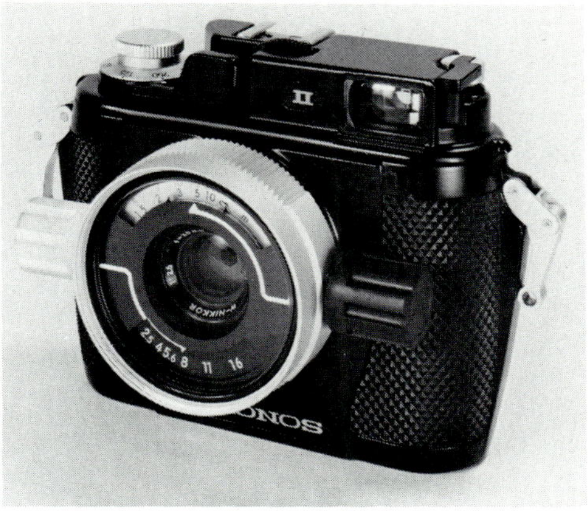

The Nikonos III

Virtually a brand-new camera, the Nikonos III vastly improved on the earlier models. Design changes such as the altering of the camera's basic size and shape and the relocating of the frame counter and tripod socket, improved handling and made the camera easier to use. The differences between the Nikonos III and the earlier cameras can best be seen by comparing the illustrations on pages 14–17. One of the most important changes, the difference in connector design, is not visible in the illustrations, but Chapters 4 and 6 include information on that change.

Basic Care

The care and periodic maintenance that a Nikonos requires are covered in detail in Chapter 9, but basic care of the camera includes thorough rinsing in tap water after exposure to the elements. This is especially important if the camera has been exposed to dust, dirt, sand, or salt water. Before the Nikonos is opened for unloading, and before any accessories are detached, the camera must be rinsed properly in tap water. It should then be allowed to air dry but can be blotted dry with a soft cloth when film must be changed quickly. Under normal conditions, the camera should never be dried with forced hot air; nor should it be left in the sun to dry. Extended periods of time in the sun could damage the camera, the lens, the film, or all three.

Nikonos II

1. Strap-attachment levers.
2. Lens positioning groove.
3. Bayonet mount.
4. Rewind crank and rewind knob.
5. Accessory shoe.
6. Safety lock.
7. Film-advance/shutter-release lever.
8. Shutter-speed control.
9. Frame counter.
10. Viewfinder.
11. Rewind shank.
12. Film-pressure plate (hinged on top edge)
13. Film-cartridge catch.
14. Film take-up spool.
15. Shutter curtain.
16. Lens.
17. Lens positioning pin.
18. Tripod socket/synchro-socket cover.
19. Main o-ring.

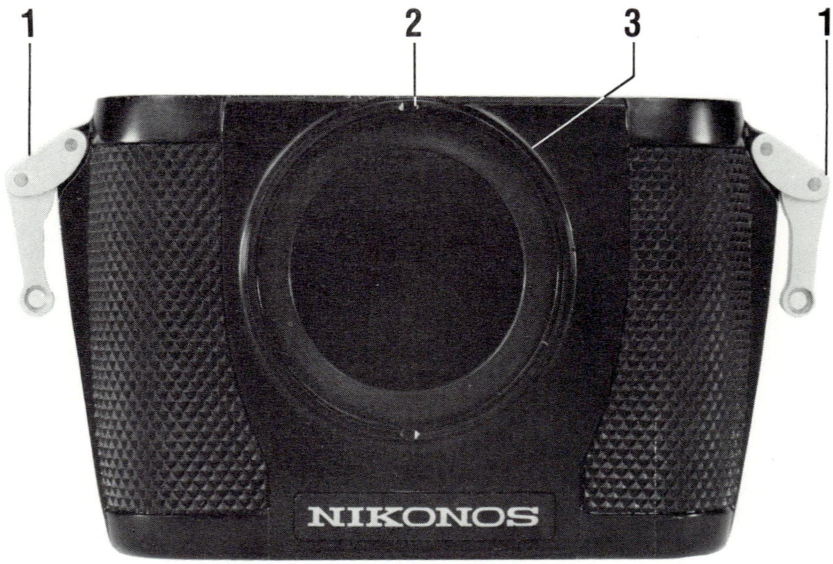

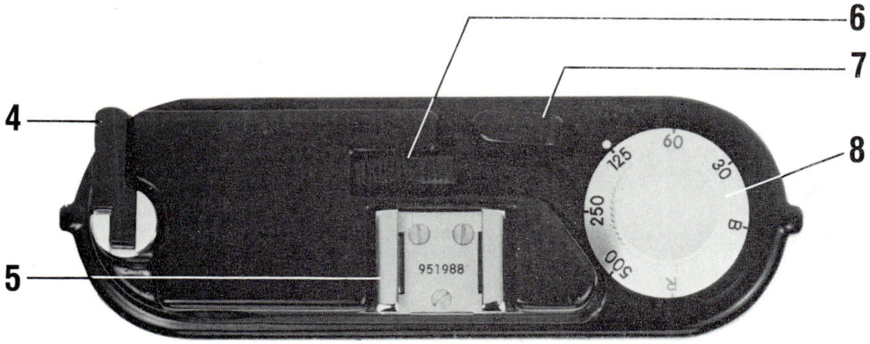

6
7
4
8
5
951988
125
60
30
250
B
500
R

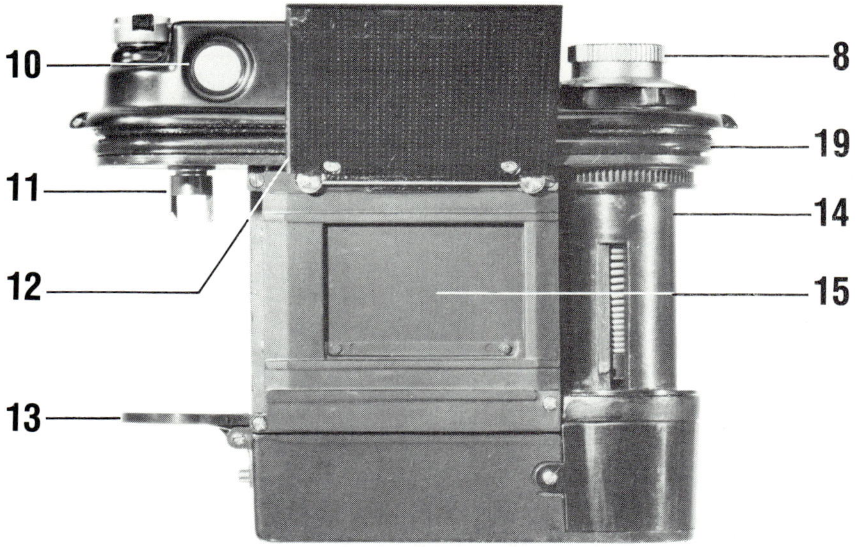

10
8
19
11
14
12
15
13

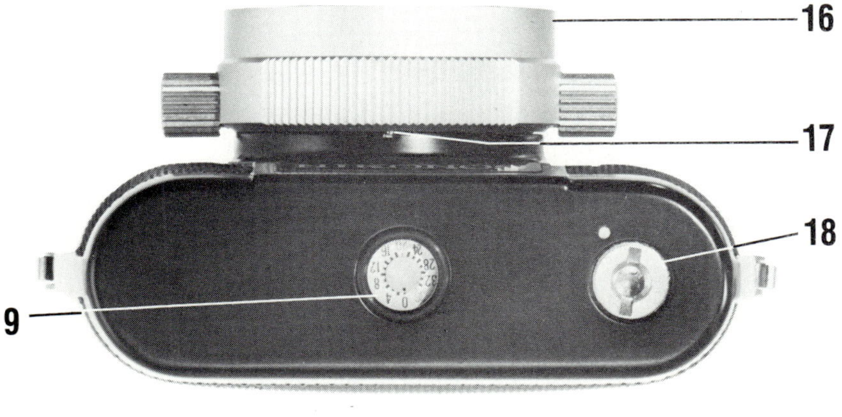

16
17
18
9

Nikonos III

1. Strap-attachment levers.
2. Lens positioning groove.
3. Stainless steel bayonet mount.
4. Rewind crank and rewind knob.
5. Accessory shoe.
6. Safety lock (built into lever).
7. Film-advance/shutter-release lever.
8. Shutter-speed control.
9. Frame counter and built-in film-advance indicator.
10. Bright-line type viewfinder.
11. Rewind shank.
12. Film-pressure plate (hinged on bottom edge).
13. Film-pressure-plate latch.
14. Film take-up spool.
15. Shutter curtain (vertical travel, metal focal plane).
16. Lens.
17. Lens positioning pin.
18. Tripod socket (independent of synchro-socket cover).
19. Synchro-socket cover.
20. Film-advance sprockets.
21. Main o-ring.

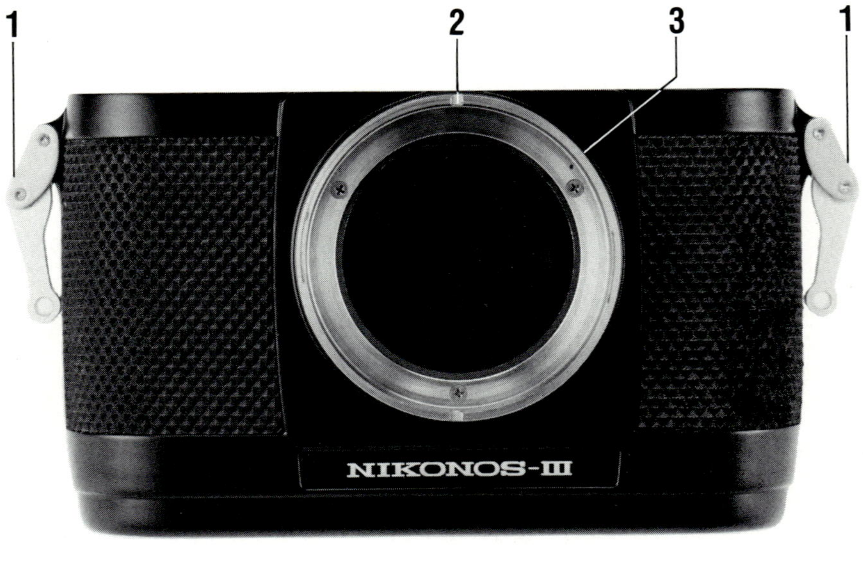

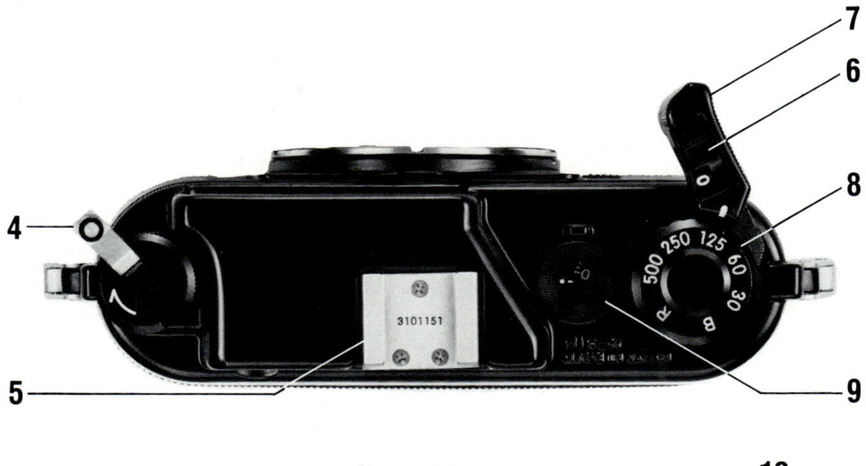
7
6
8
4
500 250 125 60 30 B R
3101151
5
9

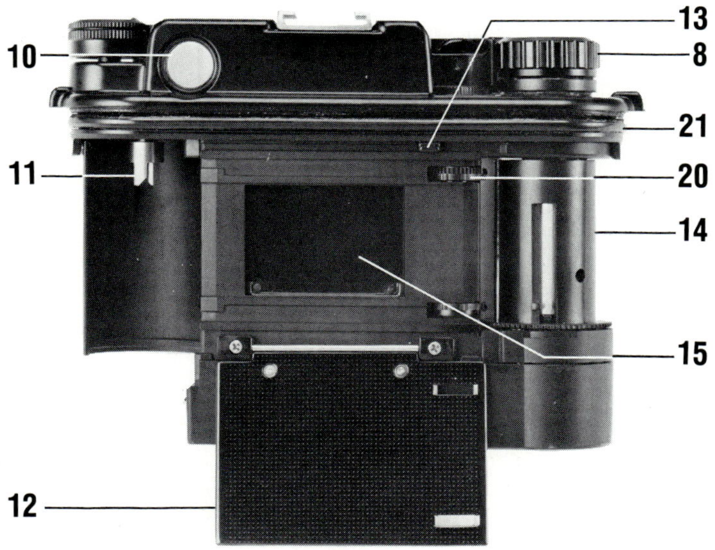
13
10
8
21
11
20
14
15
12

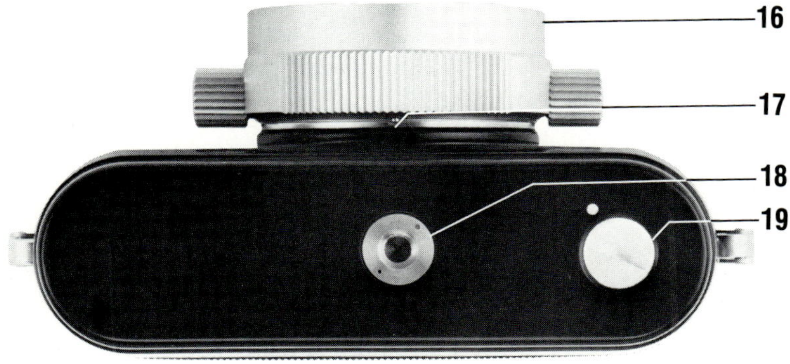
16
17
18
19

CAMERA DISASSEMBLY

Removing the Lens

To open the camera for loading, you must first remove the lens because it locks the entire camera together.

Grasp the lens by the ribbed surface and pull it firmly away from the body until the positioning pins on the lens mount are free of the grooves on the camera body. Next, rotate the lens 90 degrees (in either direction) and pull the lens gently away from the camera body. The lens will slip out of the bayonet mount.

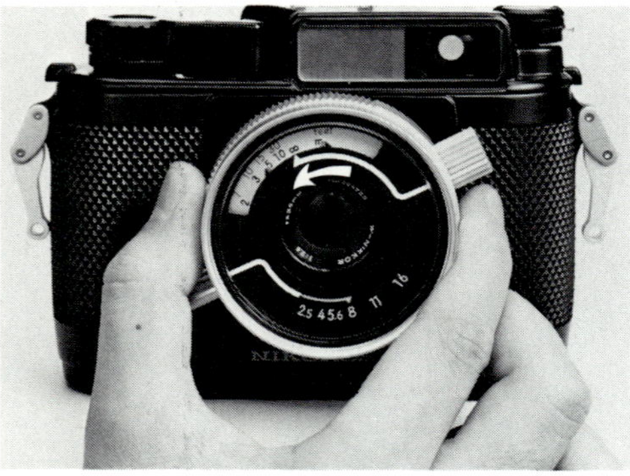

To remove the lens, pull it away from the body until the positioning pins are clear of the grooves on the body and rotate the lens.

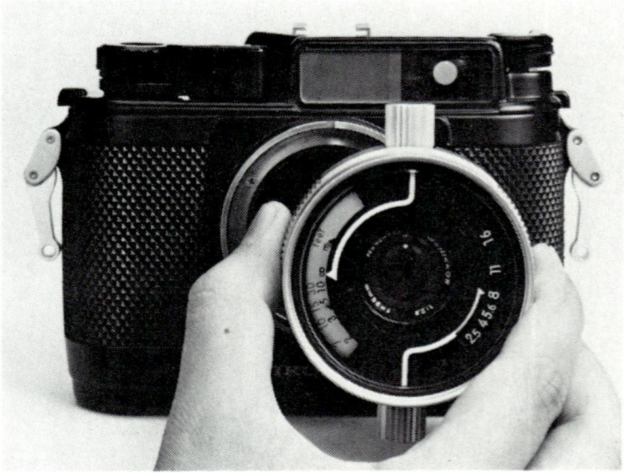

Rotate the lens 90° and gently pull it away from the camera body.

Removing the Inner Body

NEVER ATTEMPT TO REMOVE THE INNER BODY WITHOUT FIRST REMOVING THE LENS. Also, before removing the inner body from the outer body, be sure to rewind any film in the camera into its cartridge. Film in the camera will not be exposed by removing the lens—this makes it possible to change lenses in mid-roll—but film will be exposed if you separate the inner body from the outer body without first rewinding all the film into its cartridge.

To remove the inner body, position the strap-attachment levers under the protruding lips at each end of the camera. With the levers seated against the lips, push firmly downward and pry the inner body free of the housing. This is most easily accomplished by standing the camera on a flat surface and using your thumbs to apply the pressure to the levers. Once the inner body is unseated, it can be lifted from the housing.

Position the strap-attachment levers under the projecting lips on the camera body and apply downward pressure with your thumbs. This will unseat the inner body.

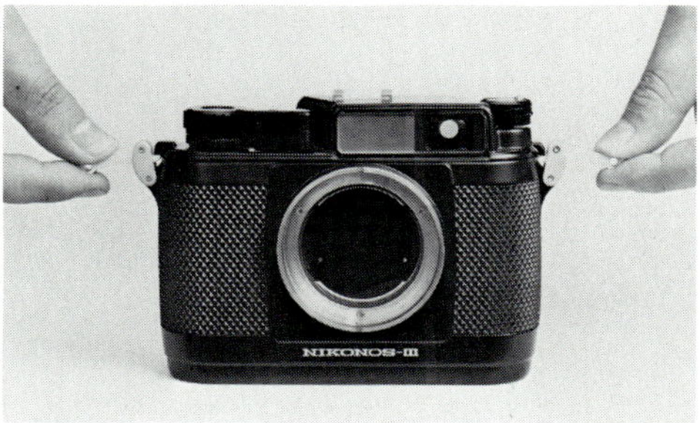

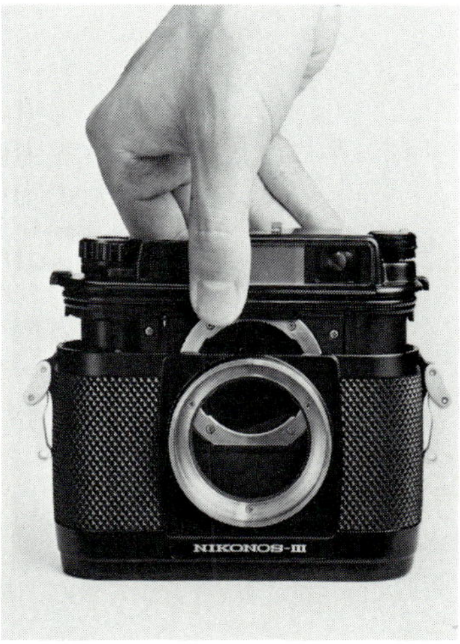

When the o-ring seal is broken, lift the inner body straight out of the camera's outer shell.

Loading the Nikonos III

With the inner body free of the housing, release the film-pressure-plate latch by pushing it upward. This will permit the film pressure plate to swing downward and away from the camera. Next, fit the film cartridge on the shank of the rewind shaft; the spool end of the cartridge should point downward, and the film leader should be as shown in the accompanying illustration. Align the film with the guides and insert the leader into one of the slots on the take-up spool (the spool can be rotated to facilitate insertion). Advance the film lever slowly, checking to see that the film is leaving the cartridge smoothly and is winding onto the take-up spool. Be sure that both the upper and lower film-advance sprockets are transporting the film, then close the film pressure plate. You should feel the pressure plate "click" into place.

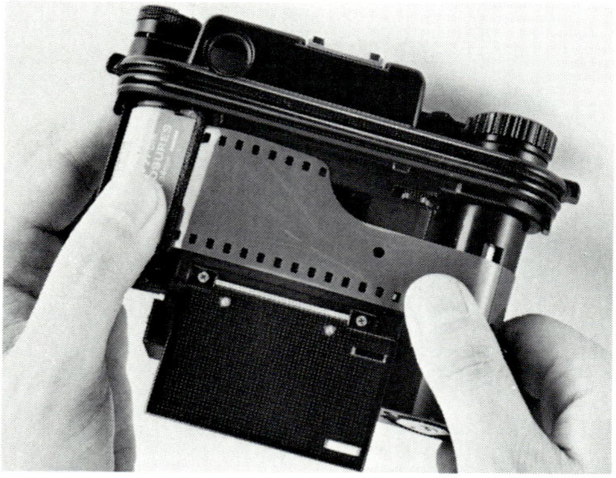

To load the Nikonos III, release and swing down the pressure plate, then follow the instructions above.

Loading the Nikonos II

On the Nikonos II, the film pressure plate is hinged along its *upper* edge, and no latch holds it in place. To load the camera, first lift the pressure plate up and away from the camera body. Next, position the film cartridge on the shank of the rewind spool while holding the film-cartridge catch down. Release the film-cartridge catch and it will hold the roll of film in place. Align the film on the guides and insert the film leader into the slot in the take-up spool (the spool can be rotated to ease insertion). Advance the film and check to see that the tooth in the take-up slot catches a sprocket hole on the lower edge of the film. Lower the film pressure plate into position.

To load the Nikonos II, follow the detailed instructions above.

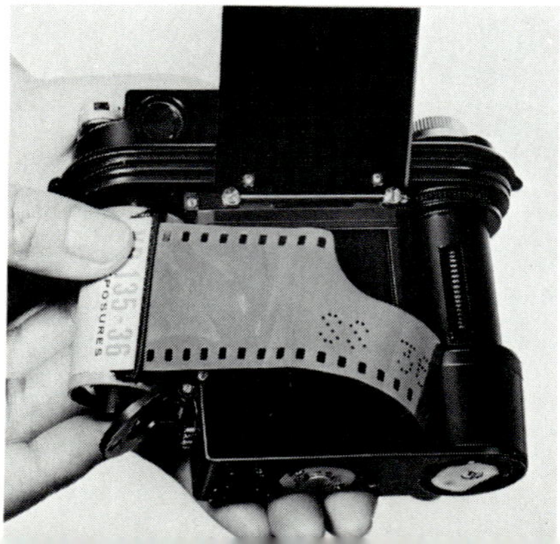

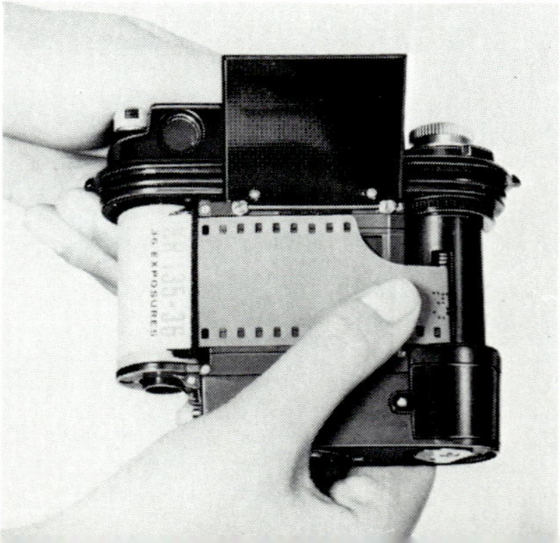

Loading the Original Nikonos (or Calypso)

Loading the original Nikonos (or Calypso) is similar to loading the Nikonos II, but the film pressure plate on the original Nikonos (and Calypso) is stationary. Because the pressure plate is not hinged, the film leader must be slipped under it once the film cartridge is on the rewind shaft. If the film is not slipped under the pressure plate, it will not be exposed when pictures are taken.

To load the Nikonos I, the film leader must be slipped under the stationary film-pressure plate (right). With all models, be sure the tooth in the take-up spool catches a film sprocket hole (below) and that both the top and bottom edges of the film are spooling (below right).

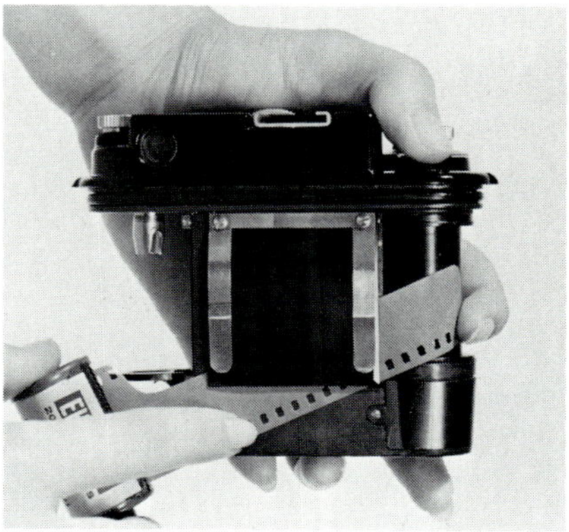

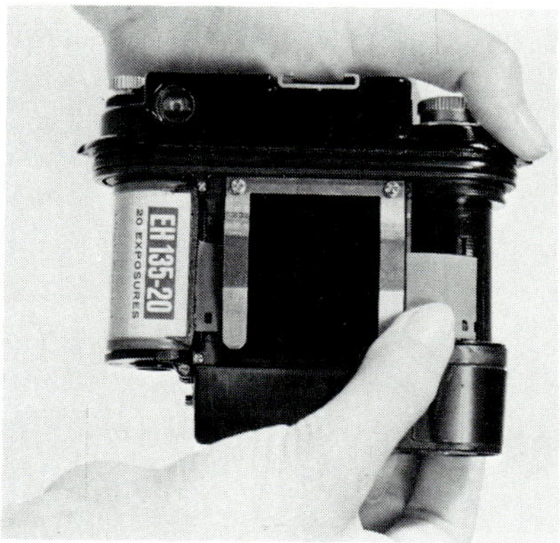

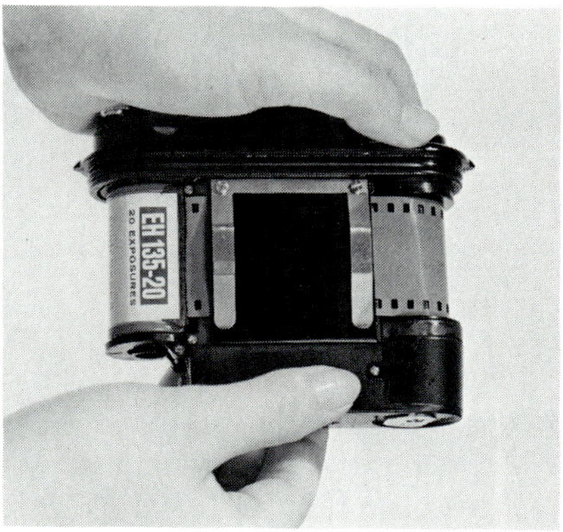

Checking the Advance

At this point, before placing the loaded inner body into the outer shell, check again to be sure the film you have just loaded is advancing properly. Advance the film so that both the top and bottom edges are past the pressure plate and spooling onto the take-up reel. Trying to squeeze 37 or 38 frames from a 36-exposure roll of film is foolish if you run the risk of not having the film advance at all.

CAMERA ASSEMBLY

Installing the Inner Body

With the film loaded and checked, slide the inner body vertically into the outer shell until the main o-ring makes contact. Next, press the two parts of the camera together by applying pressure to the central portion of the camera as shown in the accompanying illustration. The inner body will now be solidly within the outer shell. During installation, do not apply pressure to the rewind knob, film-advance/shutter-release lever, or shutter-speed dial.

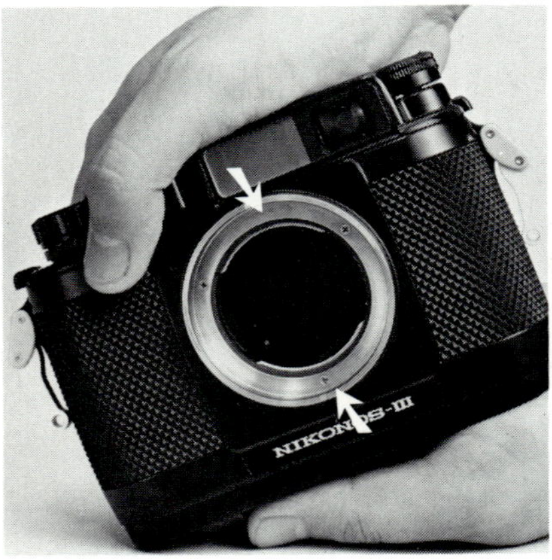

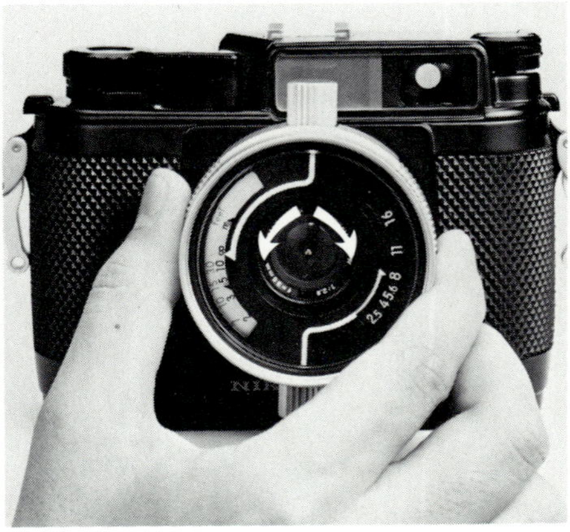

Install the inner body as shown (left). Install lens (right) normally by turning it clockwise; to install it upside down, turn counterclockwise.

Installing the Lens

To install the lens, position it in the camera body's bayonet mount so the lens focusing knob is pointing toward the top of the camera. Next, push inward and rotate the lens 90 degrees clockwise. The lens positioning pins should now be in place in the grooves on the camera body.

Install the lens in this way if you do not plan to use the camera around your neck. However, if you do plan to carry the unit around your neck, it is a good idea to install the lens upside down. In this position, you will be able to read the distance scale, depth-of-field scale, and aperture settings by simply tilting the camera back toward you. To install the lens in the upside-down position, follow the same procedure as above, but begin by positioning the lens aperture knob toward the top of the camera.

Before Shooting

Before making your first exposure, set the shutter-speed dial to any position except "R," lift the rewind knob, and unfold its crank. Turn the knob back and forth slightly to engage the shank, and gently turn the crank in the direction of the arrow until you feel a slight drag, which indicates that the slack in the film cartridge has been removed.

With the Nikonos III, before disengaging the rewind knob, advance the film two frames to dispose of the film exposed during loading and to set the counter at "0." (The frame counter on the Nikonos III is located on top of the camera between the shutter-speed dial and accessory shoe.) Advance the film by squeezing the film-advance/shutter-release lever until it springs forward. When the lever comes to rest, bring it back to its original position, then squeeze it again. Once more return it to its original position.

While advancing the film, be sure the rewind crank is turning in the direction opposite the engraved arrow. This indicates that the film has been loaded properly and is advancing. The index dot in the frame counter on the Nikonos III will also revolve if the film is advancing properly. Finally, drop the rewind knob back into its recessed position and fold the rewind crank flat. (The original Nikonos does not have a rewind crank, so simply push the knob down into its normal position.)

With the models I and II, the film exposed during loading can be advanced by making short strokes with the film-advance/shutter-release lever, but not actually completing each stroke. In this way, the

When the film-advance/shutter-release lever is in the "ready" position (left), the shutter is cocked. To release the shutter, squeeze the lever toward the camera. The shutter will release and the lever will swing away from the camera (right). When it comes to rest, return it to its original position by again squeezing it toward the camera.

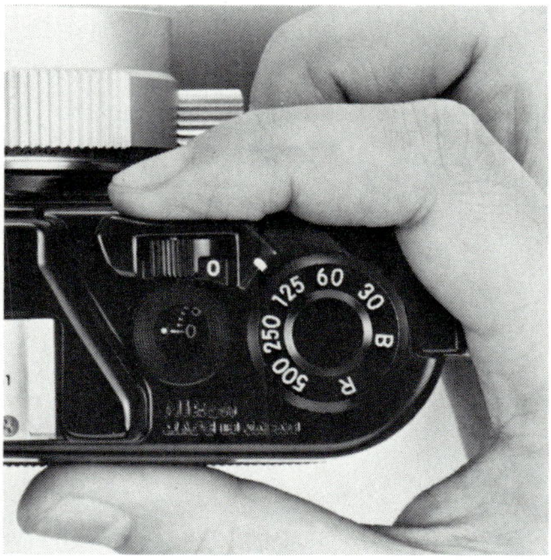

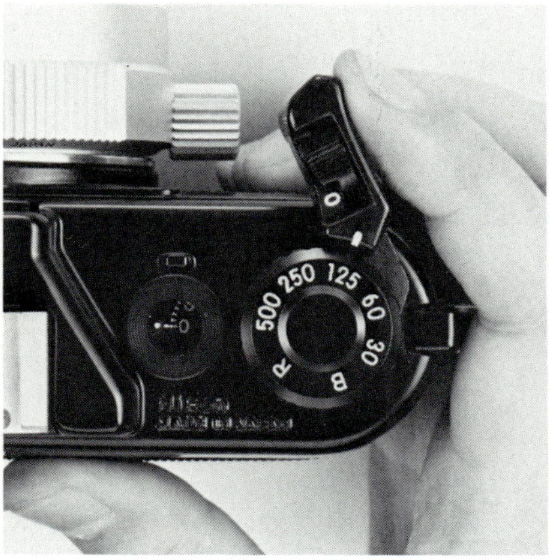

frame counter will record only actual exposures. The frame counter on models I and II is located on the underside of the camera.

With the rewind knob in position, and the frame counter at "0," you are ready to make your first exposure. But before you do that, lock the camera and familiarize yourself with its handling and controls. Locking the film-advance/shutter-release lever will prevent inadvertent exposures. On models I and II, the film-advance/shutter-release lever is secured by simply moving the safety lock into position behind it. On the Nikonos III, the lock is an integral part of the lever. To secure the lever, slide the safety lock toward the shutter-speed dial until the "L" is visible. In this position, the film-advance/shutter-release lever cannot be activated. To unlock the lever, slide the lock away from the shutter-speed dial until the "O" is visible.

USING THE CAMERA

Holding the Camera

Learning to hold the camera properly is an essential part of good picture-taking. The most common cause of unsharp pictures is camera movement during exposure. This is especially so at slow shutter speeds.

To hold the camera steady, you must have a comfortable grip on it. Study the accompanying illustrations and modify the demonstrated method of holding the camera until it is comfortable for you. Try holding the camera vertically and horizontally. It should be noted that because of the camera's compact size, it is very easy to place a finger over the lens. To avoid having the tips of your fingers turn up in your pictures, try to keep them on the camera body.

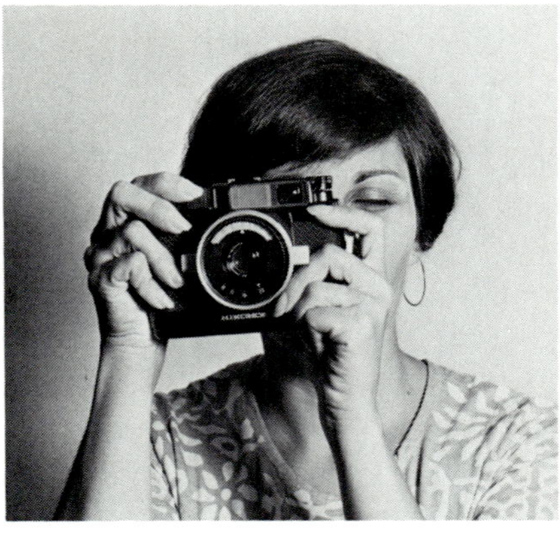

Hold the camera steady as shown and keep your fingers on the camera body to avoid the chance of your fingers blocking the lens.

When taking pictures while standing, distribute your weight evenly and hold your arms in, against your body. If at all possible, brace your camera and/or your arms against a solid object. Underwater, it is especially important to try to brace yourself, particularly when shooting at slow shutter speeds.

Using the Built-In Viewfinder

When using the Nikonos in air, use the camera's built-in viewfinder to frame your subject. (Viewfinders for use underwater are discussed in Chapter 2.) Hold the camera up to your eye and view the subject through the eyepiece on the camera back. In addition to your subject, you will see framing lines within which you should compose your picture. These framing lines indicate the image you will get on your film although the total viewfinder shows a bit more area.

In the viewfinder of the Nikonos III, you will see two framing lines: one for the 35mm lens, the other for the 80mm lens. In the viewfinder of models I and II, there is one framing line, corresponding to the picture area for the 35mm lens alone.

The built-in viewfinder in the Nikonos III shows framing lines for the 35mm lens (outer lines) and 80mm lens (inner lines). At minimum focusing distances use the parallax correction marks for framing your subject.

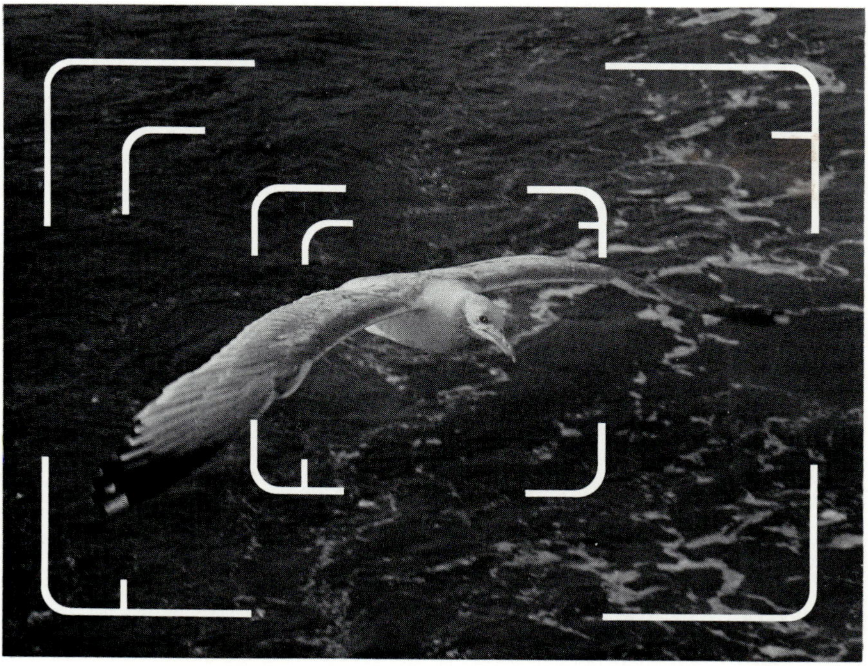

In addition to the main framing lines, you will see framing-correction marks. These marks should be used when framing a picture at the minimum focusing distance of the particular lens you're using. Correction marks are necessary because the Nikonos is not a single-lens reflex camera, which means, you do not view your subject through the camera lens. Subsequently, what you see in the viewfinder is not *exactly* what the camera lens "sees" and records on your film. This occurrence is known as parallax. This "problem" of parallax is only a genuine problem at close focusing distances, or when using a lens with a narrow angle of view (like the 80mm). The viewfinder in the Nikonos III corrected somewhat the parallax problem of the earlier models by moving part of the viewfinder closer to the lens. You can see this if you cover the front of the viewfinder with your finger, then uncover first one half then the other.

Despite the improved viewfinder and correction marks, parallax can be a problem with the 80mm lens. It is best to use the auxiliary optical viewfinder provided with the 80mm lens when using this lens in air.

Not viewing your subject through the camera lens presents another problem: Looking through the viewfinder will not tell you if the lens cap is in place or not. Always check to be sure you've removed it before shooting.

BASIC CAMERA CONTROLS

The amount of light that will be allowed to fall on the film and expose it is determined by two factors you can control: shutter speed and aperture. The shutter speed determines how long the shutter will remain open to allow light to enter, and the aperture determines the size of the opening through which the light will pass. The proper combination of the two determines "correct" exposure.

Shutter Speed

While holding the camera in the normal picture-taking position, the shutter-speed dial can be turned easily between the thumb and forefinger of your right hand. To select a shutter speed, rotate the dial until the desired speed is opposite the index line on the film-advance/shutter-release lever. When rotating the dial, you will feel a "click" when the speed is selected correctly. Do not use intermediate positions.

Nikonos shutter speeds range from 1/30 sec., the slowest—allowing the most light to enter the camera—to 1/500 sec., the fastest—

allowing the least amount of light to enter the camera. (Note that only the lower half of the fraction appears on the shutter-speed dial.) Between these two are the shutter speeds 1/60 sec., 1/125 sec., and 1/250 sec. The "60" (for 1/60 sec.) is marked in red because it is the shutter speed that must be selected for proper synchronization when using electronic flash and certain types of flashbulbs. Synchronization is explained in Chapters 4 and 5.

In addition to synchronization, many other factors determine shutter speed selection: overall light, the kind of film being used, and the focal length of the lens on the camera. When beginning photography, two general rules of thumb should be kept in mind when selecting an appropriate shutter speed—in addition to correct exposure, of course. They are: (1) Select a fast shutter speed to stop a moving object. (2) Brace the camera or hold it steady at slow shutter speeds. Underwater, because of currents, surge, and your own buoyancy, try to avoid using a shutter speed slower than 1/60 sec. Even using 1/60 sec. requires good breath control and a steady hand.

In addition to the speeds mentioned above are two other settings on the shutter-speed dial: "R" and "B." The "R" setting (Note: There is no "R" setting on the Nikonos I or Calypso) is selected when film is being rewound into its cartridge. When the "B" setting is selected, the shutter remains open for as long as the film-advance/shutter-release is held against the camera body. The shutter closes when the lever begins to swing away from the camera body. With the camera braced on a tripod, this setting can be selected when making long exposures at night. Exposures from 1 second to as-long-as-you-can-hold-the-lever can be made with "B."

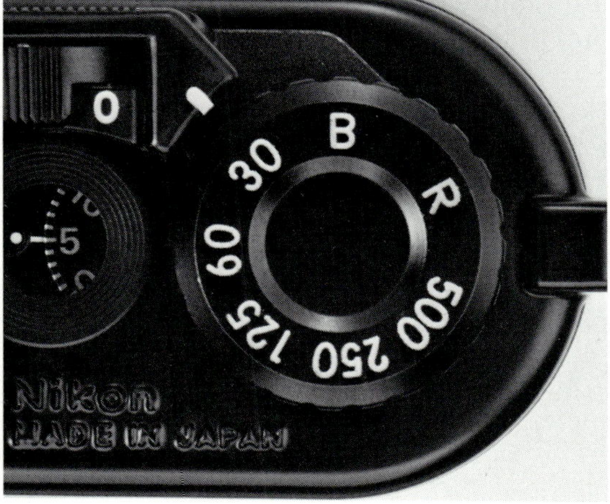

Shutter-speed dial set at 1/30 sec. Frame counter indicates 5 exposures have been made.

This lens is focused at 10 ft. and its aperture is set at *f*/16. Depth of field is from 5 ft. to infinity.

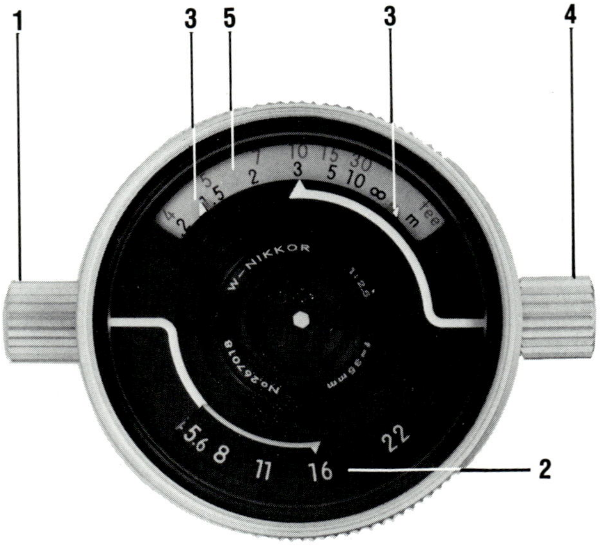

1. Aperture-control knob.
2. Aperture scale.
3. Depth-of-field indicators.
4. Focusing knob.
5. Distance scale (feet and meters).

Aperture (*f*/Stop)

With the lens in the normal position, and viewing the front of the camera, the aperture-control knob is located at the left side of the lens. The white line connecting the knob and the aperture index makes positive identification easy. Aperture, or *f*/stop, is selected by rotating the knob until the desired *f*/number and the index align. Depending on the lens being used, apertures can range from *f*/2.5, a wide opening that admits a lot of light into the camera, to *f*/22, a small opening that allows little light to enter the camera. As with shutter speed, many factors determine the selection of an aperture that will yield proper exposure. One factor that may influence aperture selection is depth of field.

2.5 4 5.6 8 11 16 22

The above *f*/numbers may help you remember which ones represent large lens openings and which ones represent small openings.

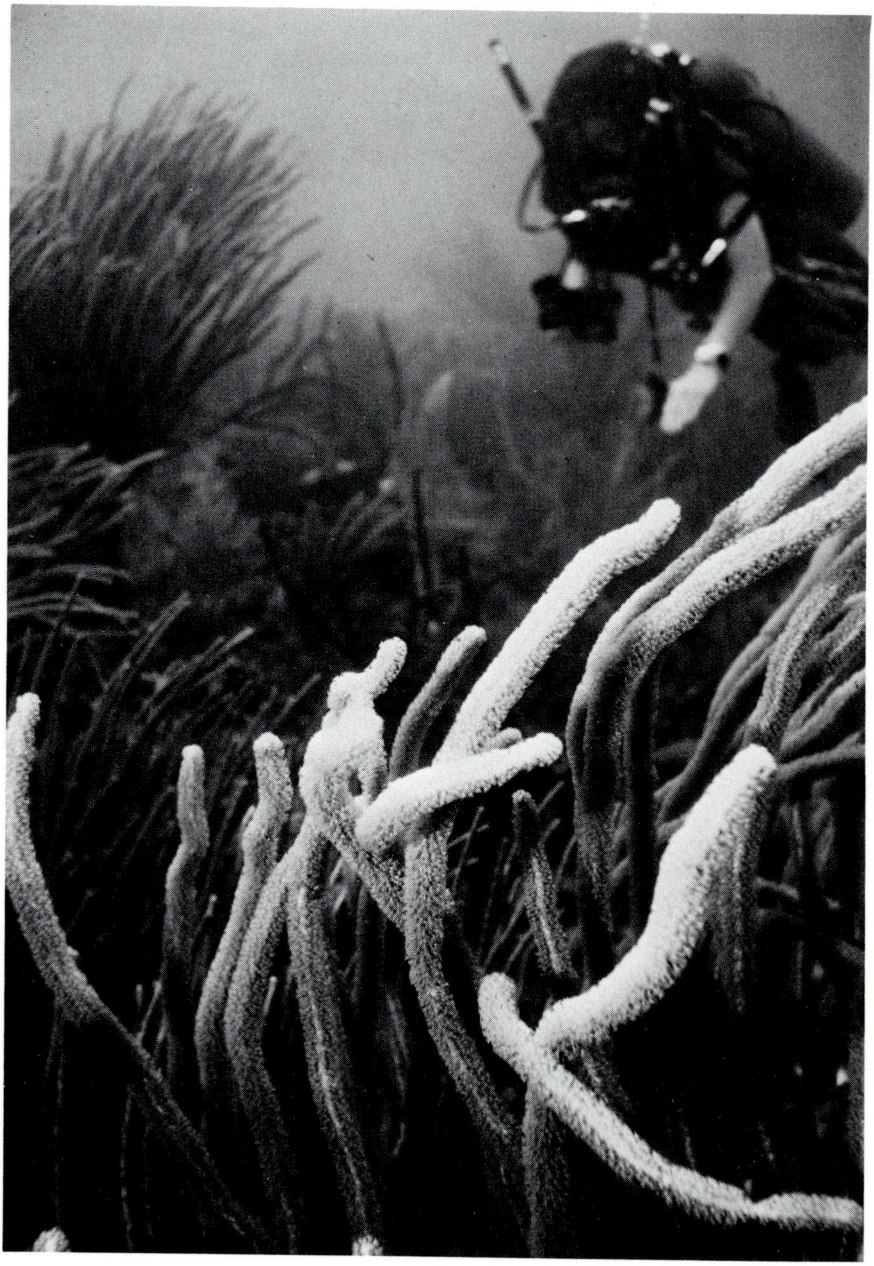

Depth of field can be used to emphasize different elements in a picture. Here the soft coral in the foreground is in sharp focus while the diver in the background is not.

Depth of Field

Depth of field, simply stated, is the area of sharp focus in front of and behind the principal point of focus of the lens. Aperture selection greatly influences depth of field. Nikonos lenses are equipped with the easiest to read depth-of-field indicators on any lens. As you turn the aperture knob to select your lens opening, the depth-of-field indicators move over the distance scale—closer together as you select wider openings, and farther apart as you select smaller openings.

At the same focused distance, the wider the aperture, the narrower the depth of field; and the smaller the aperture, the greater the depth of field. For example, with the 35mm lens focused at 10 ft., and the aperture set at *f*/16, the depth-of-field indicators would show that the area of sharpness extends from about 5 ft. to infinity (∞). But with the aperture changed to *f*/2.5, the depth of field would extend only from 8 ft. to 11 ft.

In addition to lens aperture, two other factors greatly affect depth of field: the focal length of the lens being used, and the distance at which it is focused. Effects with different focal-length lenses are illustrated in Chapter 2, but briefly, short focal-length lenses (wide-angle lenses) always yield a great depth of field while long focal-length lenses (telephoto lenses) yield a shallow depth of field. Regarding

Depth of field is very great with wide-angle lenses. Here the Nikonos 15mm lens records excellent depth of field even though the focused distance was only 3 ft. and the aperture was *f*/5.6. Visibility was 4 ft.

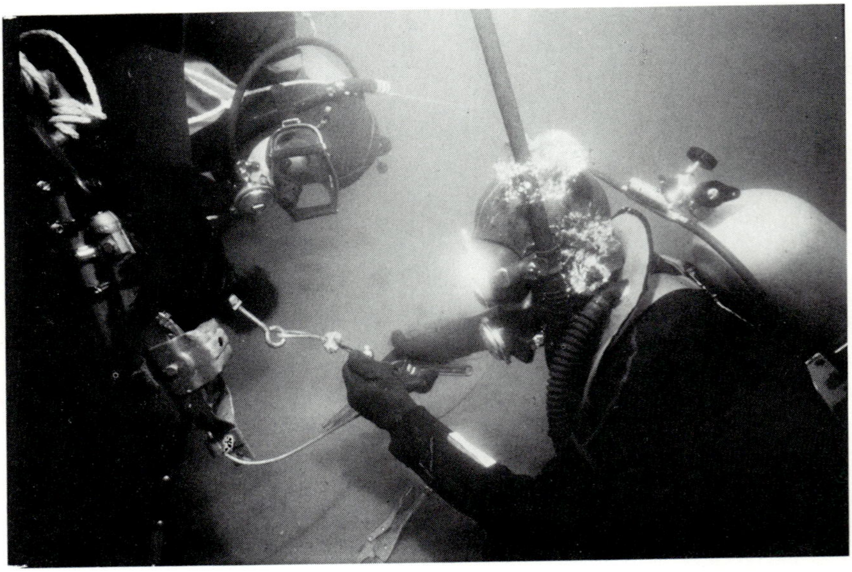

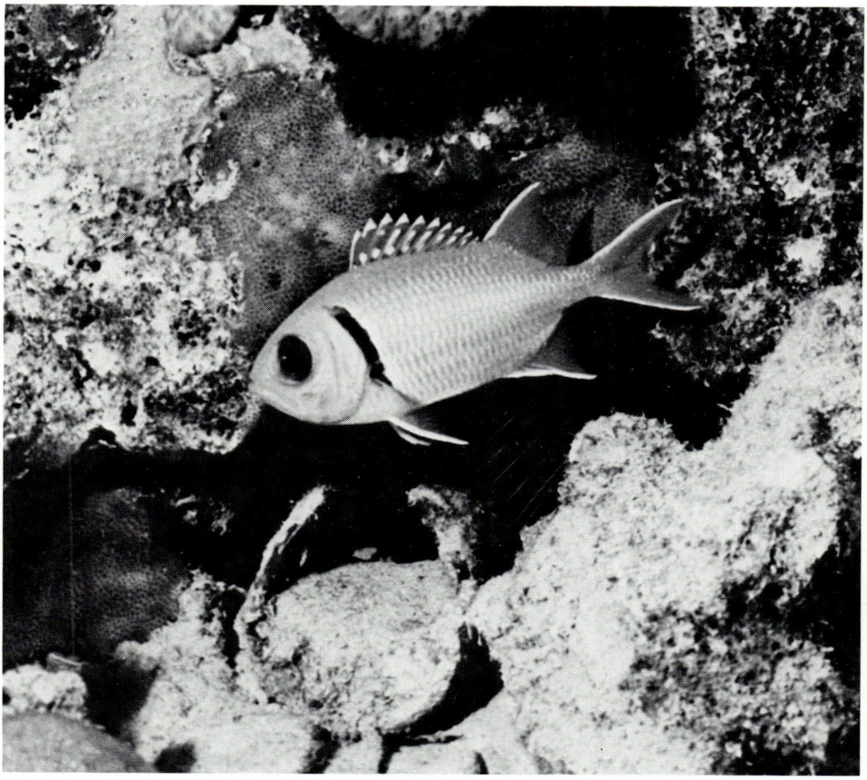

At close focusing distances depth of field becomes shallow. Here the subject plane is virtually two-dimensional to avoid having areas out of focus.

focused distance, depth of field changes as it does. When a lens is focused close, depth of field is very shallow as compared to the same lens focused at a great distance or infinity. Shallow depth of field is especially apparent in close-up photography, which is covered in Chapter 8.

Focusing the Lens

Since the Nikonos is not equipped with a device for visual focusing (such as a rangefinder or focusing screen), the camera lens is focused by estimating the distance from the camera to the subject and then setting that estimated distance on the distance scale of the lens. This is known as scale focusing. (In air, you can measure the distance to your subject for greater accuracy.) The knob opposite the aperture knob controls the focusing scale. To focus the lens, rotate the focusing knob until the estimated distance appears over the wedge-shaped index mark.

Underwater, you should follow this same procedure. Estimate the camera-to-subject distance and set that apparent distance on your camera lens. If you actually measure the camera-to-subject distance underwater, you must multiply that distance by 3/4 and then set the calculated distance on the distance scale. For example, if the measured camera-to-subject distance underwater was 10 ft., you would set the focusing scale at 7.5 ft. (10 × 3/4 = 7.5).

Refraction, the bending of light rays as they pass from one medium to another (as from water to air), is the phenomenon that makes objects appear closer underwater. Refraction is explained further in Chapter 7. For the time being, keep in mind that estimates of apparent distance underwater will be as accurate as your estimates of distance on land.

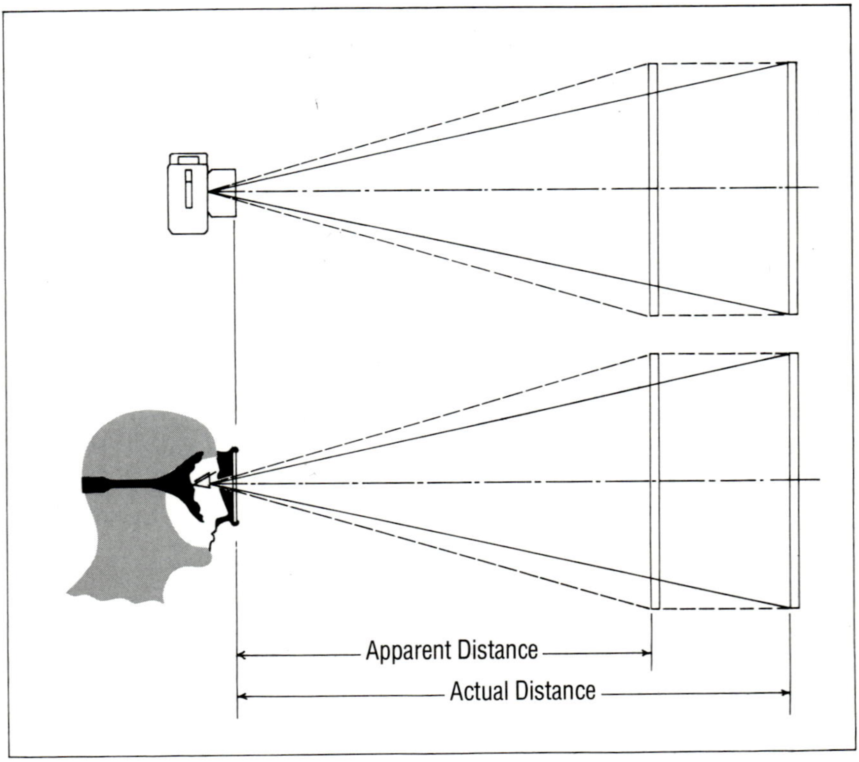

To focus the Nikonos underwater, estimate the distance to the subject and set that *estimated distance* on the distance scale. The effect of refraction makes objects underwater appear closer than their actual distance, but the effect is the same at the lens port and your face mask so no calculations are necessary to correct for refraction when you use estimated distances.

The band of lettering above the waterline is exactly the same size as the band of lettering below the waterline yet the lower one appears closer (larger) than the one above because of refraction. Your estimates of distance underwater will be as accurate as your estimates of distance in air. Set *estimated* distances on the camera lens.

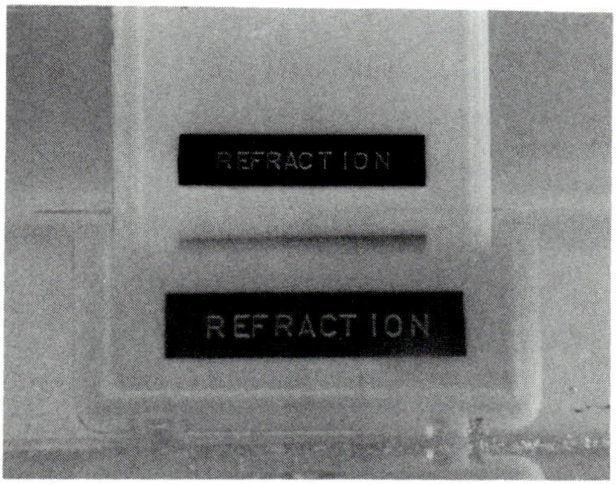

Exposure

Correct exposure for any given kind of film is determined by particular combinations of apertures and shutter speeds and the amount of light on a scene. Apertures and shutter speeds are calculated in such a way that an increase in one can be compensated for by a decrease in the other. For example, if 1/60 sec. at *f*/11 yields a correct exposure, so will any of the combinations below:

1/30 sec.	1/60 sec.	1/125 sec.	1/250 sec.	1/500 sec.
f/16	*f*/11	*f*/8	*f*/5.6	*f*/4

Most often, you will be "locked into" a narrow range of usable *f*/stops and shutter speeds because of the kind of film loaded and the amount of light on your subject.

A film's sensitivity to light, or its speed, is indicated by its ASA number. From a practical point of view, films for underwater use range from ASA 25 to ASA 400, but the high end of the scale can be extended by special processing methods. Films in the ASA 25 range are considered "slow" because they need more light than "fast" ASA-400-range films to produce usable images. The ASA scale was established in such a way so that when a film's ASA number is doubled, its sensitivity is increased by one *f*/stop. Thus, an ASA 50 film is twice as fast as an ASA 25 film, which sounds like a lot, but if the two films were being used to photograph the same subject from the same location, the difference in exposure would be only one *f*/stop.

There are methods for estimating exposures in air and underwater, but none is completely satisfactory. Accurate exposures using available light can best be attained with an exposure meter. Chapter 3 deals with available light underwater and exposure meters.

Taking a Picture

With the exposure and distance determined, and the controls appropriately set, you are ready to take a picture. Compose your subject in the viewfinder and slowly squeeze the film-advance/shutter-release lever toward you. The frame counter will advance as you make exposures. Continue making exposures until the frame counter indicates you've exhausted the film, or until you feel resistance on the lever. The counter will indicate 20 or 36 exposures, depending on the length of the roll loaded.

Rewinding the Film

When the film is exhausted, you must rewind it back into its cartridge. Do not attempt to rewind film underwater, as you run the risk of flooding the camera. When you're ready to rewind the film (after washing and drying is best), set the shutter-speed dial to "R" (if you have an "R" setting) and lift the rewind knob up. Turn the knob until it locks in place and cannot be pushed back into the camera.

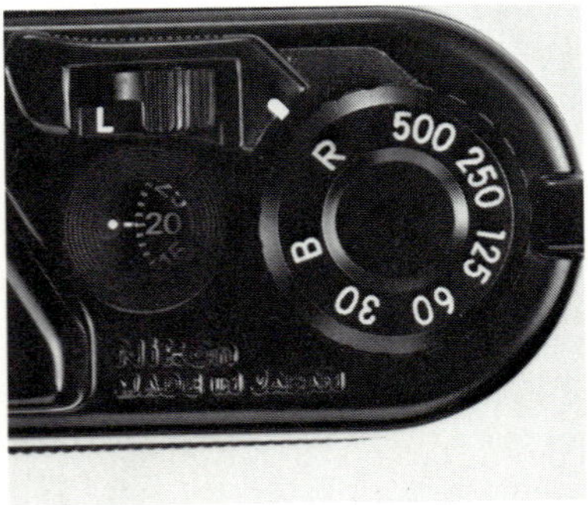

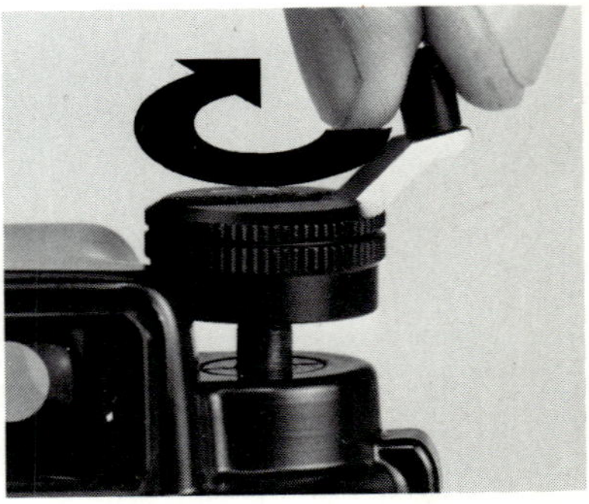

When film is exhausted, set shutter speed dial to "R" (left), lift rewind knob and crank, and rewind film (right).

Next, unfold the rewind crank and smoothly turn it in the direction of the arrow; the white dot in the frame counter on the Nikonos III should rotate as the film is being rewound. When it stops rotating and you feel an easing of the tension, the film is rewound into its cartridge. An extra turn or two will ensure that the film leader is completely within the cartridge; doing so will prevent you from mistakenly loading your camera with an already exposed roll of film.

With the film completely in the cartridge, remove the lens and open the camera as outlined earlier.

2

Lenses and Lens Accessories

The very core of any camera system is its lenses, and Nikonos users have at their disposal the finest camera optics on the market. Nikkor lenses are unsurpassed in their performance and are recognized around the world as the very best that can be had. The four Nikkor lenses made for use with the Nikonos are:

UW-Nikkor 15mm *f*/2.8 (for use underwater only)
UW-Nikkor 28mm *f*/3.5 (for use underwater only)
W-Nikkor 35mm *f*/2.5 (for use in air and underwater)
Nikkor-Q 80mm *f*/4 (for use in air and underwater)

In almost every shooting situation underwater, one of these four lenses will be perfect. In air, the coverage of the 35mm and 80mm dual-purpose lenses will prove to be more than adequate for many commonly encountered situations. The 15mm and 28mm lenses were designed for use in water only, and since their focusing characteristics and color-correction qualities are at their optimum in water, photographs made in air will prove unacceptable in most cases. This is not to say that the lenses will not record a scene; should you happen upon a once-in-a-lifetime event, or even if you simply want to make a personal record of something, by all means use whatever lens is available to you at the time. For a once-in-a-lifetime event, anything is better than nothing. And for jogging the memory, a picture, even a poor-quality one, is better than a page full of notes.

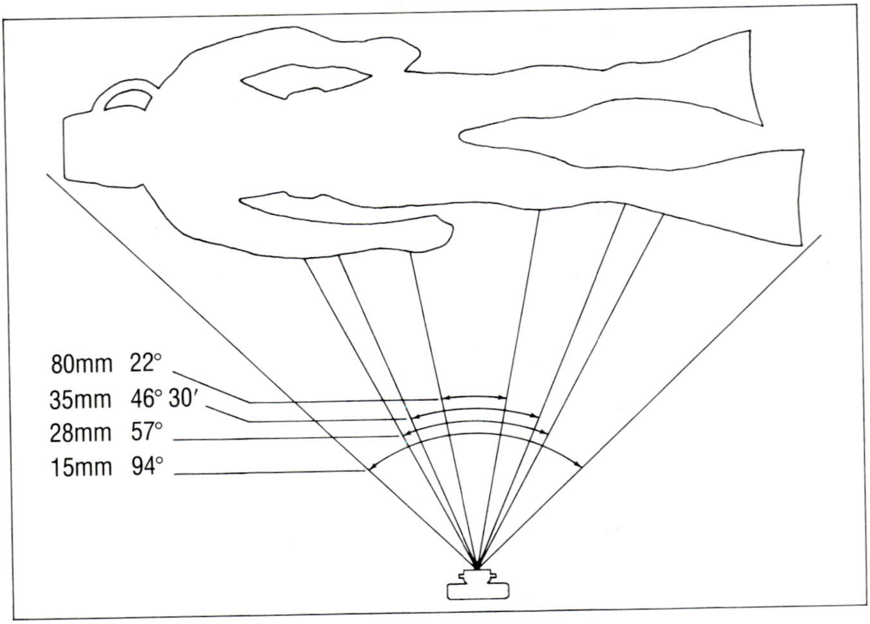

Various underwater angles of coverage for the Nikonos lenses.

At present, with the exception of Nikon, the only manufacturer that produces a lens for the Nikonos is Seacor, Inc. (Note: All the manufacturers mentioned are listed in Appendix B with their addresses as of this book's press date.) Seacor manufactures and distributes its Sea-Eye, a 21mm *f*/3.3 lens for underwater use. Seacor also makes the Super-Eye, a housing for adapting fisheye lenses (and extreme wide-angle lenses) to the Nikonos body.

W-NIKKOR 35mm *f*/2.5 LENS

The Nikkor 35mm *f*/2.5 lens is the lens most often supplied with the Nikonos when purchased new. It is the camera's "normal" lens. In air, the 35mm focal length provides an angle of coverage of 62 degrees. It is an excellent general-purpose lens, and the 35mm focal length is the first choice among press photographers and photojournalists. When the lens is used underwater, its angle of coverage is reduced to 46 degrees because of refraction, but even with the reduced coverage, the lens is perfect for many shooting situations. The lens is very often abandoned in favor of wider-angle lenses, but at its closest focusing distance, it is good for recording schools of fish and small coral heads. At longer distances, it is good for photographing divers and overall views, providing visibility permits, of course. The fact that the 35mm lens can be used in air as well as underwater makes it the ideal lens to have if you like to travel light. It is by far the most popular of the Nikonos lenses.

W-Nikkor 35mm *f*/2.5 (for use in air and underwater)

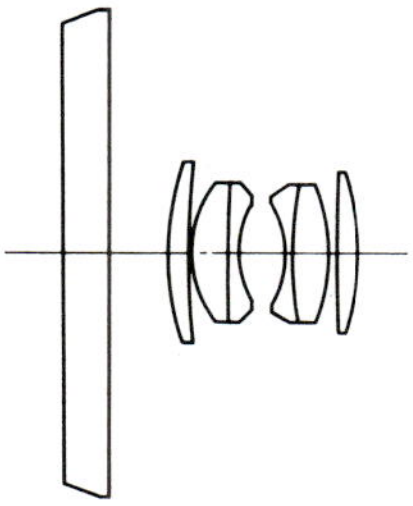

Focal Length:	35mm (air) 50mm (effect underwater)
Aperture Range:	*f*/2.5–*f*/22
Angle of View:	62° (air) 46°30′ (water)
Focusing Range:	2.75 ft.–∞
Attachment Diameter:	58mm
Lens Hood:	Screws-in and slip-on
Dimensions:	See diagram.
Weight:	5.5 oz.
Auxiliary Viewfinder:	Underwater finders available.

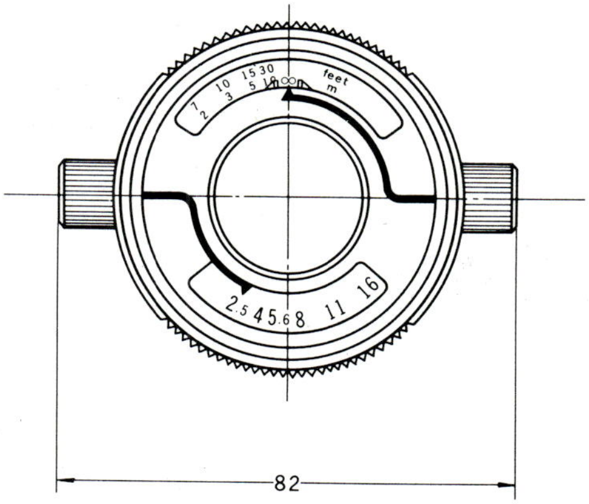

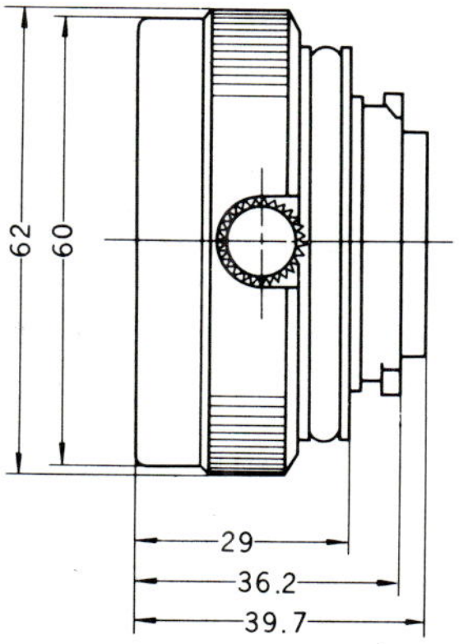

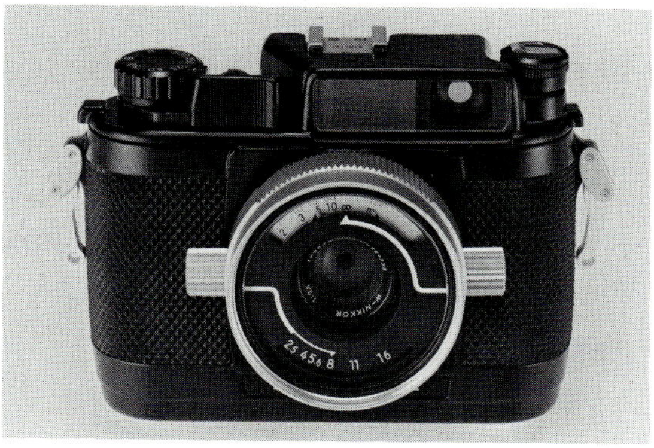

The 35mm *f*/2.5 lens on a Nikonos III.

UW-NIKKOR 28mm *f*/3.5 LENS

The 28mm lens is the second most popular of the Nikonos lenses. It is designed for underwater use only (although some photographers occasionally use it in air), and it is usually the first additional lens a diver buys when wishing to expand the camera's capabilities. The 28mm lens is the choice because it can focus down to about 2 ft., and because its angle of coverage underwater is about 59 degrees. With this angle of coverage, a diving photographer can get within 5 ft. of fellow divers and still record them from mask to flippers. As you will see later, keeping the camera-to-subject distance as short as possible is the key to successful underwater photography. The 28mm lens is probably the most useful lens for general-purpose underwater photography.

A look at the accompanying lens diagram shows that the front of the 28mm lens is actually a ground optical element and not simply a flat port as in the 35mm and 80mm lenses. It is this element which improves the underwater characteristics of the lens, but it also creates slight barrel distortion when the lens is used in air. The distortion is most noticeable at the outer edges of a scene photographed in air, but the central portion shows virtually no distortion. By using only the central portion of a negative or slide, fair results can be obtained.

The 28mm lens is excellent for recording large fish like this stoplight parrotfish.

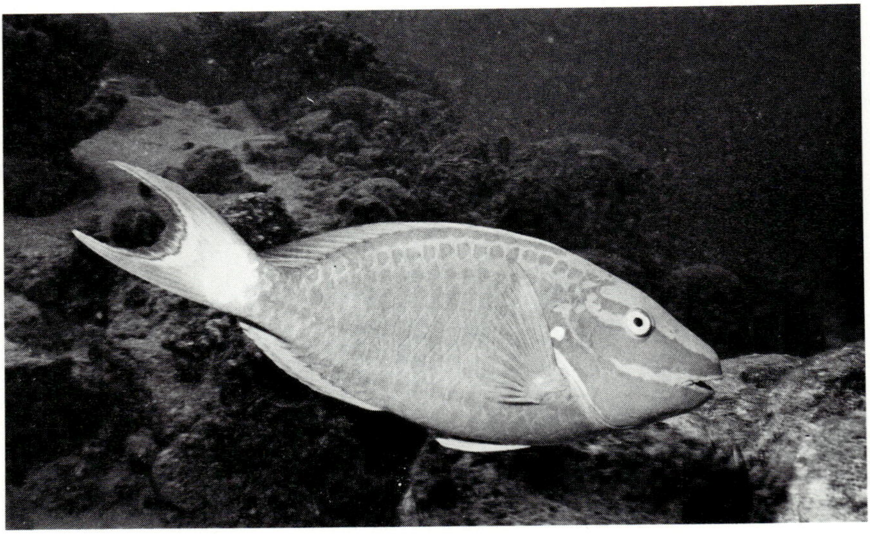

UW-Nikkor 28mm *f*/3.5 (for use underwater)

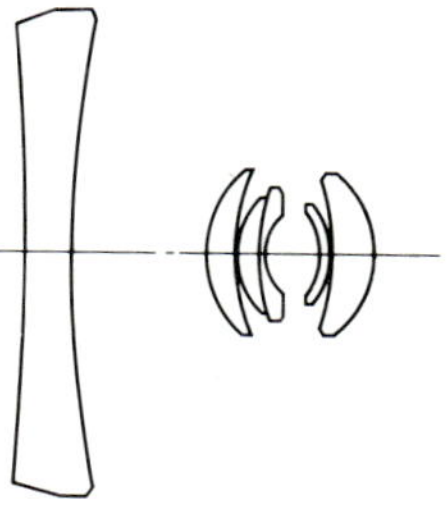

Focal Length:	28mm (water)
Aperture Range:	*f*/3.5–*f*/22
Angle of View:	57° (water)
Focusing Range:	2 ft.–∞
Attachment Diameter:	58mm
Lens Hood:	Screw-in type available.
Dimensions:	See diagram.
Weight:	5.6 oz.
Auxiliary Viewfinder:	Underwater finders available.

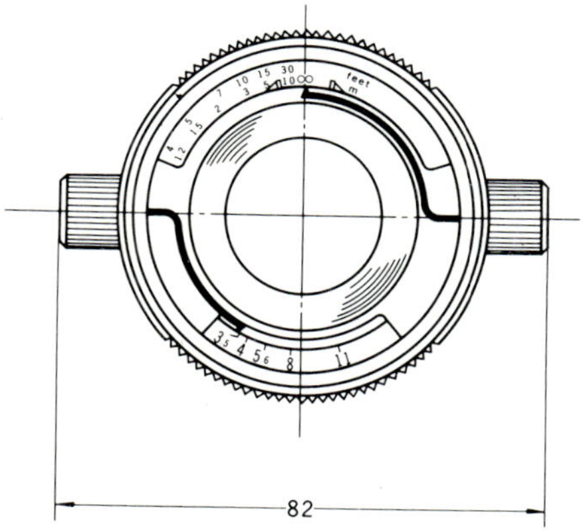

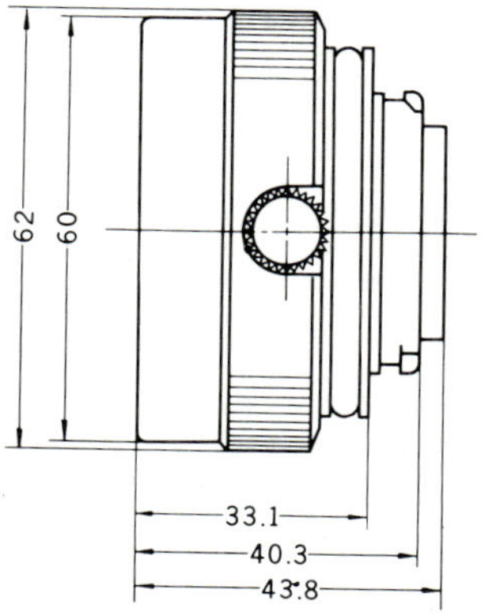

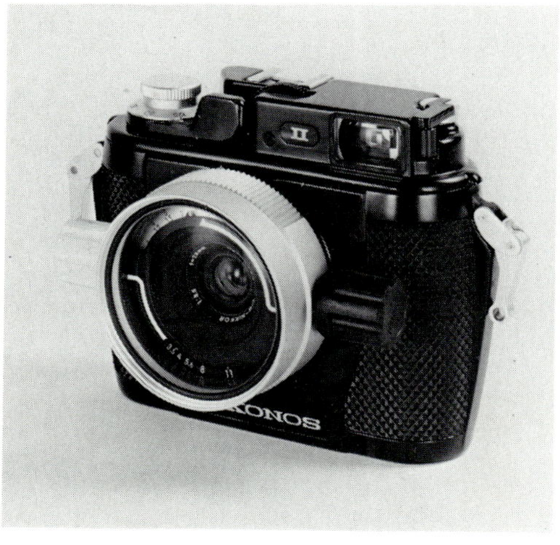

The 28mm *f*/3.5 lens on a Nikonos II.

UW-NIKKOR 15mm *f*/2.8 LENS

The 15mm underwater-only lens is the lens most diving photographers would like to add to their equipment list, but its price tag (approximately $1000 at this writing) makes its purchase difficult to justify for all but professional photographers and the most serious amateurs. Its extreme wide-angle of coverage (94 degrees), incredible depth of field, and the fact that it is virtually distortion-free (it is a rectilinear lens) make it a highly desirable lens. This is particularly so for those who do much of their photography in murky water.

Even in water where the visibility is less than 3 ft., the 15mm performs amazingly. Focused at 2 ft. and stopped down to *f*/16, everything from 11 in. to infinity (or the limit of visibility) will be in focus, distortion-free, and as detailed as water clarity permits.

UW-Nikkor 15mm *f*/2.8 (for use underwater)

Focal Length:	15mm (water)
Aperture Range:	*f*/2.8–*f*/22
Angle of View:	94° (water)
Focusing Range:	1 ft.–∞
Attachment Diameter:	84mm
Lens Hood:	Built-in.
Dimensions:	See diagram.
Weight:	11.3 oz.
Auxiliary Viewfinder:	Supplied with underwater optical finder.

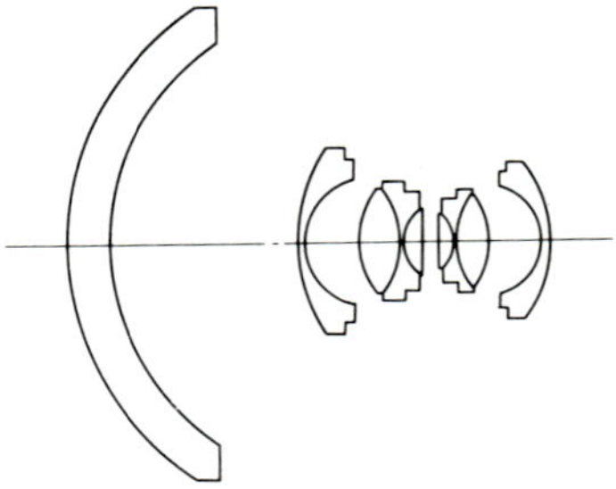

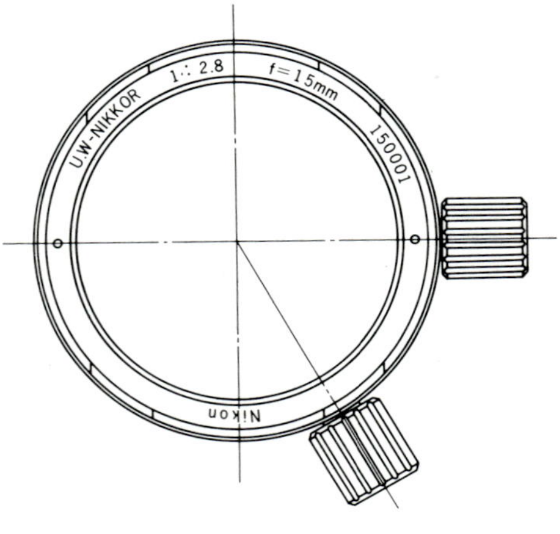

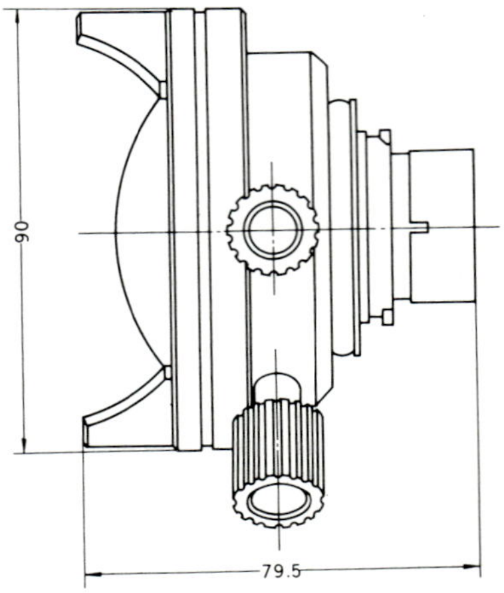

The 15mm *f*/2.8 lens and its underwater viewfinder mounted on a Nikonos III.

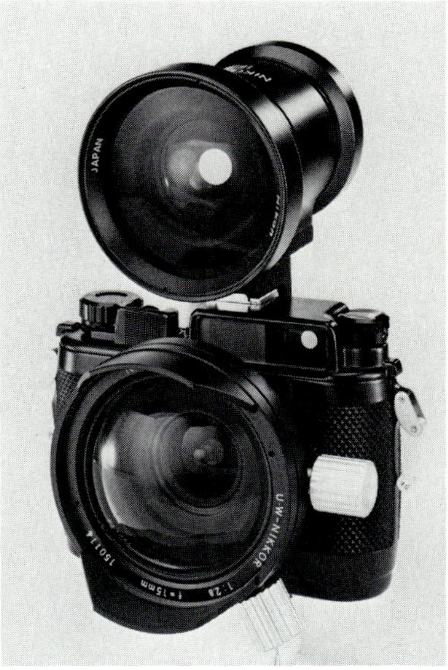

The 15mm lens is constructed somewhat differently than the other Nikonos lenses. The first obvious difference is the large correction dome that covers the other lens elements. The dome makes it possible for the lens to record distortion-free images and to maintain its great angle of coverage. More on dome optics in Chapter 7.

Another difference between this lens and the other Nikonos lenses is the placement of the lens controls. The aperture and focus knobs on the 15mm lens are at almost 90 degrees to each other, whereas on the other lenses, they are in line on opposite sides of the lens barrel.

Still another difference is the placement of the distance scale, depth-of-field scale, and the aperture settings. On the 15mm lens, these settings are located around the barrel of the lens rather than on the face of the lens as with the others. Thus positioned, it is possible to adjust settings without having to turn the camera completely around to point it at yourself.

The lens mounts on the camera in the same way the other lenses do, but it is possible to mount this lens in a way that makes it difficult to read the settings and scales. When mounted correctly, the focusing scale and aperture settings will point toward the film-advance/shutter-release lever. In this position, the lower control knob will control the aperture, and the other knob will control the focusing. Distance and aperture are set at the black index mark at the center of

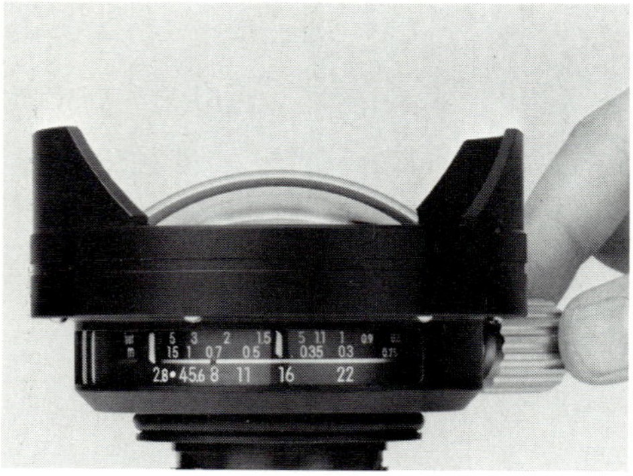

On the 15mm lens the distance scale, depth-of-field scale, and aperture settings are located on the lens barrel. This lens is set at *f*/8 and focused for a distance between 2 and 3 ft.

the scales, and, as with the other lenses, depth of field is clearly indicated with guides that move as the aperture is selected.

To protect the dome, which projects in front of the lens, a metal screw-type lens cap is provided. This cap should be removed before you enter the water or, while on the surface, before you begin your dive. Once below the surface, the increased pressure will make it difficult to unscrew the cap. If you force the cap while deep underwater, you could unseat the lens.

15mm Underwater Optical Viewfinder

Supplied with the 15mm lens is an optical viewfinder that shows the photographer almost exactly what the lens will record on film. The viewfinder corrects for parallax at a distance of 5 ft., as the accompanying diagram illustrates. At distances closer than 5 ft., especially at 3 ft. and under, the top portion of a subject may not be recorded by the lens even though visible in the viewfinder. To avoid losing an important part of your subject, keep this in mind when in turbid water where working distances are less than 3 ft.

The accompanying diagram also shows the correct position for your eye when using the viewfinder. Even with the largest face masks, it should be easy to position your eye at the correct viewing distance.

Correct eye position with 15mm lens and viewfinder.

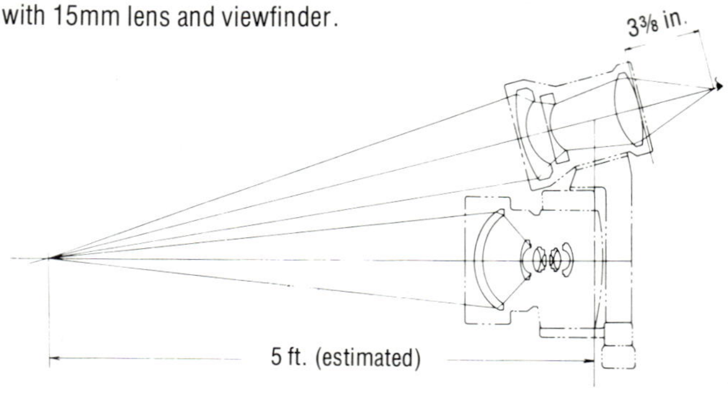

Attaching the Viewfinder

The viewfinder is attached to the camera in a manner somewhat like a C-clamp. First, unscrew the finder-attaching knob and lower the fork portion of the finder. Next, slip the finder into the accessory shoe on top of the camera. Finally, tighten the attaching knob. On the Nikonos models I and II, be sure the frame counter is visible in the slot of the viewfinder's forked end. On the Nikonos III, the tripod socket will be in the slot. When accessory brackets are used with the camera (as explained in Chapter 6), attaching the viewfinder may be a problem because the clearance between the base of the camera and the lowest position of the attaching fork is only ¼ in. Most of the simple accessory brackets on the market can be used with the viewfinder.

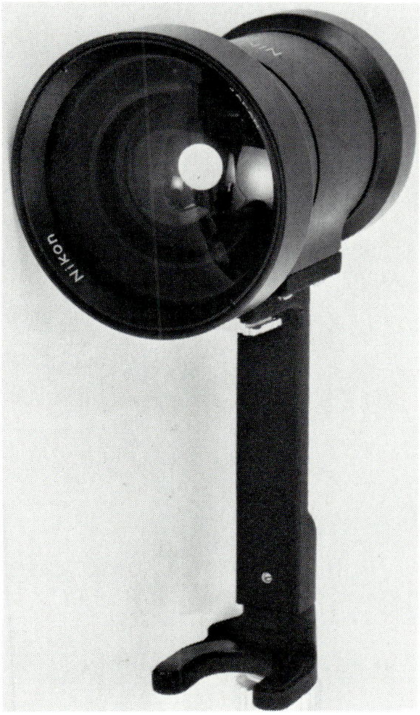

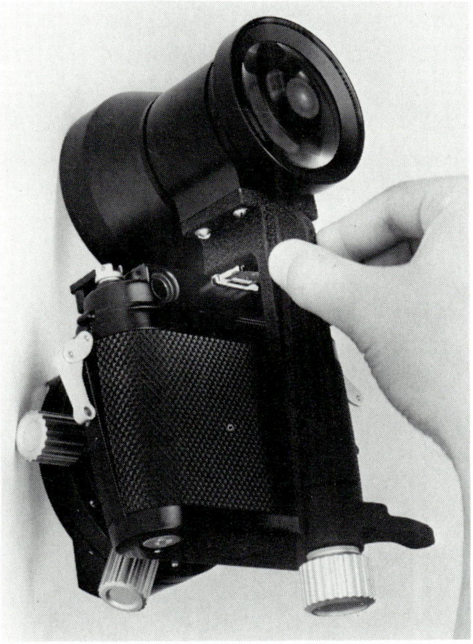

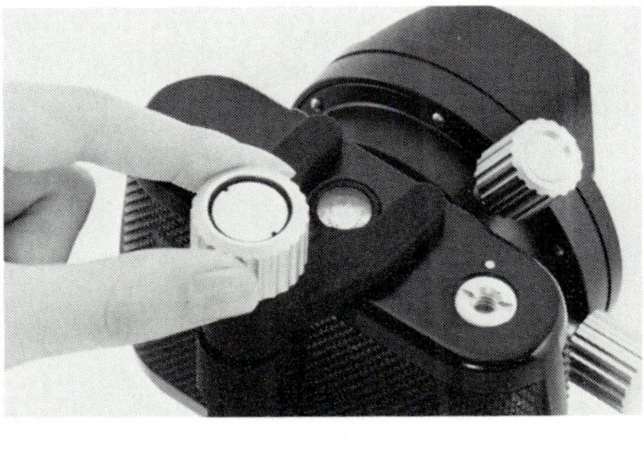

Optical viewfinder for 15mm *f*/2.8 underwater lens (top left). To attach the viewfinder slip it into the accessory shoe on top of the camera (top right) and then tighten the attaching knob (bottom right). When mounted on the earlier model cameras, the frame counter should be visible in the fork portion of the bracket.

NIKKOR-Q 80mm *f*/4 LENS

The 80mm lens is the longest lens available for use with the Nikonos. It is what is generally called a moderate-telephoto lens, and it can be used both in air and underwater. On land, it is ideal for portraits. Underwater, it is good for photographing fish that are normally somewhat difficult to approach. At a focus distance of 5 ft., it is possible to fill your film frame with a fish 18 in. long. As with all long lenses, depth of field is considerably less than with wide-angle lenses, hence it is particularly important focusing be as accurate as possible.

Because the key to successful underwater photography is keeping the camera-to-subject distances at a minimum, you will probably use the 80mm lens underwater at its close focusing distances—3.3 ft. to 6 ft. For your subjects to be sharp, your distance estimation will have to be accurate within inches because at 6 ft. at *f*/11, the depth of field is only about 13 in. When using the 80mm, you will also have to take

Nikkor-Q 80mm *f*/4 (for use in air and underwater)

Focal Length:	80mm (air) 100mm (effect underwater)
Aperture Range:	*f*/4–*f*/22
Angle of View:	30°20′ (air) 22°45′ (water)
Focusing Range:	3.3 ft.–∞
Attachment Diameter:	58mm
Lens Hood:	Screw-in.
Dimensions:	See diagram.
Weight:	9.75 oz.
Auxiliary Viewfinder:	In-air optical and underwater types available.

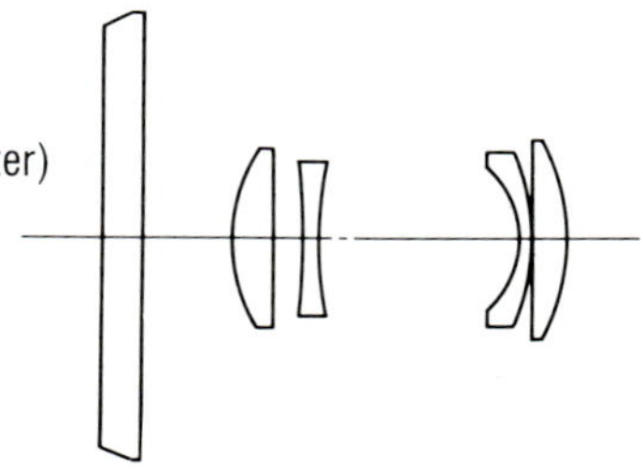

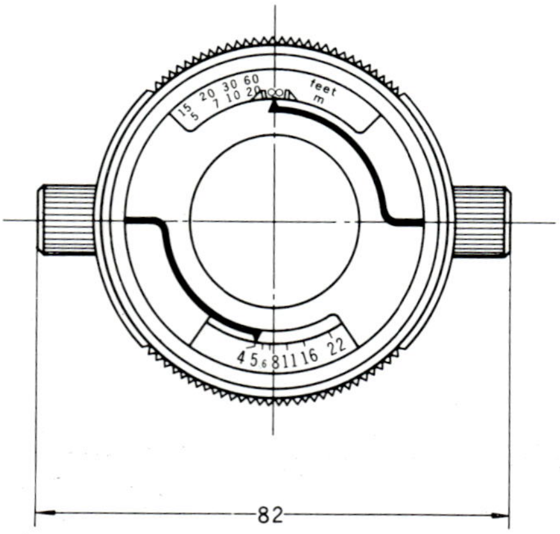

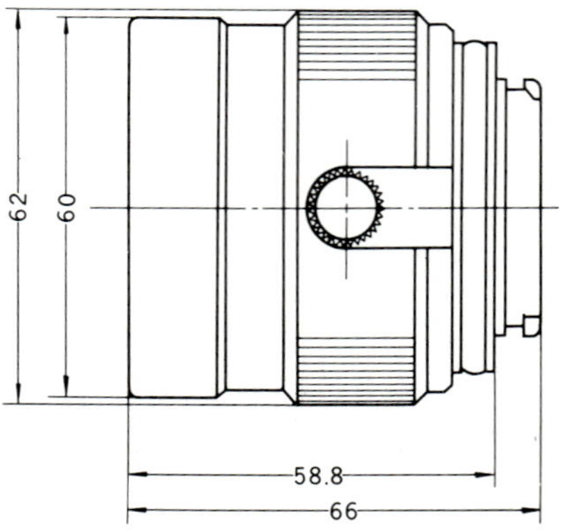

The 80mm *f*/4 lens on a Nikonos II.

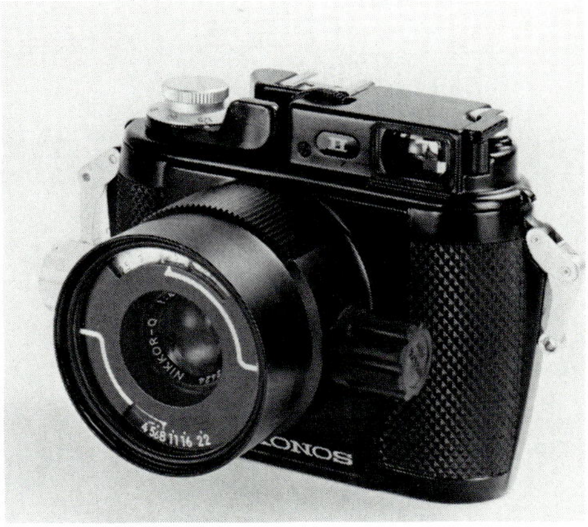

special care in framing your subject because the angle of coverage of the lens is only 22 degrees underwater. This creates a parallax problem more difficult to solve than with the other lenses. Sportsfinders, to be explained shortly, will help you frame your underwater subjects.

80mm Air-Only Optical Viewfinder

In air, the parallax problem is best solved by using the auxiliary optical viewfinder for the lens. Though it can only be used in air, it is weatherproof. If it is exposed to rain, dust, or salt spray, it can be rinsed in tap water. The finder can be adjusted to properly frame subjects at different camera-to-subject distances by rotating the distance-scale ring and setting the estimated distance at the index mark on top of the finder.

To use the finder, slip it into the accessory shoe, estimate the camera-to-subject distance, set that distance on the finder *and the lens*, frame the subject in the finder, and make your exposure.

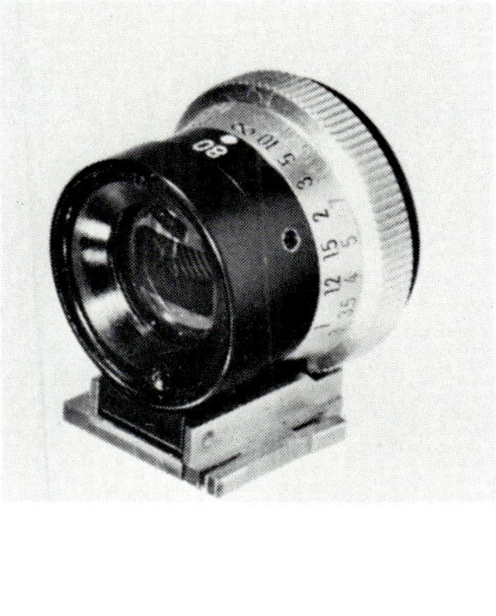

The in-air optical viewfinder for the 80mm lens solves the parallax problem created because of the narrow angle of coverage of that lens.

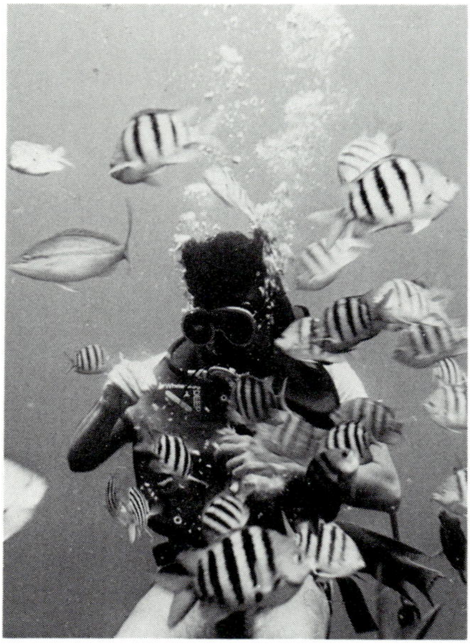

80mm

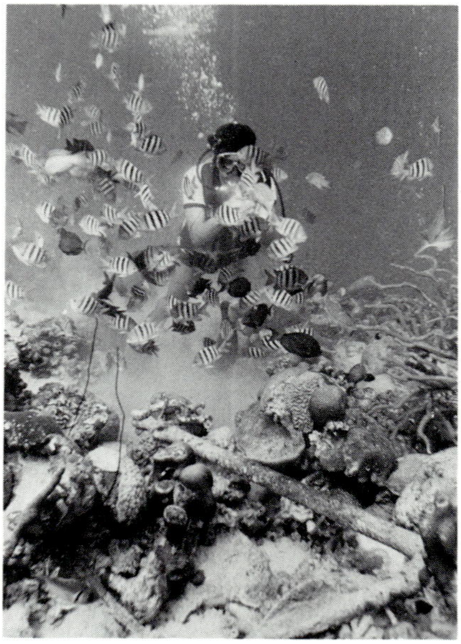

35mm

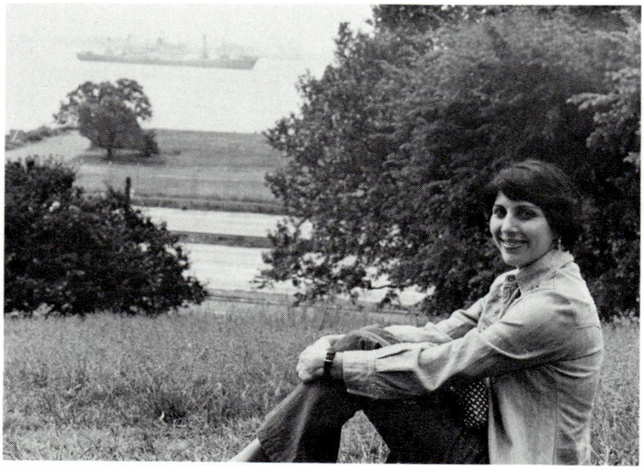

The 80mm lens and the 35mm lens are designed for use in air and underwater. Excellent results can be achieved in both mediums. Both the in-air and underwater sequences were taken at estimated distances of 10 ft.

80mm

35mm

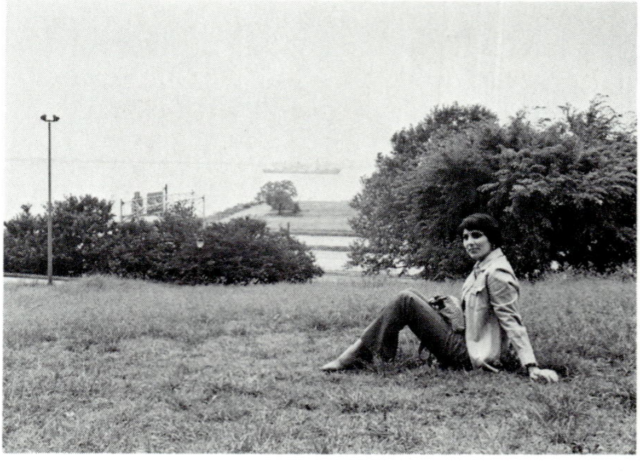

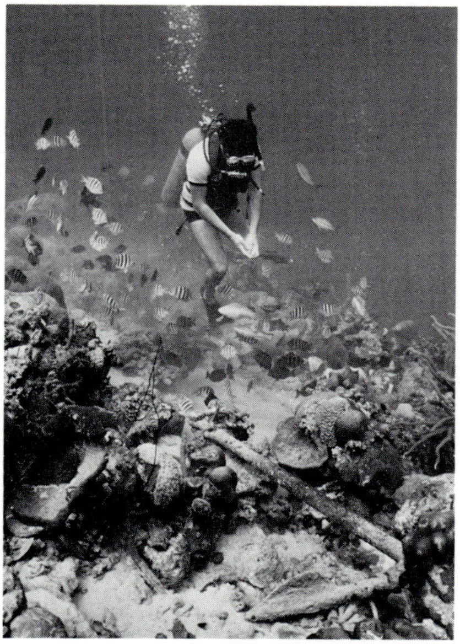

28mm

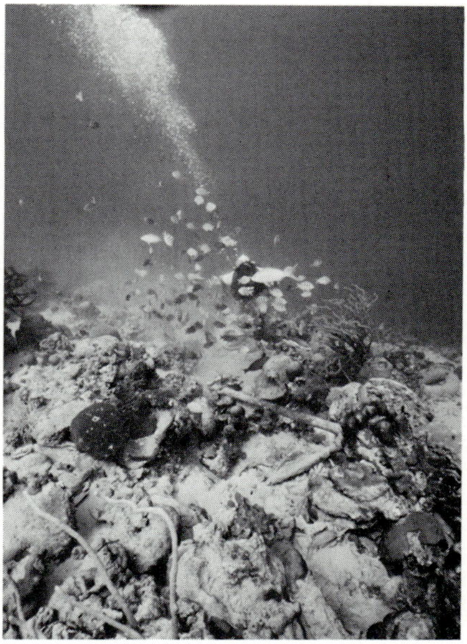

15mm

The 28mm lens and the 15mm lens are designed for use underwater. In air the 28mm will show slight barrel distortion and lack of sharpness at the edges of the frame. The 15mm cannot be focused in air, as the photo shows.

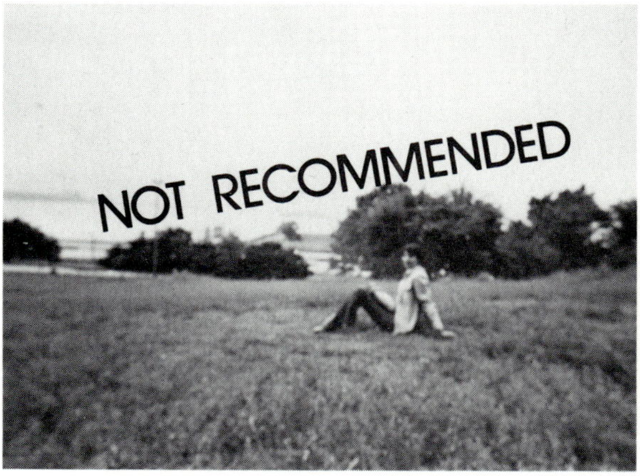

15mm

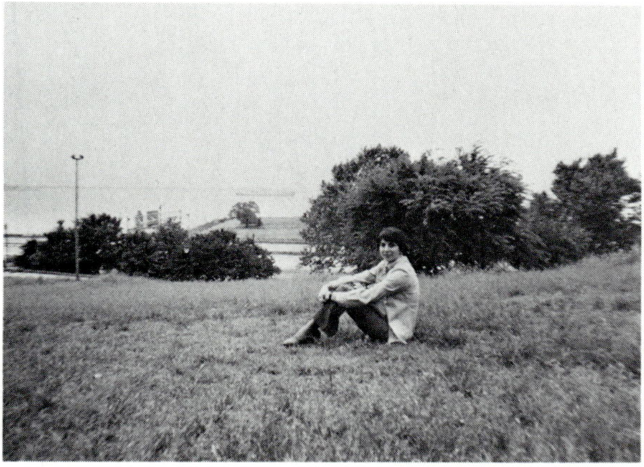

28mm

SEACOR SEA-EYE 21mm *f*/3.3 LENS

With its wide angle of coverage and close focusing distance, the Seacor Sea-Eye is capable of producing images that are virtually distortion-free. It is a good lens for working in murky water and for keeping camera-to-subject distances at a minimum in clear water because of its wide angle of coverage.

The Sea-Eye lens is constructed of a high-impact plastic, making it extremely light in weight and, of course, completely corrosion-resistant. It mounts on the camera in the same way the Nikonos Nikkor lenses do. Its control knobs are located on opposite sides of the lens barrel, and aperture and distance settings are read directly off the face of the lens as the control knobs are adjusted. Depth of field is not indicated. The lens comes equipped with a front and rear lens cap, and the front cap should be left in place until you're ready to use the lens because the dome, though made of a tough optical-quality plastic, can be scratched.

21mm Viewfinder

The Sea-Eye lens should be used with an optical viewfinder that is also made by Seacor. Called the Sea-View Universal, because it can be used with different lenses if its front mask is changed, the finder slips into the camera's accessory shoe. The mask for use with the 21mm lens covers a field of 80 degrees, a bit less than the 92-degree angle of coverage of the lens. This is an advantage, though, because even at close distances where parallax might be a problem, the lens will record a bit more than you're actually seeing.

Seacor 21mm *f*/3.3 (for use underwater)

Focal Length:	21mm (water)
Aperture Range:	*f*/3.3–*f*/16
Angle of View:	92° (water)
Focusing Range:	2.5 ft.–∞
Attachment Diameter:	NA
Lens Hood:	NA
Auxiliary Viewfinder:	Sea-View Universal.

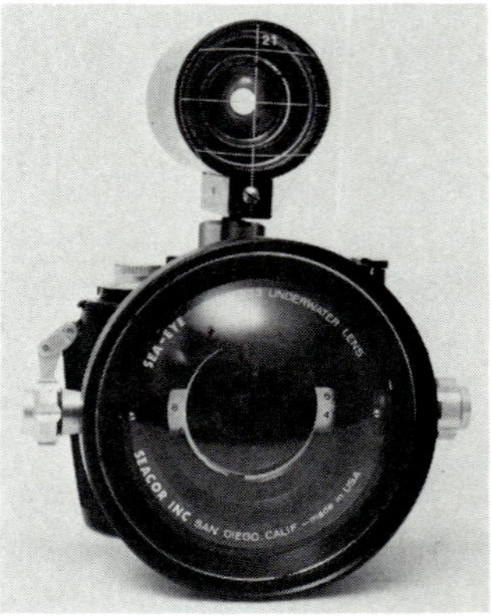

Seacor Sea-Eye 21mm *f*/3.3 lens and Sea-View Universal viewfinder mounted on a Nikonos II.

The Sea-Eye lens should be used with the Sea-View Universal viewfinder. With its 21mm mask in place, the viewfinder will present a field of view of 80°—just 12° less than the 92° coverage of the lens.

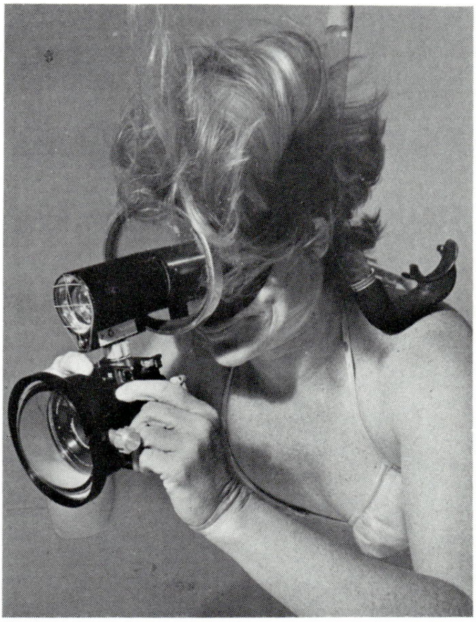

This gray whale was photographed with a Sea-Eye 21mm lens in a holding tank at Sea World in San Diego. The wide angle of coverage makes it possible to work at minimal shooting distances.

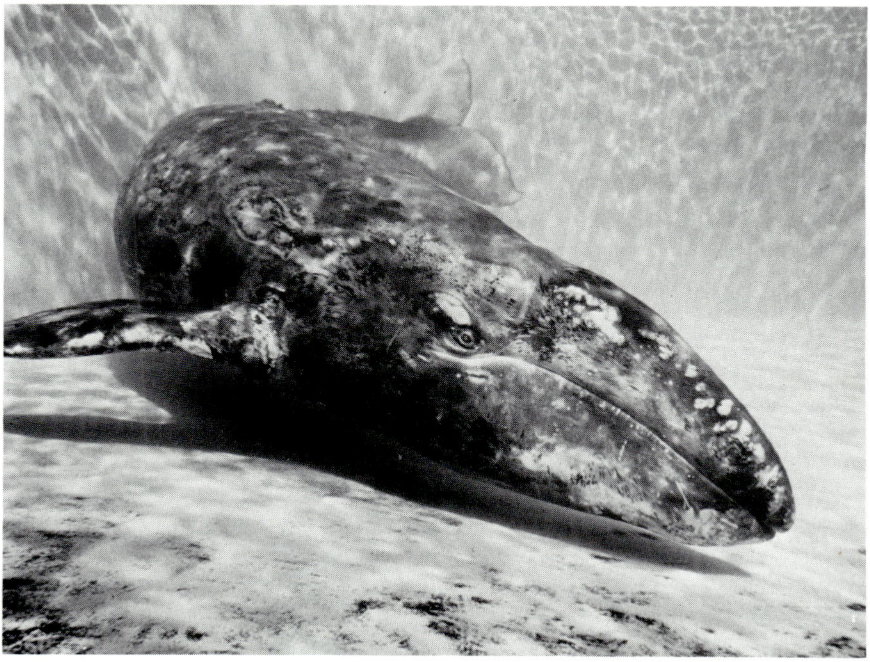

SEACOR SUPER-EYE

The Seacor Super-Eye is not a lens, but it is included in this section because with it a variety of lenses can be adapted to the Nikonos. The Super-Eye is actually an aluminum housing that encloses a lens behind a fully corrected dome of optical-quality plastic. Most often, fisheye lenses are used with the Super-Eye, but in fact almost any lens with a Nikkor bayonet mount can be used.

When fisheye lenses are used with the Super-Eye, all their fisheye qualities are retained, and the results can be quite dramatic, as the accompanying illustration shows. Fisheye lenses are known for their amazing depth of field (even at wide apertures) and their ability to focus close—two qualities that make them ideal for use in water with poor visibility. The accompanying table shows the Nikkor fisheye lenses that can be used successfully with the Super-Eye.

NIKKOR FISHEYE LENSES FOR USE WITH THE SUPER-EYE

Lens	Angle of View	Image Size
8mm *f*/2.8 Fisheye-Nikkor Auto	180°	23mm diam. full-circle image
10mm *f*/5.6 OP Fisheye-Nikkor	180°	20mm diam. full-circle image
16mm *f*/3.5 Fisheye-Nikkor Auto	170°	full-frame image

Note: Some of the discontinued Nikkor Fisheye lenses can be used with the Super-Eye.
Since the corrective dome covers an angle of acceptance of 180°, fisheye lenses with greater angles of acceptance should not be used.

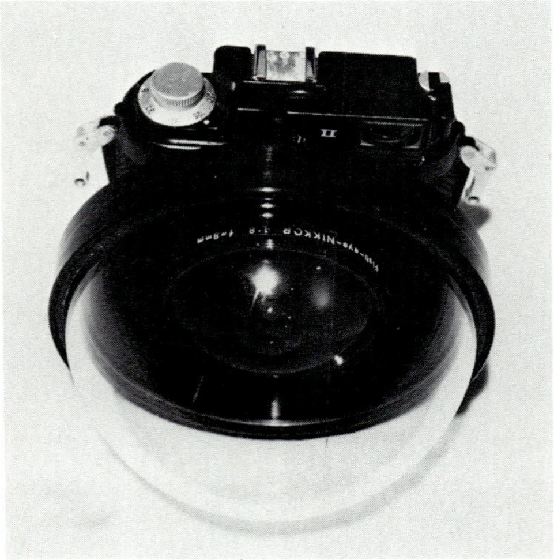

Seacor Super-Eye housing and Nikkor fisheye lens mounted on a Nikonos II.

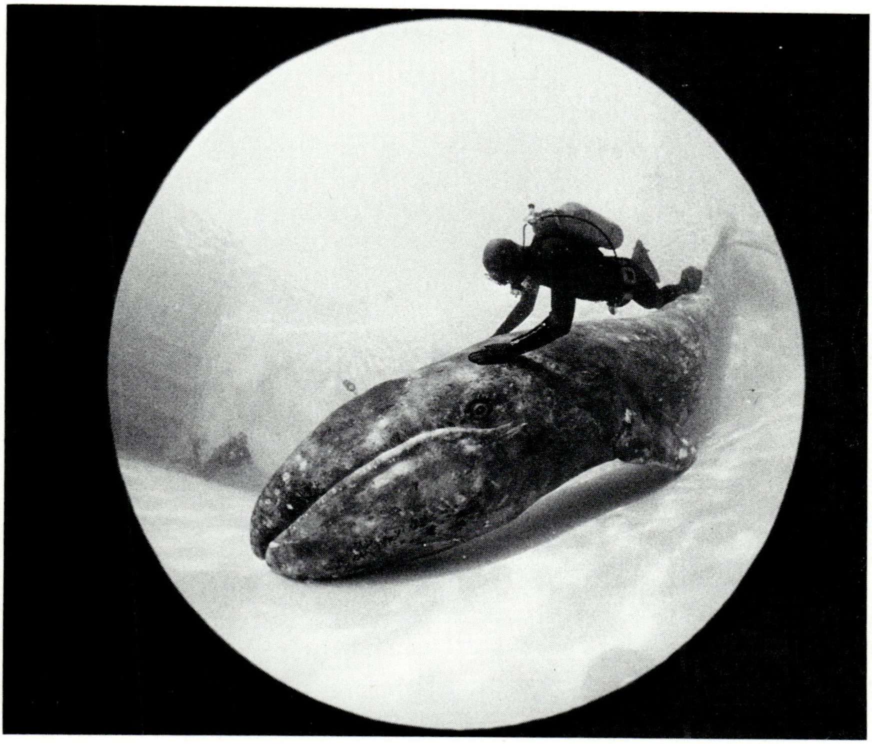

Spectacular fisheye photographs can be taken underwater by housing a fisheye lens in Seacor's Super-Eye. This gray whale is the same one pictured on page 49; compare the results the different lenses yield.

Viewfinder

The Super-Eye should be used with an optical viewfinder that approximates the effect of the lens being used in it. But currently Seacor does not make one that approximates the angle of coverage of a fisheye lens—the type of lens most often used in a Super-Eye. Seacor recommends using their Sea-View Universal viewfinder. It will give you an angle of coverage of approximately half that of a 180-degree fisheye lens. Keep that in mind when using this finder with a fisheye lens—with an extreme angle of coverage of 180 degrees, it is very easy to inadvertently include part of yourself in the film frame.

AUXILIARY VIEWFINDERS

The need for an auxiliary viewfinder will be apparent as soon as you try to compose a picture through the camera's built-in viewfinder while wearing a face mask. It is difficult. The two types of auxiliary viewfinders available, sportsfinders and optical finders, can make the job of properly framing your subjects easier. Sportsfinders are simple metal, plastic, or hard rubber frames that mount on the camera and aid in composition. They are generally inexpensive and compact while optical finders are more expensive and bulkier. Optical finders, though, better approximate the angle of coverage of the lens with which they are being used.

Sportsfinders

The sportsfinders made by Nikon for use with the 28mm, 35mm, and 80mm lenses are simple framing devices that slip into the accessory shoe on top of the camera body. The combination finder, which can be used with the 35mm and 80mm lenses, has a central frame for viewing with the 80mm lens and an outer frame for viewing with the 35mm lens. It is made of plastic. The finder for use with the 28mm lens is made of hard rubber. Both finders are corrected for parallax at 6 ft. If you use them to frame subjects closer than 6 ft., make some compensation so that you do not cut off the top portion of your subject.

To use the finders effectively, view the subject through the central portion of the finder and let the outer frame indicate the area that will be recorded on film. Your eyes should be approximately 3¼ in. from the finder and exactly behind the finder's crossbar. If you position your eye too high, too low, or too far to one side, you will not see the same image that will be recorded. The accompanying diagram will

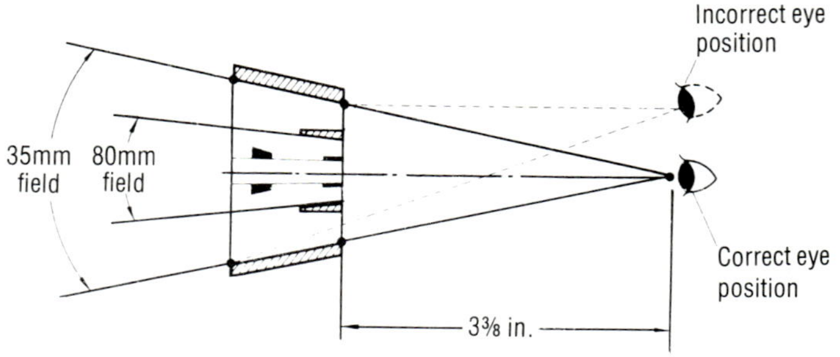

Correct eye position when using the Nikonos sportsfinder for the 35mm and 80mm lenses.

show you the proper way to use the auxiliary finder for the 35mm and 80mm lenses.

The sportsfinders were designed for use underwater. In air, the camera's built-in finder and the auxiliary optical finder for the 80mm lens provide a better means for framing your subjects. Should you try to use a sportsfinder in air, be aware that the angle of coverage indicated by the finder is less than that of the lens. Because of refraction, the angle of coverage of the lens is greater in air.

Sportsfinders can, and easily do, slip out of the accessory shoe while diving. To avoid losing a viewfinder, place a wedge under it, or use a short piece of line to attach it to the camera.

Optical Viewfinders

Optical viewfinders provide the diver with a somewhat faster and easier method of framing subjects than with sportsfinders. Ikelite and Seacor both make optical finders for use with the Nikonos. The finders slip into the camera's accessory shoe and tighten in place with a knurled nut on the base of the finders. These units have front masks that can be changed so that the finders can be used with different focal-length lenses.

With optical finders, you view, compose, and shoot. Using optical finders is the next best thing to actually viewing your subject through the taking lens of a camera because they are fast, easy to use, correct for parallax (to a degree), and they make it difficult to misframe a picture.

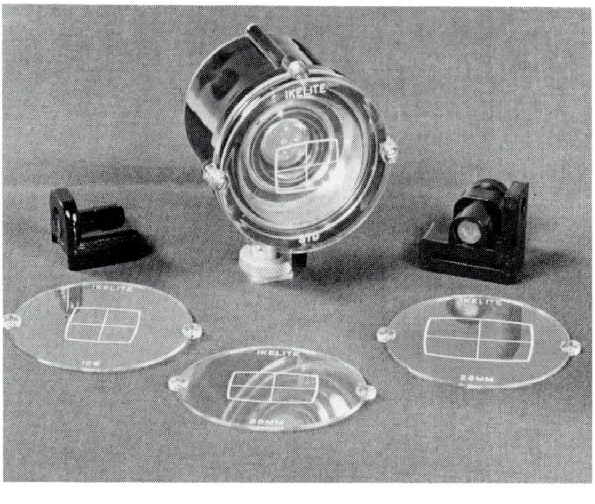

Ikelite optical viewfinder, interchangeable front masks, and adapter shoes.

Lens Shades (Hoods)

Using a lens shade, or lens hood, underwater is as important as using one on land. With a hood, you avoid the possibility of having extraneous light rays strike the front of your lens and register on the film. Lens hoods on the Nikonos also serve to protect the lenses. The rubber, slip-on lens shade for use with the 35mm lens is excellent for protecting the lens because it wraps the lens in a soft rubber that absorbs shocks. It is easily attached by slipping it over the lens and pulling down the attachment tabs until the aperture and focusing knobs pass through the holes provided for them. The hood is a good accessory to use when you expect difficult entries and exits or a strong surge.

The plastic lens hood has a 58mm screw thread for attachment to the front of the 28mm, 35mm, and 80mm lenses. In addition to acting as a lens shade, it is also a filter holder, accepting 52mm screw-in filters—the standard size for most Nikkor lenses. To use the lens shade as a filter holder, first attach the filter to the hood by screwing the filter into the side of the hood that faces the lens. Next, attach the filter and hood, as a unit, to the lens. Because the lens hood is plastic, special care should be taken when attaching it to the lens; it is easy to cross-thread the hood and strip its threads. Oceanic Products makes a metal lens hood/filter holder that lessens the chance of stripping threads. It too accepts 52mm screw-in filters.

If you don't use a lens hood, you should keep the white nylon protecting ring in place on the front of the lens. The ring keeps the threads around the front of the lens from becoming damaged, and it also gives added protection to the lens itself.

It is not a good idea to change filters or lens shades underwater unless absolutely necessary. Should the threads jam, the torque on the shade could turn the lens and unseat it.

The use of filters underwater is covered in a separate section in Chapter 3.

Lens-Knob Extenders

Oversized knobs that slip over and attach to the knobs of the 28mm, 35mm, and 80mm lenses are available from Nikon and other manufacturers. They are useful because they make the lens knobs easier to grasp by extending them away from the lens. If you're wearing bulky gloves or rubber mittens, these extenders may be especially helpful.

Extenders made by Hydro Photo have graduated markings that indicate *f*/stops and distance settings. This makes it possible to adjust the camera settings without having to turn the camera completely around to make the face of the lens visible. Knob extenders made by Beall are specially treated so that they can be written on with pencil or ballpoint pen. These can be marked with preselected *f*/stops and distance settings to avoid turning the camera when making adjustments.

Wide-Angle Attachments

Aqua-Craft manufactures a number of different attachments that have the effect of shortening the focal length and increasing the angle of coverage of the lens with which they are being used. The devices, known collectively as "Green Things," can be slipped on and off the front of the lenses underwater, making it convenient to try different effects with the same subject. The accompanying table shows the effect each adapter produces. For optimum quality with accessory lenses, read the manufacturers' instructions carefully.

AQUA-CRAFT ACCESSORY LENSES (GREEN THINGS)

	Underwater Angle of Coverage	
Attachment	With 35mm	With 28mm
Marine View 50	63°	NR
Opal Eye	95°	NR
Fish Eye	150° (partial circular image)	160° (full-circle image)

Lens Caps

It is a good idea to keep a lens cap on your lens until just prior to going in the water. This is particularly true when on a boat with other divers, each one preparing to enter the water, or when on a beach. The lens cap will protect the lens from accidental bumps, and it will keep sand off the lens.

Front and rear lens caps are supplied with the Nikonos lenses when purchased new. Replacement caps can be purchased directly from Nikon; they are also available from Beall. A rear lens cap should be placed on the lens as soon as it is removed from the camera body unless the lens is going back into the camera immediately.

For lenses with a large front element, it is a good idea to make a lens cap of neoprene rubber. You will be able to keep the cap on the lens underwater and stuff it into your safety-vest pocket when not in use. If you make your own lens cap, you can add a tab that covers the viewfinder to remind you when the cap is in place.

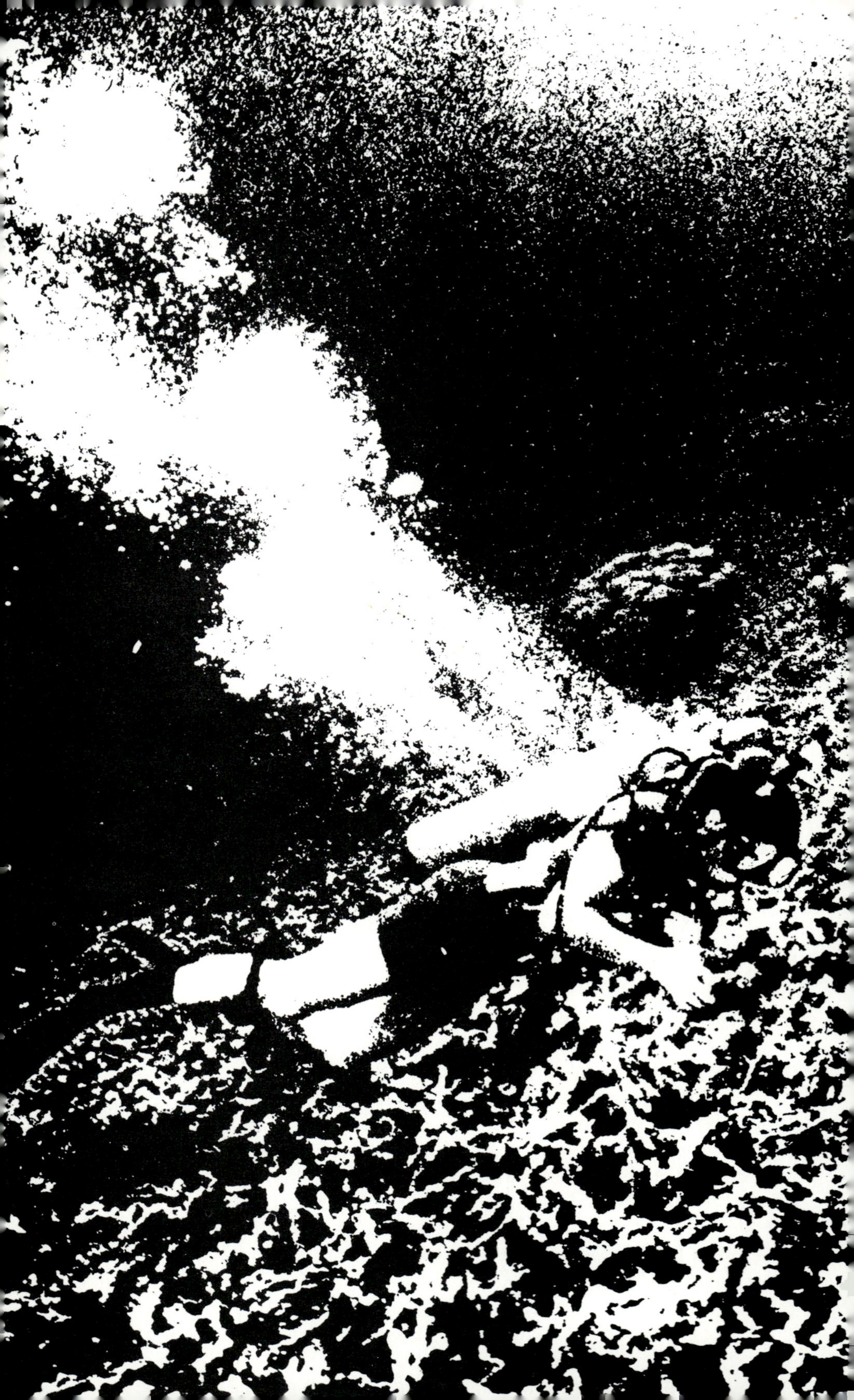

3

Available Light Underwater

With the equipment discussed so far, you will be able to take pictures underwater using available light. Using available light underwater successfully is no easy task, and mastering it can occupy many, many dives.

Underwater, available light (also referred to as ambient, or natural, light) is the light from the sun that reaches a subject after passing through the atmosphere, the surface of the water, and finally the water itself. Since water is approximately 600 times more dense than air, light traveling through it behaves differently than light traveling through air. You've probably noticed that there is always much less light underwater than on the surface at any given time, and that the quality of the light is soft and diffused. This is because of the combined effects of the reflection, refraction, scattering, and absorption of light.

PROPERTIES OF LIGHT UNDERWATER

Reflection

When the sun is directly overhead, little light is reflected off the surface of the water. The best light penetration occurs during the hours around noon. When the sun is closer to the horizon, some of its light does not penetrate the water because it is reflected off the surface. Surface conditions as well as the angle of the sun also affect how much light is reflected. When the sea is calm, little light is reflected; but when the sea is choppy, many small surfaces that reflect light are formed. The least amount of light will be lost to reflection on bright, calm days between the hours of 10 A.M. and 2 P.M.

Refraction

Light that is not reflected off the surface of the water passes down into it, but as it does, it is refracted. Refraction is the bending of light rays as they pass from one medium to another. The least amount of light ray bending occurs when the sun is directly overhead, but as the sun approaches the horizon, light ray bending increases. This causes light rays to travel farther to reach a given depth, and the increased distance the light must travel reduces its intensity. Light lost to refraction will be least around noon.

Scattering

The number of suspended particles and minute organisms in a body of water will vary greatly with geographic location, time of year, weather, and other factors. Light passing through a medium filled with floating debris is scattered and diffused as it makes its way through the mixture. In addition to reducing the overall amount of light, suspended particles also greatly affect flash photography underwater. To know when suspended particles will be at their lowest concentrations, you must learn about the weather and biological activity in the bodies of water in your area.

Absorption

When doing available-light color photography, one of the first things you will notice is that your pictures will have an overall blue or green cast. This is because of the selective absorption of sunlight by the water. Light coming from the sun consists of all the colors of the spectrum, but when the colors are mixed, the light appears white. Water acts as a filter and selectively absorbs some of the colors that make up "white light." Most of the colors that make up white light are absorbed by the time they reach 60 ft.; only the blue and green components of white light penetrate the water to any appreciable depth (see the accompanying diagram). If you want your photos to maintain all the colors you know are present, you'll have to do your photography close to the surface or add auxiliary lighting.

The combined effects of all the above factors point the way to one

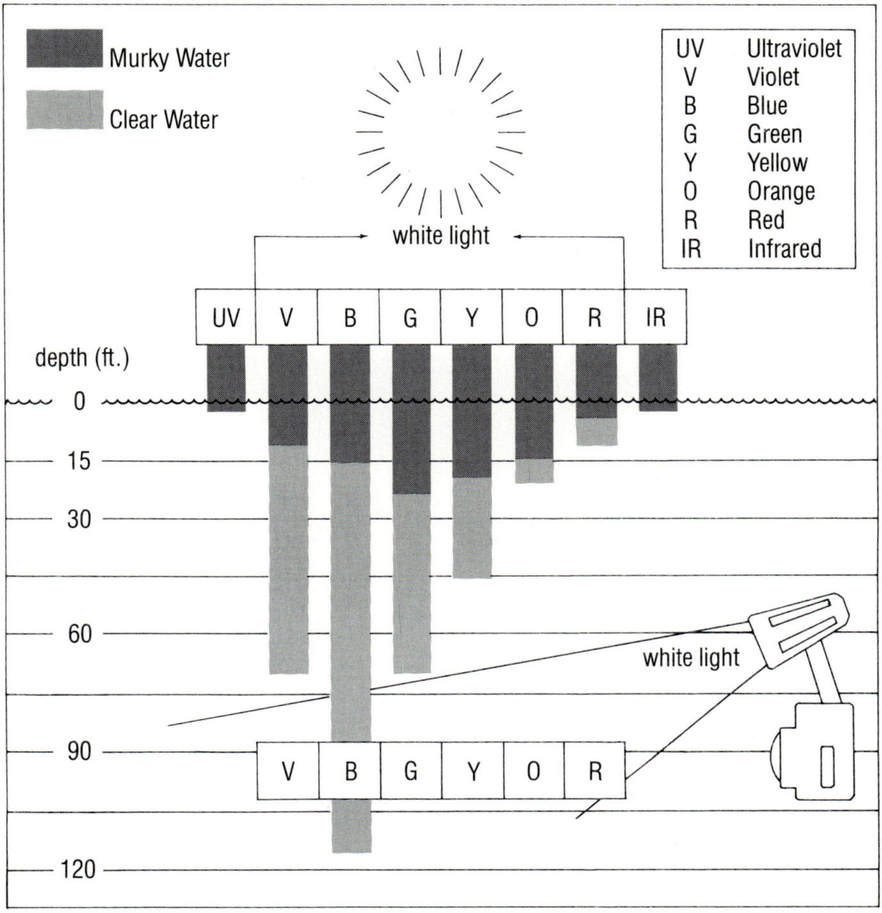

Water acts like a filter that selectively absorbs some of the colors that make up "white light." Selective absorption varies in different bodies of water: In clear water yellows may be seen as deep as 45 ft., while in murky water yellows are seen only to about 20 ft. To record colors underwater you must use auxiliary lighting.

of the most important things you can learn about underwater photography: The key to consistently good underwater pictures is to keep the distance between your camera and your subject to the very minimum. This reduces the amount of water through which light from your subject must travel to record itself on your film. Even in the clearest water, these four factors act, to a degree, and make it difficult to record sharp images with good contrast and detail. To get good contrast and detail, you will have to stay as close to your subjects as possible for the particular kind of picture you want. A rule of thumb for general underwater shooting is: Do most of your photography at distances within 1/5 of the limits of visibility. If the visibility is 100 ft., work between 0 and 20 ft; if the visibility is 10 ft., work between 0 and 2 ft.

Even in very clear water it is difficult to record images with good contrast at great shooting distances. Here visibility was about 100 ft. and shooting distance about 75 ft. For the photo on the opposite page, visibility was the same, but the shooting distance was only about 12 ft.

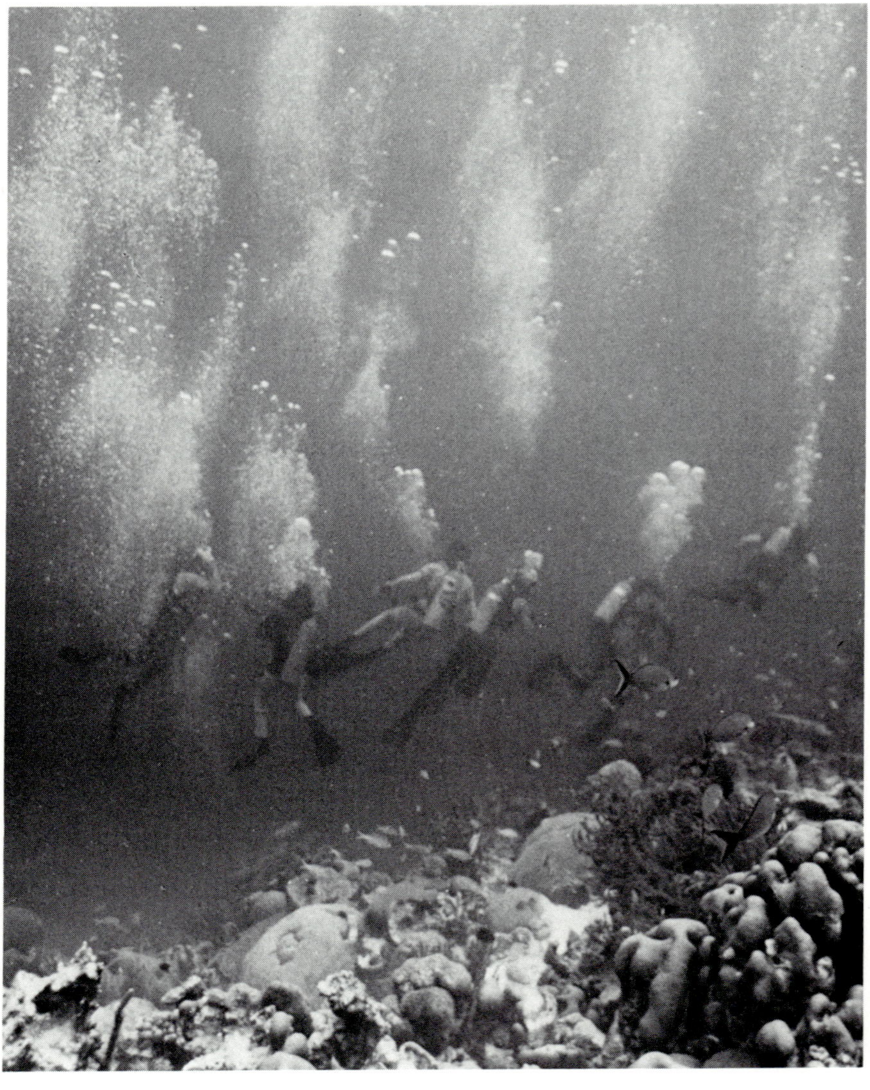

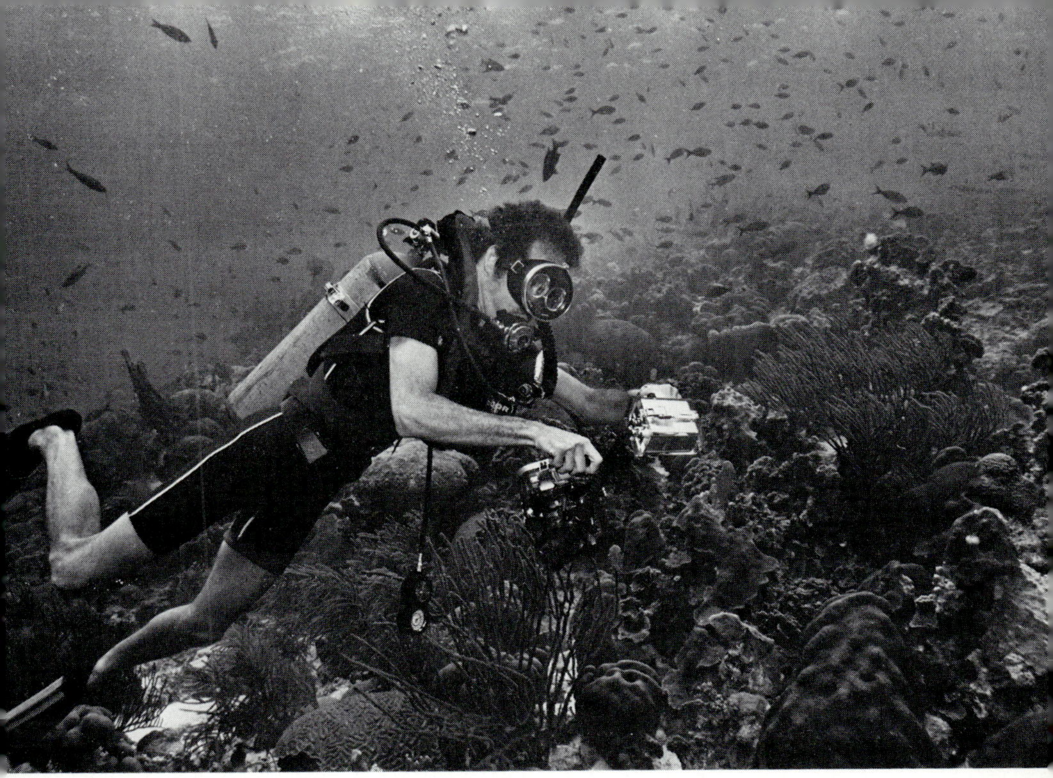

For best results keep camera-to-subject distance to a minimum. Here visibility was about 100 ft. and the shooting distance about 12 ft. Even in exceptionally clear water the closer you can get to your subject, the better your results will be.

EXPOSURE

Once you establish your working distance, one of your first concerns will be to determine proper exposure. If too much light reaches your film, it will yield prints and slides that are washed out and overly bright. If too little light reacts with your film, the result will be prints and slides that are too dark. Proper exposure is somewhat in-between. In properly exposed pictures, the intensity of the light in the image closely resembles the intensity observed in the original scene. For most purposes, properly exposed pictures are those which please you and most of the people whom you show them to.

Estimating Exposure

Estimating how much light is present in any given scene in air is difficult. Underwater, it is even more so.

In bright daylight, in air, exposures can be estimated by using the one-over-ASA method. Simply set your aperture at *f*/16 and set your shutter speed to the reciprocal (1/50 is the reciprocal of 50) of the ASA of the film you're using. For example, in bright sunlight, in air, with the films at the left, you could use the exposures at the right.

		Exposure	
Film Speed	Reciprocal	Closest Shutter Speed	Aperture
ASA 400	1/400	1/500	*f*/16
ASA 160	1/160	1/125	*f*/16
ASA 64	1/64	1/60	*f*/16

This method of exposure determination will yield a photograph which many people consider "OK," but by no means is it a way to get accurate exposures consistently. The method only works in bright daylight; when taking pictures on cloudy days or in open shade, you must make exposure adjustments. To determine the exact adjustments with any regularity is nearly impossible. Underwater, using the above method and making adjustments for depth and all the other factors that reduce light underwater reduces the accuracy of exposure estimating still further.

Measuring Exposure

Using an exposure meter is essential for getting consistently accurate exposures on land and underwater. The basic technique for using any reflection-type exposure meter (the type most often used underwater) is simply a matter of setting the appropriate film speed (ASA) on the meter, pointing the meter at the subject, and then aligning a dial or pointer with the indicator needle. When this is done, you will have a selection of shutter-speed and *f*/stop combinations that will yield correct exposure.

When measuring the light reflected off subjects near the surface, your meter needle may waver over a range of exposures because of surface ripples or chop. For good exposure, average the readings and use the average setting or a setting between the average and lowest light level.

As you go deeper, the amount of light will stabilize, but it will still change should passing clouds block the sun. Deeper still, and your exposures will not vary with fast-changing surface conditions, but of course light values will fall as the sun approaches the horizon.

For accurate exposures, you must meter the portion of the total picture that is most important. Get as close to your subject as possible for metering, set the appropriate shutter speed and *f*/stop on the camera, then move back to compose and take your picture.

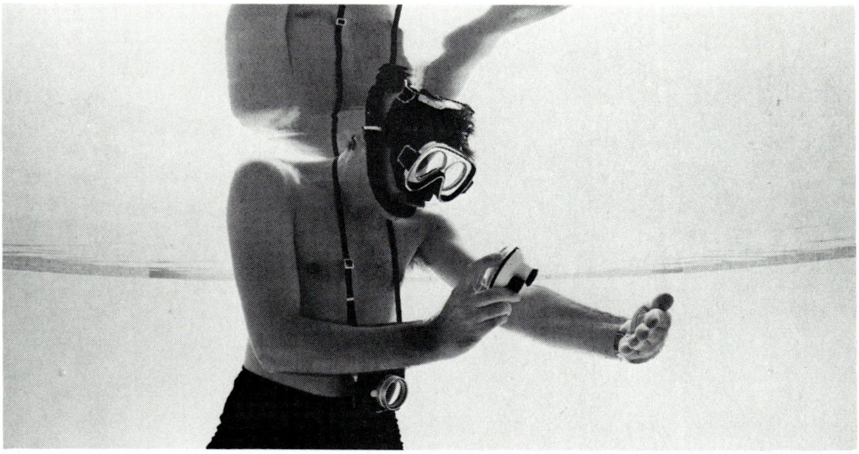

When using the substitute-metering technique, be sure the reflectance of the substitute you meter matches the reflectance of your subject.

Whenever measuring the light off an overall scene, again measure the most important parts and try to avoid having the meter influenced by a sandy bottom or the bright surface of the water. Try to be aware of the angle of acceptance of your exposure meter and aim it to measure what you want it to.

You can use a substitute metering technique when you can't get close to your subject. For example, you can meter the reflectance of your hand if you're photographing people in bathing suits, but you can't expect to get good exposures if you measure the light from a bright object near the surface and then photograph dark subjects 30 ft. below the surface.

Getting close to your subject and measuring the light coming off it is the best way to get accurate exposures. Bracketing (taking an extra shot that is one *f*/stop over the measured exposure, and then taking another one *f*/stop under) will help you get *perfect* exposures consistently.

The best place for your exposure meter is firmly attached to your housing or accessory tray. Special pieces of hardware designed to hold different exposure meters are available commercially and are a good investment. Attached with a bracket, you'll always know where your meter is. Attached to the end of a line, a negatively buoyant meter will be bumping into your other equipment or dragging along the bottom. On the end of a line, buoyant exposure meters usually wind up pointing toward the surface for long periods of time. If yours is a cadmium-sulfide type meter, it may give a false reading when you use it because such meters "remember" the bright reading of the surface.

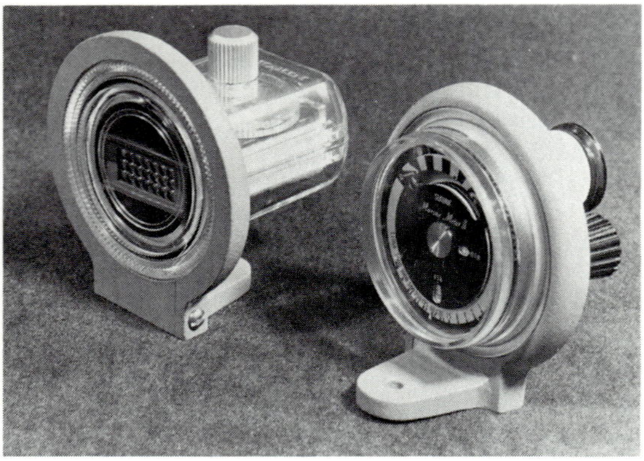

These meter brackets are made by Oceanic Products. The Sekonic meter in the housing (left) is available from Nikon. The Sekonic Marine Meter II (right), a self-contained exposure meter that can be used to 200 ft., is available from Copal.

Color Balance

In addition to proper exposure, try to attain "proper color balance" when using color films. Proper color balance in a picture means that the color values approximate the actual color values in the scene photographed. Proper color balance is a very subjective thing because colors are perceived differently: What one person calls "greenish," another may call "bluish." Proper color balance in any scene, though, is what most people call "correct." Skin tones are the areas to check when looking at a picture to check color balance; almost everyone can agree when skin tones are "off."

When films are manufactured, they are balanced to yield "correct" color values when used with specific kinds of light. Daylight-type film, also called outdoor film, is color balanced to yield pleasing results when exposed to sunlight; other types of film are matched to other light sources and are called indoor films. Blue flashbulbs and electronic flash both emit light that closely matches the color qualities of daylight, so they can be used with daylight-type films.

Any kind of film, indoor or outdoor, can be color balanced for use with any kind of light source simply by using different filters to provide the color rendition desired. When filters are used, though, exposure compensations must be made because filters reduce the amount of light reaching the film. Underwater, daylight-type films are the kind most commonly used because they can be used without filters even though natural light underwater is more blue than the natural surface light for which they are balanced.

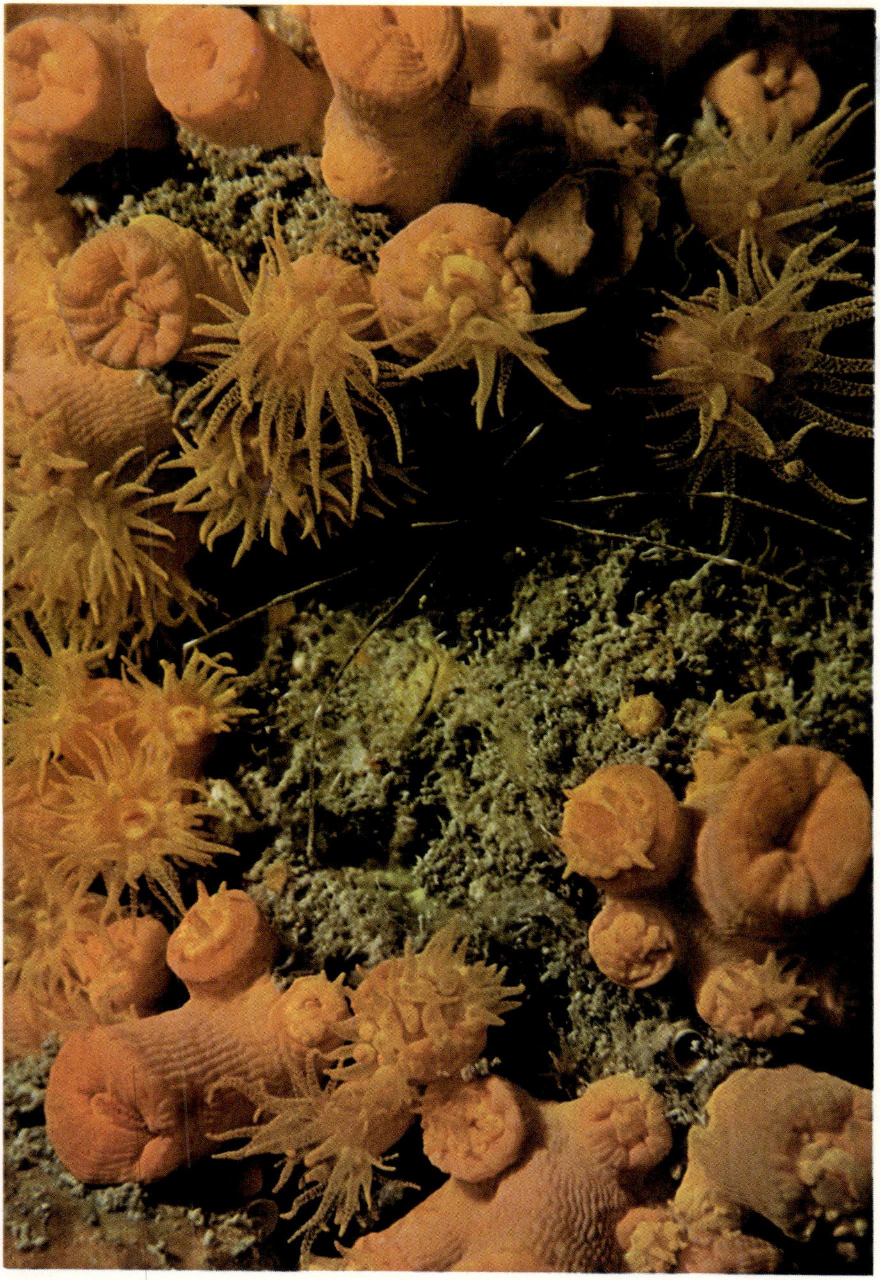

The Caribbean orange coral, above, was photographed in the waters off Bonaire in the Netherland Antilles with a Nikonos III, the 80mm lens, and the Nikonos Close-up Outfit. Close-up photography can provide the diving photographer with whole new subject areas to explore.

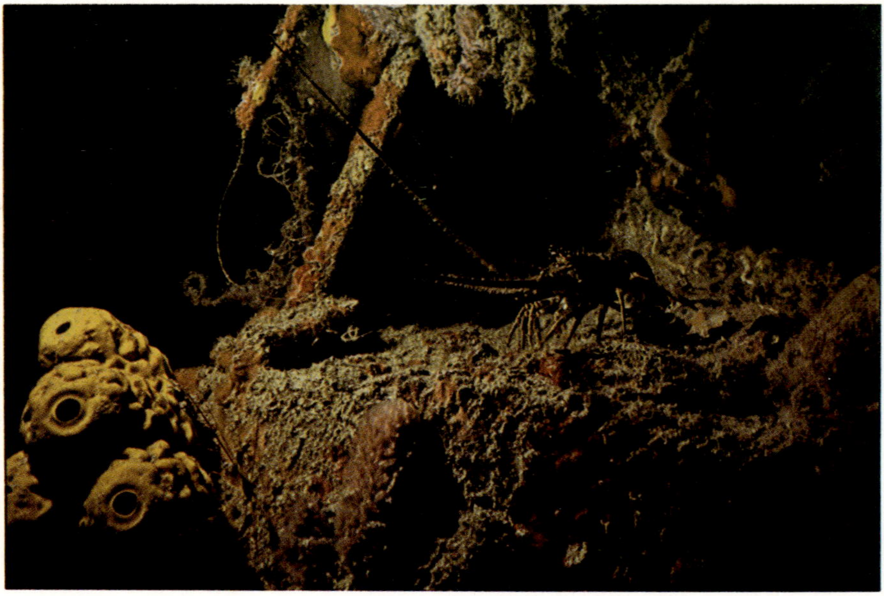

Removing your flash or strobe from your camera, and holding it far to the side or even behind your subject, can create shots like the above photo of a juvenile spiny lobster. Direct frontal lighting is illustrated below in the photo of an oyster drill on a boring sponge. At the right, in the same picture, is another cold-water species of sponge, red finger sponge.

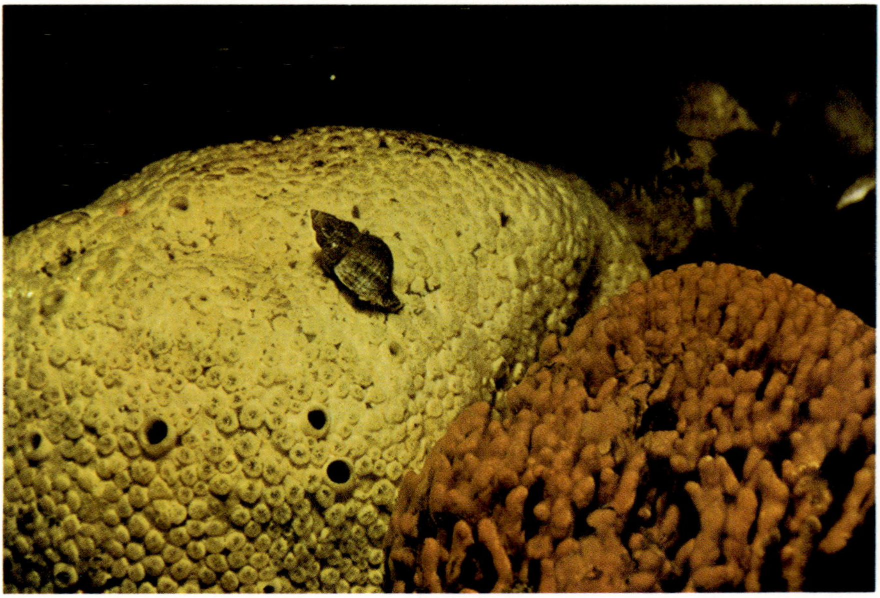

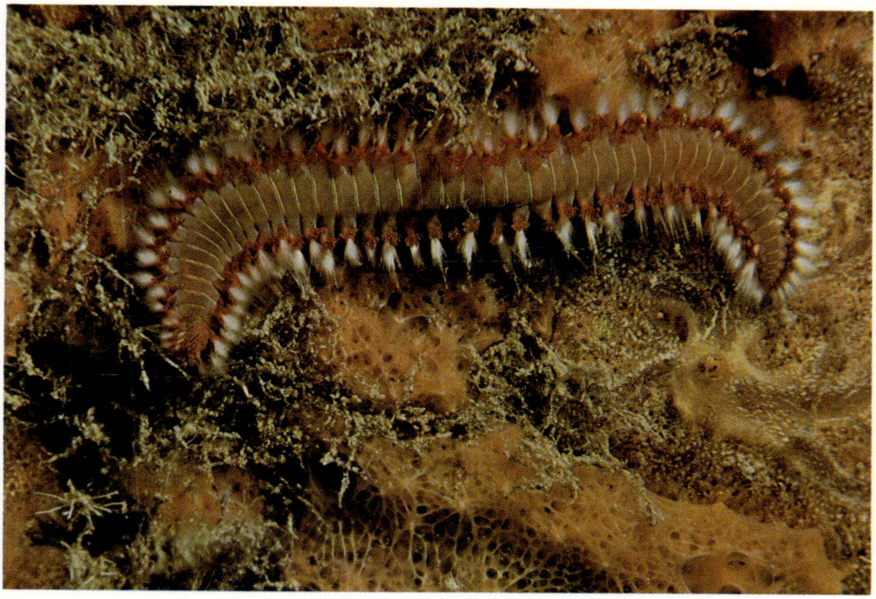

This harmless-looking fireworm, above, can leave many of its poisonous bristles in unprotected skin. Wearing gloves underwater will permit you to handle different creatures without fear of getting bitten or stung. Below, two juvenile spotted drums glide by purple sponges. Patience pays underwater; wait for all the elements in your viewfinder to arrange themselves the way you want.

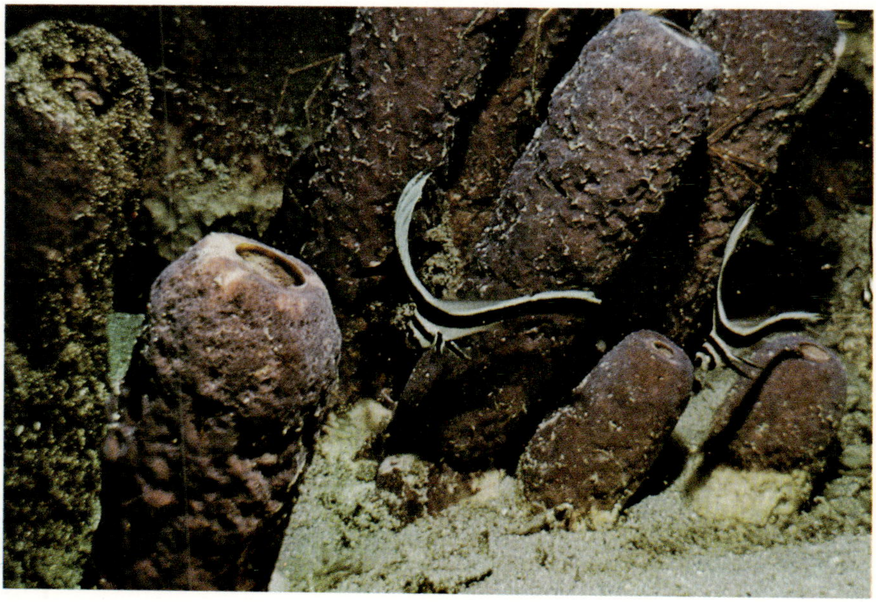

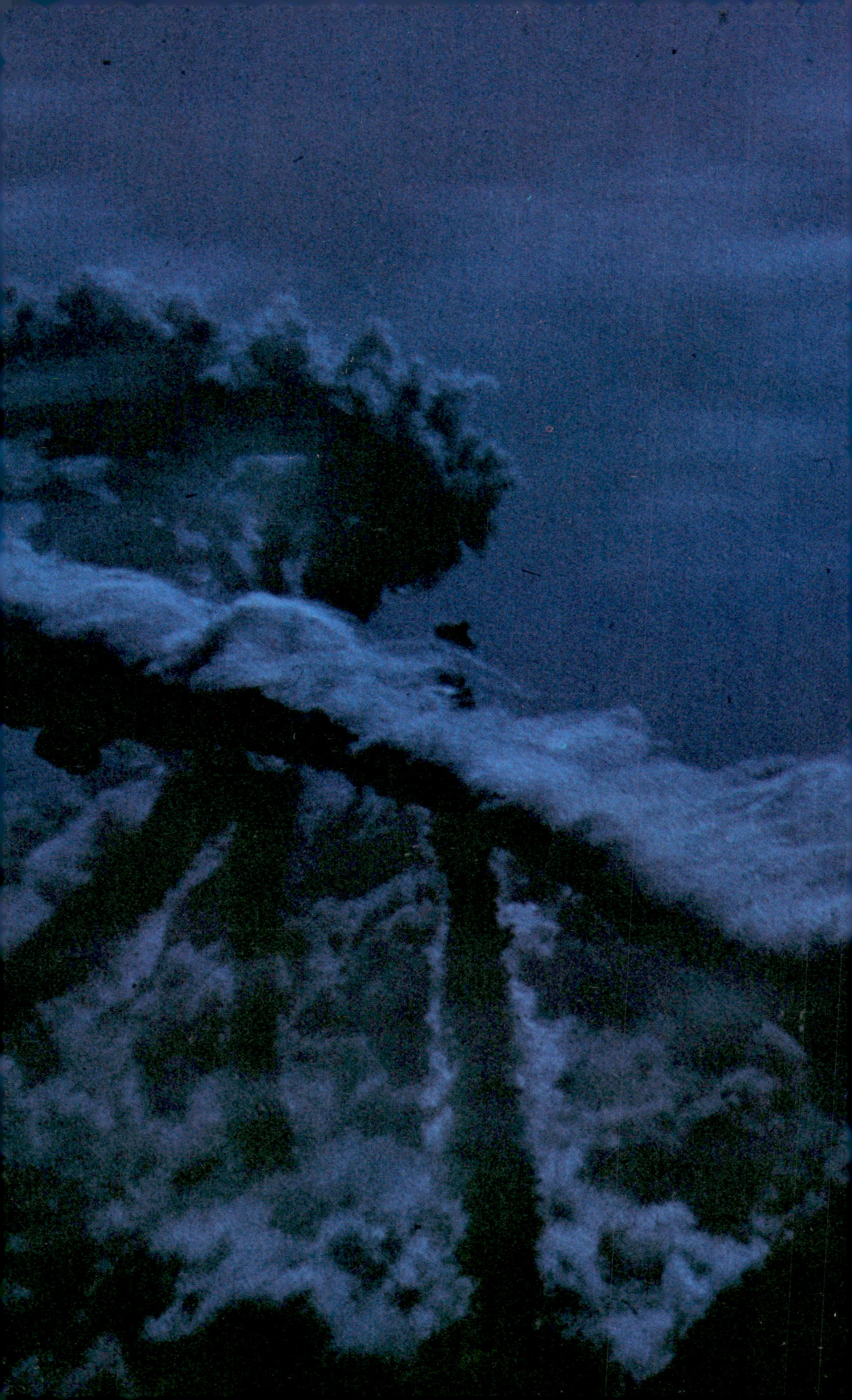

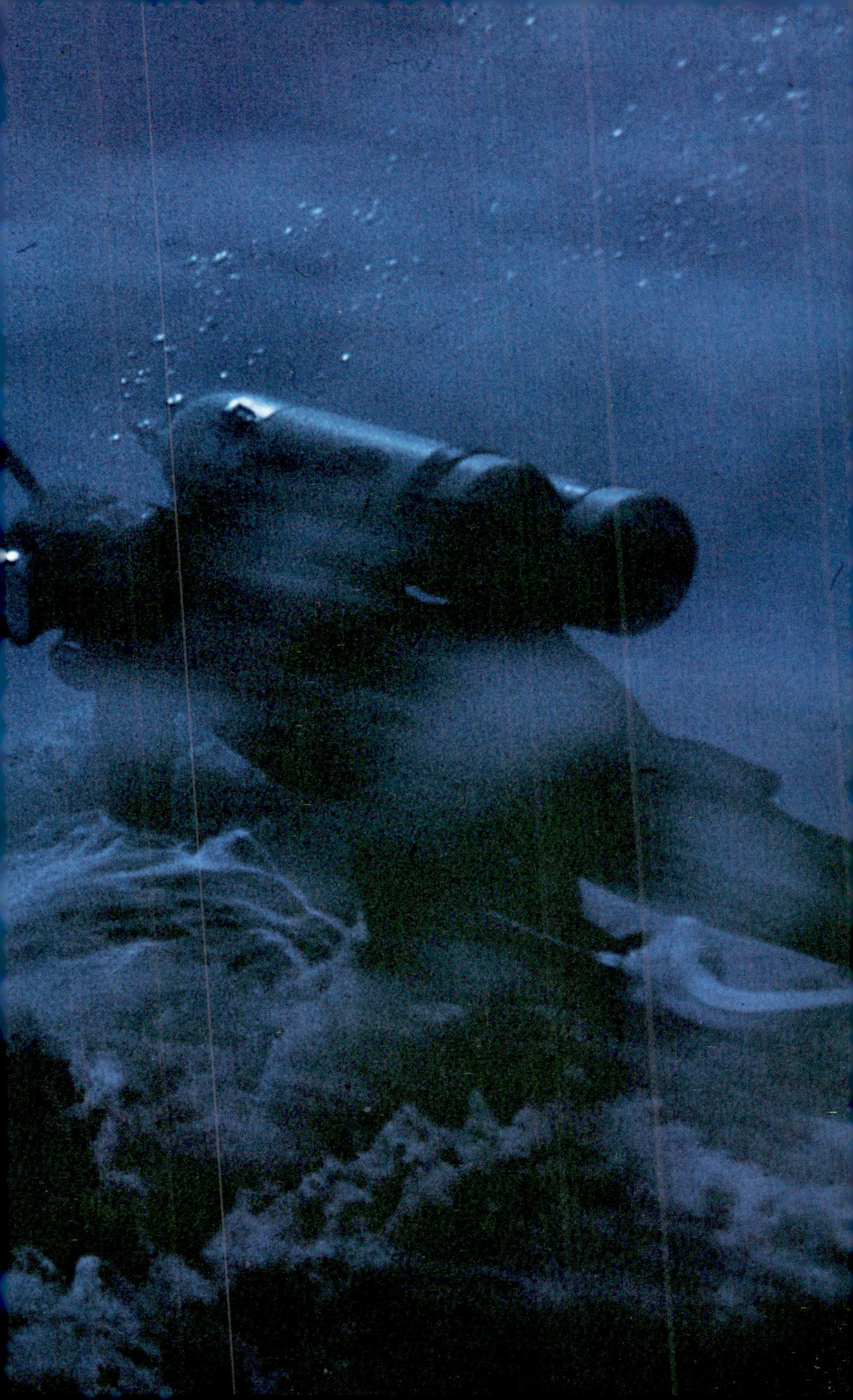

Light Underwater

◀ Using only available light can create photos like the one on the previous spread. Available-light photos reveal the true nature of the underwater world. The picture was taken at 90 ft. on the wreck of a German transport sunk during WWII off the north coast of Crete.

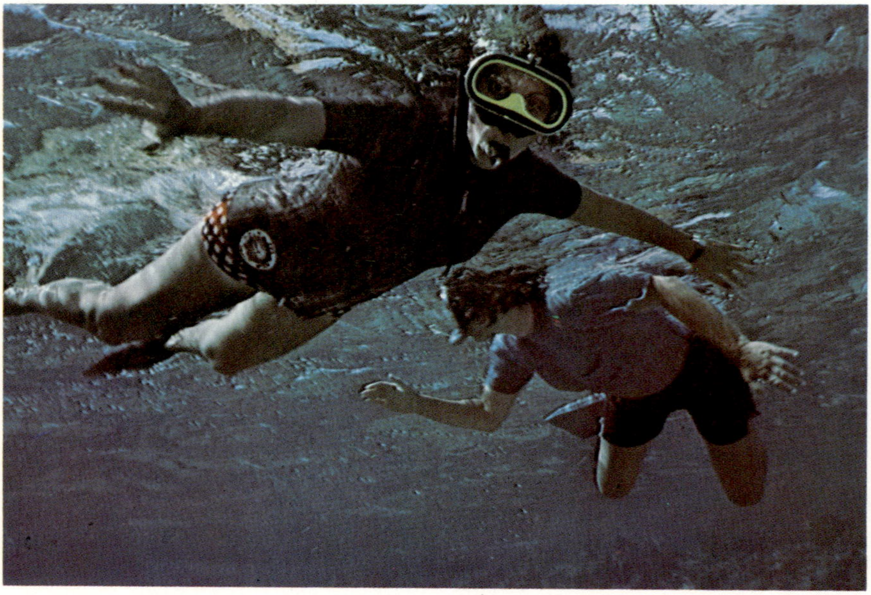

The difference in the water quality in the photo above compared to the one below illustrates why one set of underwater guide numbers and exposures can't be used in all locations. Above—near Buck Island, St. Croix, U.S.V.I. Below—near Montauk Point, New York.

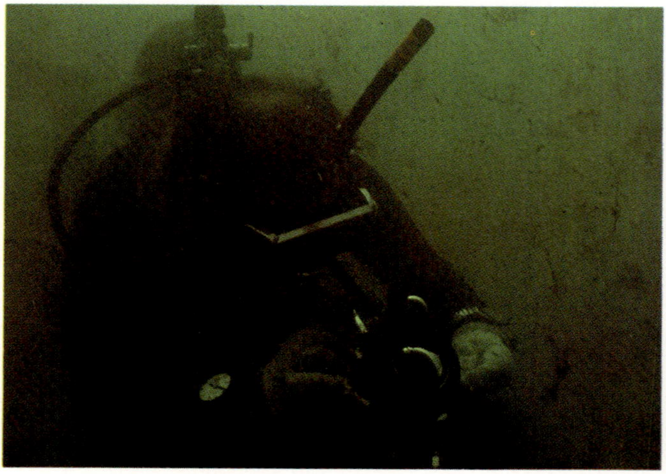

Close-Up Photography

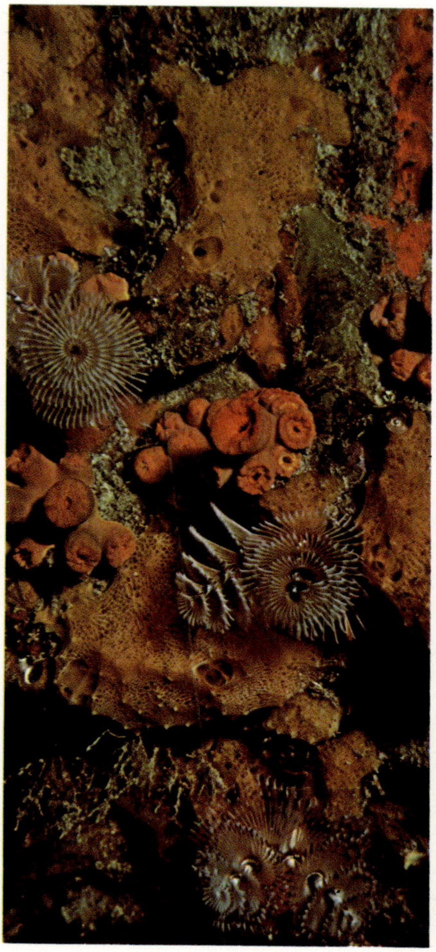

◄ Sponge

◄ Feather duster worms (opened)

◄ Caribbean orange coral

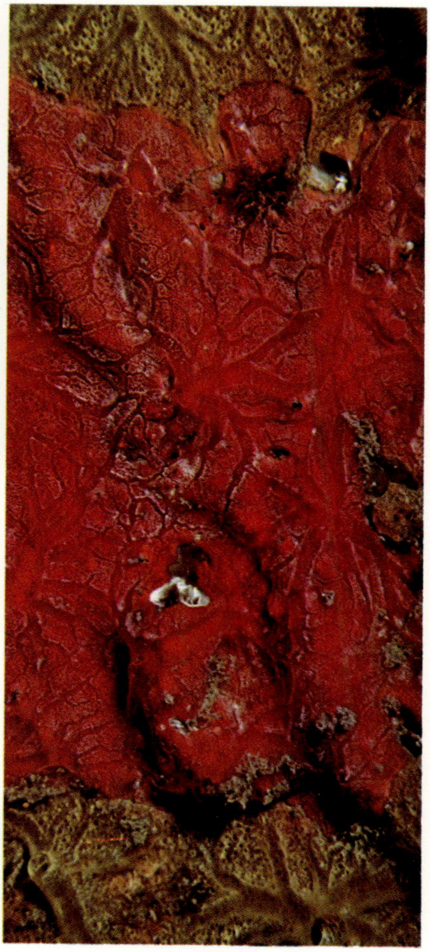

Feather duster worms (closed) ►

Piers and pilings in tropical waters are often not considered worth diving, but for a photographer interested in close-up work, they provide a wealth of potential subjects.

Species Behavior

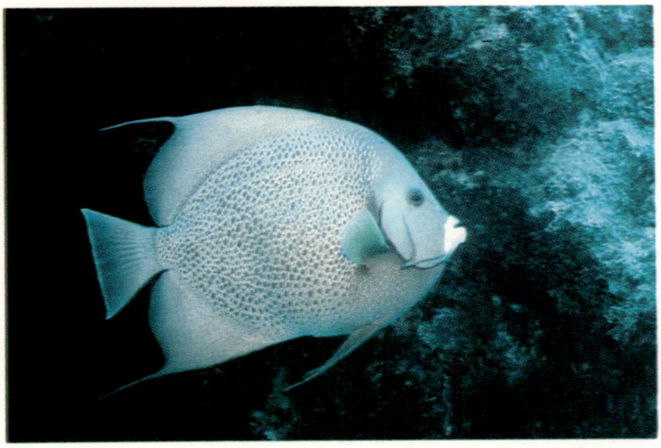

Some fish are naturally curious, so getting a picture like the one above of a gray angelfish is simply a matter of waiting for the fish to come to you to look you over. Many crustaceans, like the banded coral shrimp below, will not flee when approached slowly. Crustaceans in general are easy to photograph. Beau gregory juveniles, like the one at the right, are shy and retiring creatures. Getting a photo of one requires watching the animal's movement about its bit of coral, noting where it regularly appears, focusing on that spot, and then waiting for it to make its appearance again.

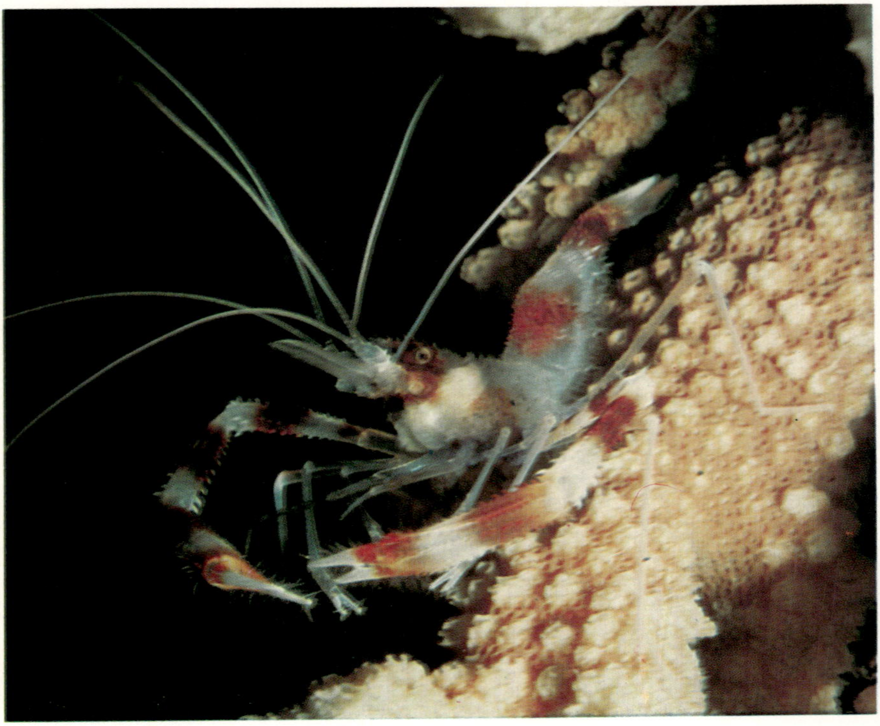

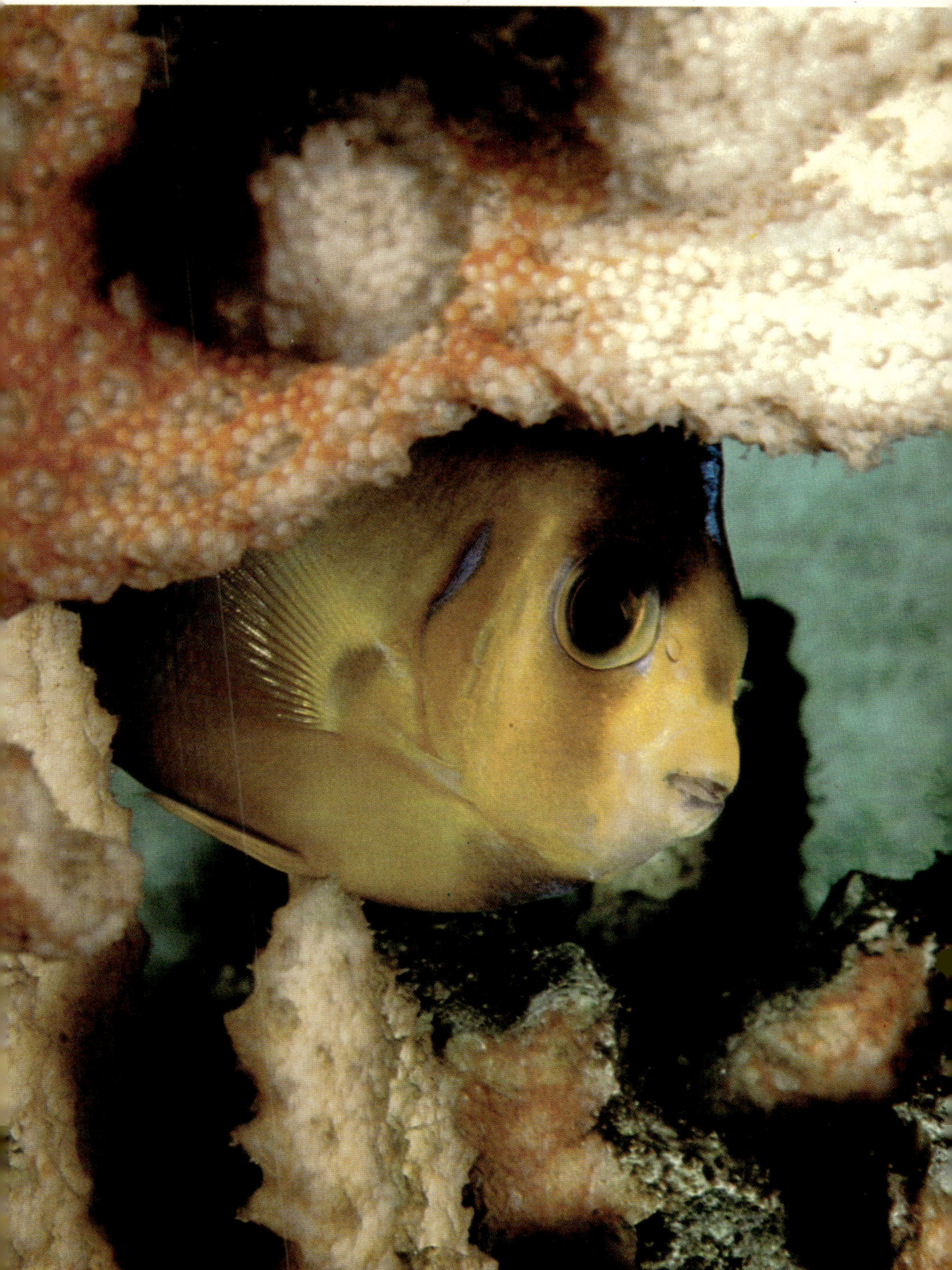

Camouflage

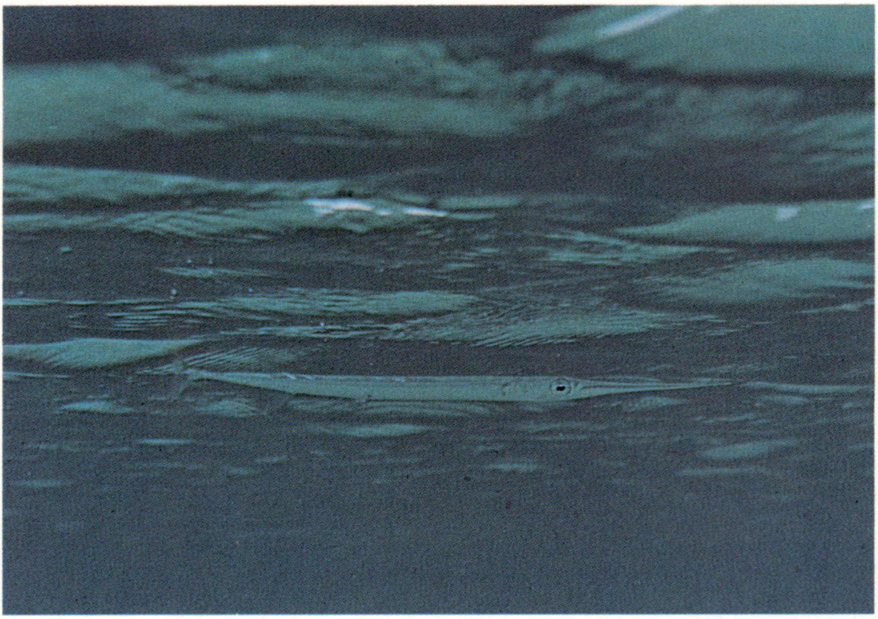

The houndfish, above, hides perfectly in the reflections near the surface as it waits for unsuspecting prey. The peacock flounder, below, blends naturally with whatever bottom it rests on, and completes the hiding process by tossing bits of sand onto itself.

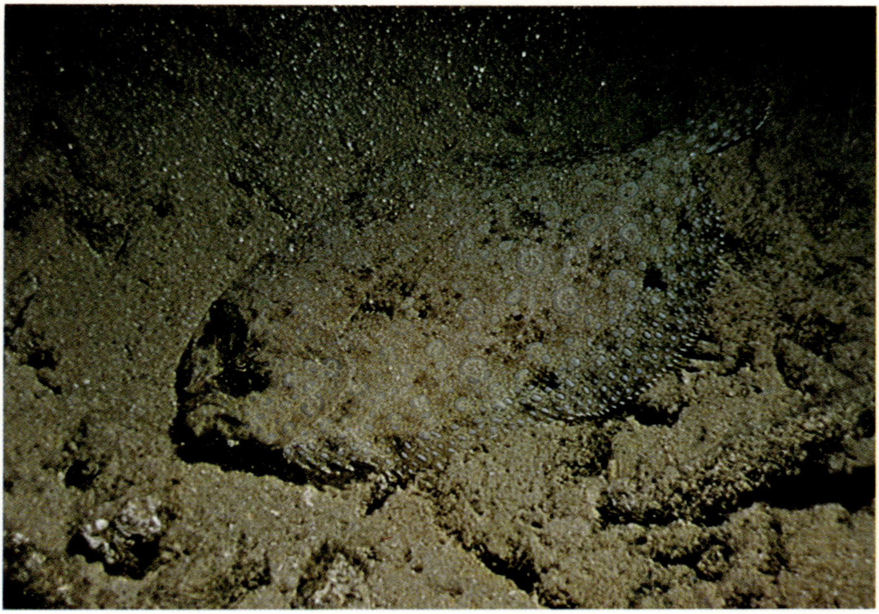

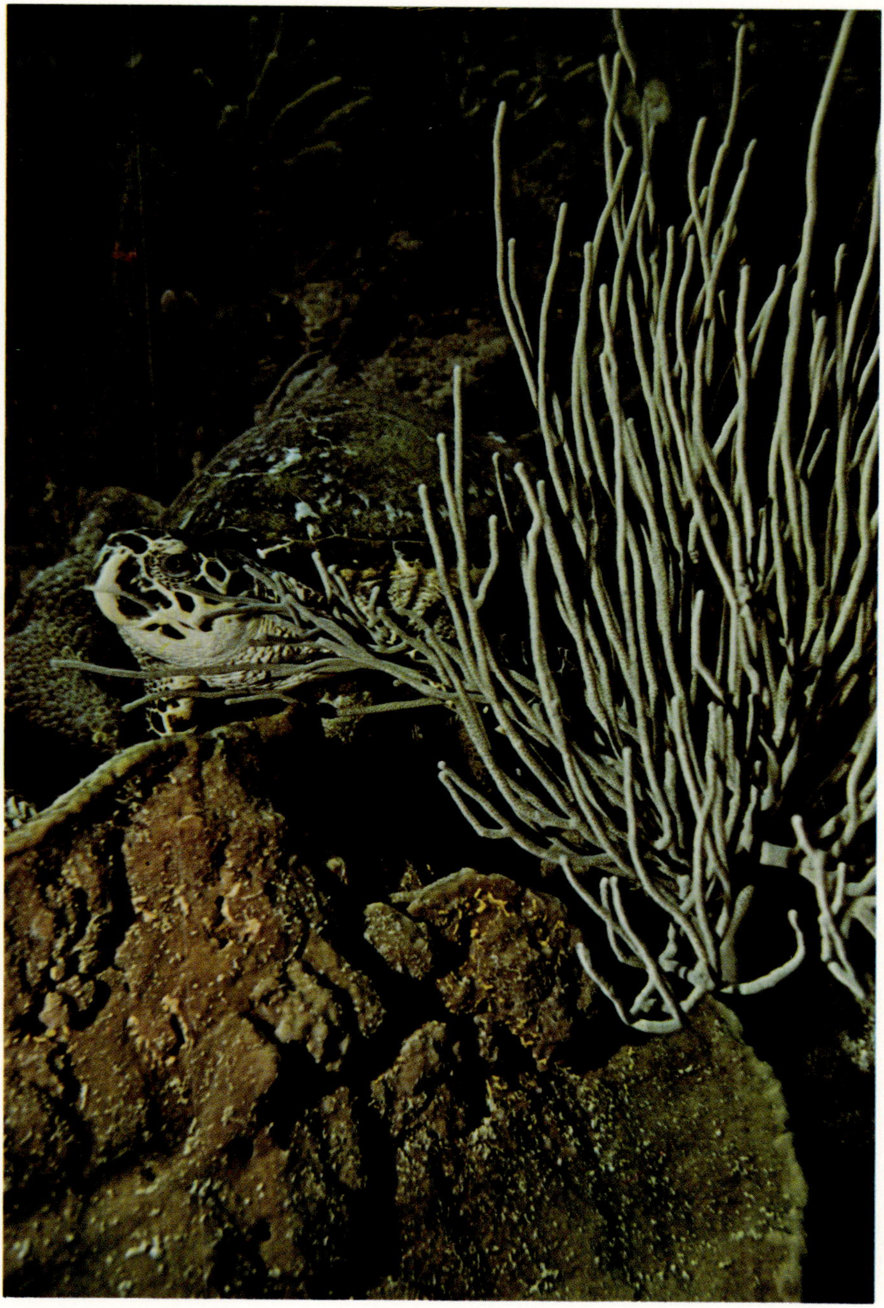

This green turtle went unseen until the photographer was almost on top of it. Did the turtle just happen to stop to rest near the branching soft coral at its right? Note the pattern on the animal's skin and its similarity to the pattern created by the coral.

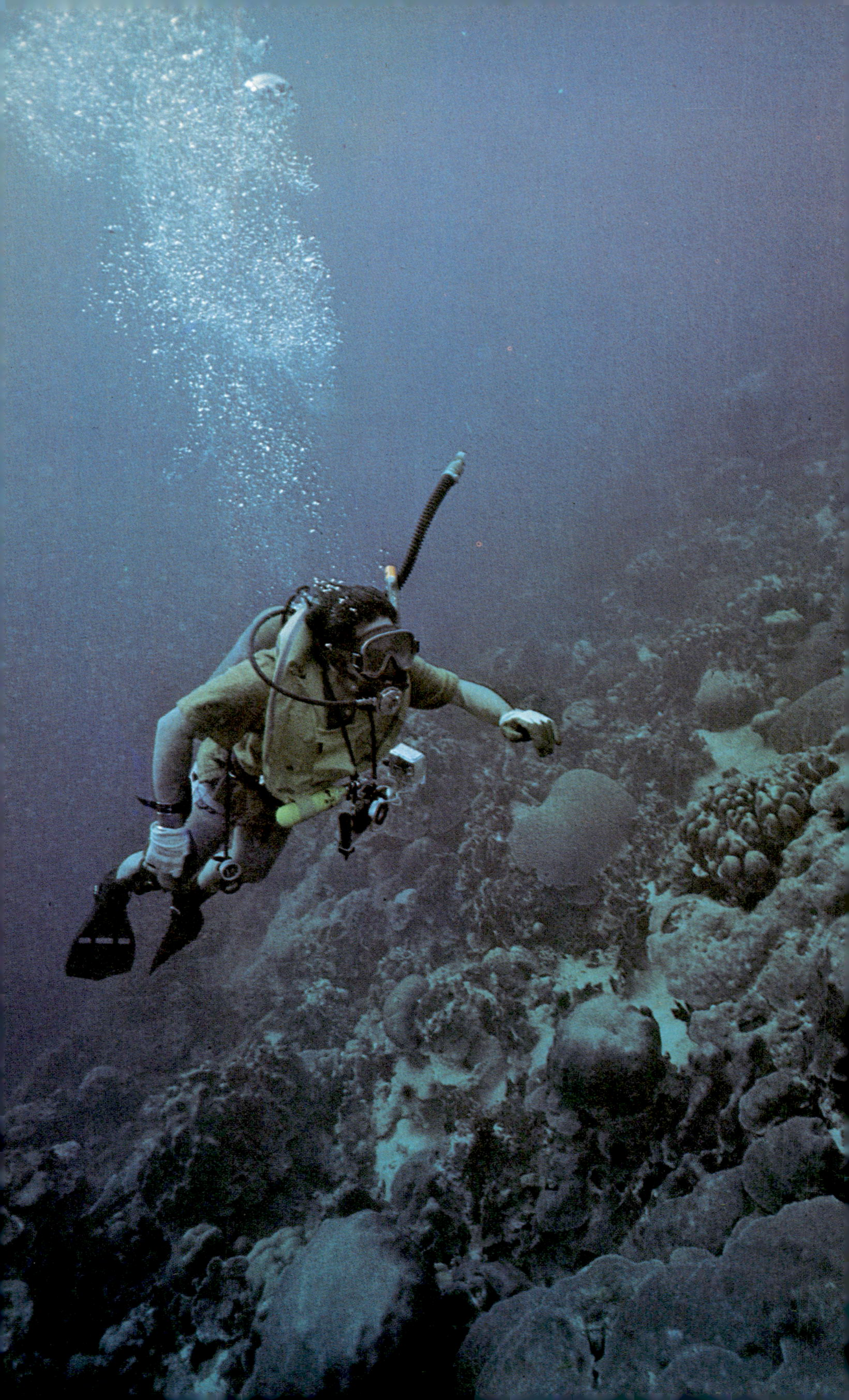

SELECTING FILM

There are many daylight-type films that can be used underwater, but often photographers get into the habit of using one or two films and staying with them. Learning about, *and trying*, different films, though, will enable you to select the "right" film for any given circumstance. For specific applications, one kind of film will often yield far superior results than another.

Before you select a film, think about how the final product will be used. If you want to show slides, use a reversal film. If you hope to sell your work and have it published, shoot reversal film also because transparencies are what most editors prefer to see. If color display prints are what you want, use a color negative film.

Reversal Film (Slides and Transparencies)

For color photography underwater, reversal film is the first choice among most divers. It is a direct-positive film, meaning that the film used in the camera becomes the final slide, or transparency. No negative is produced, therefore no image quality is lost with intermediate steps. Because of the direct process, reversal film is the cheapest film to use—even cheaper than black-and-white if enlargements are made.

Reversal films are also popular because they are available in a wide variety of film speeds. Reversal films can be purchased that range from a slow ASA 25 (Kodachrome 25) to a fast ASA 500 (GAF 500). Between these extremes are many ASA 64 films (Kodachrome 64, GAF 64, Agfachrome 64, and Kodak Ektachrome-X), an ASA 160 film (Kodak Speed Ektachrome), an ASA 200 film (GAF 200), and an

Even though you shoot color reversal film, you can have a conversion made if you occasionally want a black-and-white print. The original Ektachrome-X transparency was taken at about 60 ft. off Bonaire.

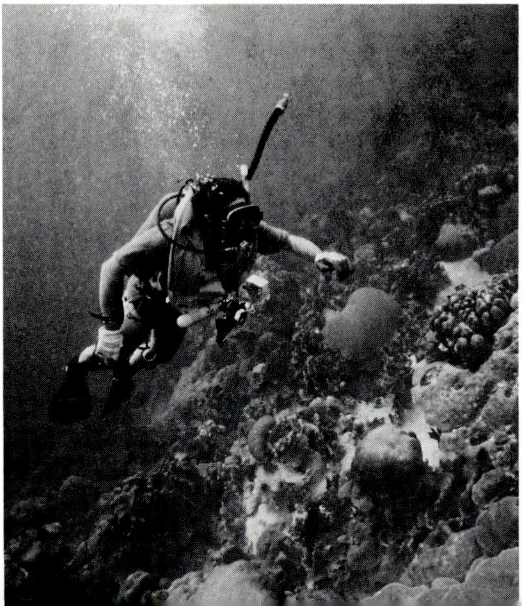

ASA 400 film (Kodak High Speed Ektachrome—pushed). The wide selection makes it easy to choose the right film to use for the amount of natural light available, or to choose the film for the best results with any size electronic flash unit.

All reversal films have very little latitude, meaning exposures must be close to perfect or very poor images will result. Most reversal films yield poor results if exposures are off by more than one-half *f*/stop. Because reversal films are so unforgiving, they are good to use when making tests to determine exposures with flashbulbs or electronic flash. When the results of a test on reversal film are lined up next to each other, it is easy to tell which exposures are correct.

The Kodachromes, GAF films, and Agfachrome tend to yield colors that are a bit warmer than the Ektachromes—a good feature for films used underwater where much cooling of tones takes place. But the Ektachromes have two advantages over the other reversal films: Exposure compensations can be made when they are processed, and they can be processed at home. This makes it possible to develop one or two rolls from a vacation shooting, process them normally, inspect the results, and then process the rest of the film to compensate for the desired increase or decrease in exposure. However, this will work only if you were consistent in your exposures from one roll to the next. Ektachrome exposures can be varied 1½ *f*/stops over and under the film's normal ASA (ASA 64 for Kodak Ektachrome-X and ASA 160 for Kodak High Speed Ektachrome) in one-half *f*/stop increments.

Color Negative Film

The selection of color negative films is not as wide as with reversal films, and the film speeds available are clustered around the ASA 80–100 range. However, good results can be had with Kodacolor II (ASA 80), Kodak Vericolor II, Type S, (ASA 100), GAF Color Print Film (ASA 80), or Agfacolor CNS Color Print Film (ASA 80).

Exposure latitude with color negative film is fairly wide, depending on the specific film, and in most cases, a usable print can be made from a negative that is over- or underexposed by an *f*/stop or two. Overexposed negatives are easier to work with than underexposed ones.

Processing your own color negative films is the best way to ensure that you get the most out of your underwater shooting. Color negative film can, of course, be processed commercially, but unless you use a custom lab, fair results are the most you can expect. By printing your own negatives, you can shift colors to achieve the balance you want.

Should a print be "too blue," you can make it warmer by controlling the filtration at the enlarger.

Black-and-White Film

Using black-and-white film underwater with available light can yield results that closely approximate what divers see. The blues and greens usually encountered lend themselves to representation on the gray scale of black-and-white film.

Black-and-white films offer, by far, the greatest choice of films and the widest range of film speeds than the other types of films, including films that can be used in almost any kind of light. If you do close-up work and have plenty of light (big flashbulbs or a powerful strobe), Kodak Panatomic-X (ASA 32) is excellent and extremely sharp. If you work with very little ambient light, Kodak 2485 High Speed Recording Film (as high as ASA 8000) can get you the negative you want. Between these extremes are many other films. Some of the more popular ones are: Kodak Plus-X (ASA 125), GAF 125 (ASA 125), Ilford HP-4 (ASA 400), Kodak Tri-X (ASA 400).

Black-and-white films have wide exposure latitudes, meaning that if your exposure calculation is incorrect, you still have a chance of getting a usable image from the exposure. Even with exposures that are one or two full *f*/stops over or under the correct exposure, an image will be deposited on the film. How usable that image is will depend on what is done in the darkroom and your personal standards of acceptance. Keep in mind that overexposed negatives are always easier to work with in the darkroom. If you're unsure about an exposure, you'll be better off if you overexpose a bit.

Black-and-white film can be home-processed easily, and doing so is the best way to achieve exactly the results you want.

Processing and Pushing

No matter what film you choose, and no matter how carefully you expose it, all can be for nothing if you do not handle the exposed film properly. As soon as the film comes from the camera, it should be placed back into its film can and stored cool until it can be processed. In the tropics, store the exposed film (sans cans) in plastic bags with desiccant packets to avoid the possibility of fungus forming. In either case, process the film as quickly as possible after exposure for best results.

Don't take chances with your investment in time, money, and equipment by using second-rate processors. Have your film processed by the film manufacturer, a competent custom lab, or do it yourself. Many films can be processed in home darkrooms, and doing your own processing will give you complete control over every phase of image production. Setting up a home darkroom is neither difficult nor expensive. Home processing will also give you the opportunity to try manipulating your images for special effects. High contrast, bias relief, and solarization are just some of the effects you can try when you have your own darkroom. (See Appendix C for a list of helpful books.)

Doing your own processing, or using a custom lab, also makes it possible to "push" film. "Pushing" film is a way to increase its light sensitivity by exposing it at a higher-than-normal film speed (ASA) and then compensating for the exposure increase by varying development times and temperatures. The Ektachromes and most black-and-white films can be pushed, but as sensitivity increases, image quality decreases. By rating a film at a higher ASA, you will be able to record an image, but the image will not be as good as other images made with another roll of the same film and exposed at its normal ASA. The same applies for films that are not pushed. Low-speed films, in general, are extremely sharp; Kodachrome 25 (ASA 25) and Kodak Panatomic-X (ASA 32) can be greatly enlarged with little image deterioration. High-speed films such as Kodak Tri-X (ASA 400) and GAF 500 (ASA 500) tend to be less sharp and grainy, and they do not enlarge as well as the lower speed films.

FILTERS

As mentioned earlier, the water you dive in acts as a filter. It passes more light of its own color to your film than any of the other colors that make up white light. In water that is essentially blue, more blue light will reach your film than any of the other components of white light. Filters help your underwater photography by creating contrast and improving color balance.

Filters work in the same way as the water, passing light of their color while "holding back" others in varying degrees. How much light of a particular color is held back depends on how close in the color spectrum the other color is to the color of the filter. For example, red filters will pass more yellow light than blue light because yellow is closer to red on the color spectrum. Nothing is added when filters are used; more of one kind of light reaches the film than others, but overall, the total amount of light is reduced.

Another factor that will affect how filters work underwater is depth. Since the components of light will vary at different depths because of absorption, so will the effect of any particular filter.

Filters and Color Film

Near the surface with color films, you can restore some of the reds lost through absorption by using a red filter, such as Tiffen's CC30R. The CC30R filter is the type most commonly recommended, but any of the CC (Color Compensating) red filters can be used, depending upon the amount of correction desired. Going deeper underwater, a magenta-yellow correction filter, such as Seacor's Sea Filter IV, creates a pleasing color balance.

Color photography illuminated by electronic flash (see Chapter 5) can be improved with a warming filter, such as Tiffen's 81A. By placing the filter over your flash, some of the yellow light from the strobe, filtered out by the water it must pass through to reach the subject, appears to return, and a warmer balance is attained.

Filters and Black-and-White Film

With black-and-white films, filters can be used to create the contrast that is lost because of diffusion and absorption underwater. Near the surface, contrast can be created by using a red or an orange filter, such as Nikon's R60 or O56. This will cause the red or orange portions of your subject to be lighter on your final prints than if no filter were used. Going deep with these filters diminishes their effect since no natural red or orange light is present to pass to the film.

Yellow filters, like Nikon's Y48, can create contrast deeper underwater in much the same way they create contrast in air. By passing yellow light and holding back blue light, contrast is created. In the final print, light-colored subjects will stand out against darker backgrounds. In air, blue skies can be darkened with yellow filters; underwater, blue water backgrounds can be darkened too.

Blue filters, like Nikon's B2, work the opposite way the yellow filters do. By passing the blue light of water backgrounds and holding back light from brighter colored subjects, prints will show a lightened background against which a darkened subject will appear.

When using filters, you must think about what they're doing. On a typical dive, you could easily encounter situations that would call for different filters; no one filter is good in all situations.

Almost every filter you use will reduce the amount of light that reaches your film. For proper exposure, you will have to know exactly how much light is lost because of the filter and then make an equivalent exposure increase by selecting a wider aperture or slower shutter speed, or both. Filter manufacturers supply exposure-increase information with their products.

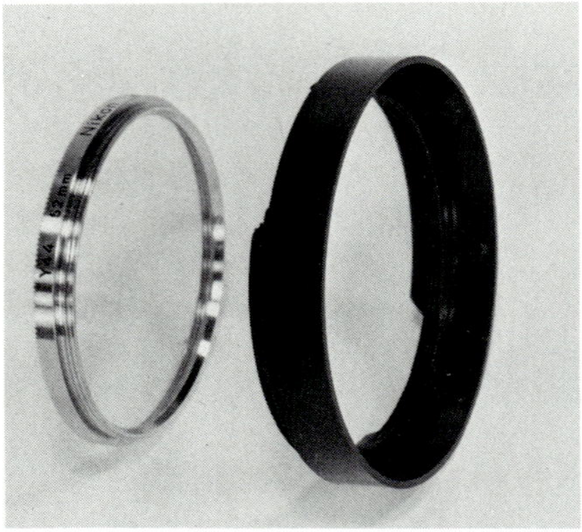

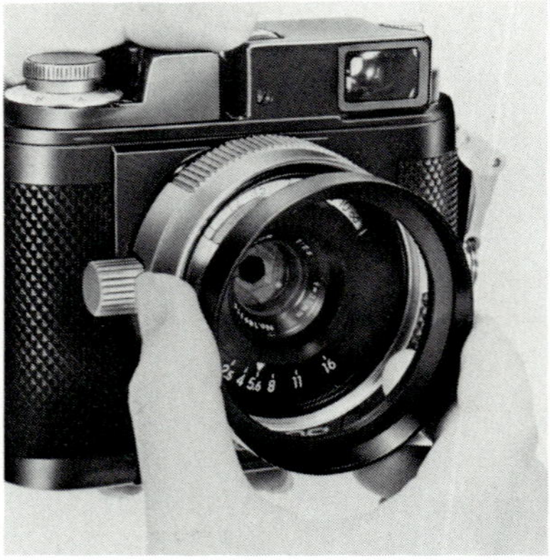

The Nikonos screw-in lens hood accepts 52mm filters. Filters are screwed into the back of the lens hood (left) and the hood, with filter in place, is screwed into the lens barrel (right).

Mounting Filters

The Nikonos lenses (except the 15mm) accept 58mm screw-in filters directly on their lens barrel. These filters should be placed on the lens while underwater to ensure that water is permitted to enter the space between the filter and the lens. An air pocket between the filter and the lens will cause distortion and at depth it could cause the filter to break because of the pressure differential created.

The Nikonos lens hood/filter holder accepts 52mm screw-in filters. With the filter in the holder, the assembly can be mounted on the lens in air because water can flow between the filter and the lens. Most of the Nikkor in-air lenses accept 52mm filters—a point to consider if you have a Nikonos and another Nikon camera.

Kodak manufactures many different filters in 2-in. square gelatin sheets. Cutting round filters from the sheets and then attaching them to the back of the Nikonos lenses with tape or silicone grease is an inexpensive way to use filters, but the process is risky. Silicone is messy and extremely difficult to remove if it gets onto the lens, and should the cut-out filter come away from the rear of the lens and work its way back to the shutter, a costly repair bill could result.

4

Flashbulbs Underwater

Beautiful photographs can be obtained using only available light, but at some point in your underwater picture-taking career, you will realize the need for auxiliary lighting. Available light, in the quantities you need, may not always be available. But the most important factor that will start you thinking about auxiliary lighting is color. Because colors are partially absorbed as light passes through water (as the diagram on page 59 shows), blues and greens will be the only colors your film will record unless you add light.

From a practical standpoint as an underwater still photographer, you can add light to a scene with either flashbulbs or electronic flash. Which one you choose is a matter of specific needs. Here are some questions you should ask yourself when trying to decide whether to use flashbulbs or electronic flash:

How serious are you about underwater photography?

How many flash pictures will you be taking?

How much money do you have for an initial outlay?

If you expect the majority of your work to be available-light photography, or if you've a limited amount of money to invest in underwater lighting, flashbulbs are probably your best bet. If you're dabbling in underwater photography, you definitely should choose flashbulbs.

The advantages associated with using flashbulbs underwater are:

1. The low initial cost of a unit.
2. The ability to vary light output by bulb selection.
3. Exposure control through shutter speed selection (with FP bulbs).
4. Color control through clear or blue flashbulb selection.
5. High light output per unit of weight.
6. The units are compact and simple.

Some of the disadvantages associated with using flashbulbs are:

1. The continuing high cost of flashbulbs.
2. Slow loading and unloading of bulbs underwater.
3. The bulkiness of many bulbs while traveling and diving.
4. Bulb disposal problems.

Some of the above points will mean more to you after reading the rest of this chapter and the following chapter on electronic flash. More important, talk with as many diving photographers as possible and try to use both types of lighting before you decide the best type for you.

Should you decide on flashbulbs, you will find that ounce for ounce, the amount of light that a bulb can deliver is unbeatable. Tiny "peanut" bulbs pack enough light for close-up photography, and big focal-plane bulbs deliver the most light a diver can easily take underwater.

THE NIKONOS FLASHBULB UNIT

One of the easiest ways to bring light to your underwater photography is to use the Nikonos Flash Unit. The unit is attached to the camera with a specially designed bracket that is held in place by the connector, which electrically links the camera with the flash unit. The lightweight bracket rotates so that the flash unit can be used in an infinite number of positions. When desired, the flash unit can be withdrawn from the bracket's clamp and used "off camera" to produce dramatic side- and backlighting.

The Nikonos Flash Unit is of the BC type, which simply means that a battery *and* a capacitor are part of the circuit that fires the flash. BC circuits offer greater reliability than battery-only circuits because the firing charge is stored in the capacitor. With the charge stored in the capacitor, the battery is drained gradually—only as it is necessary

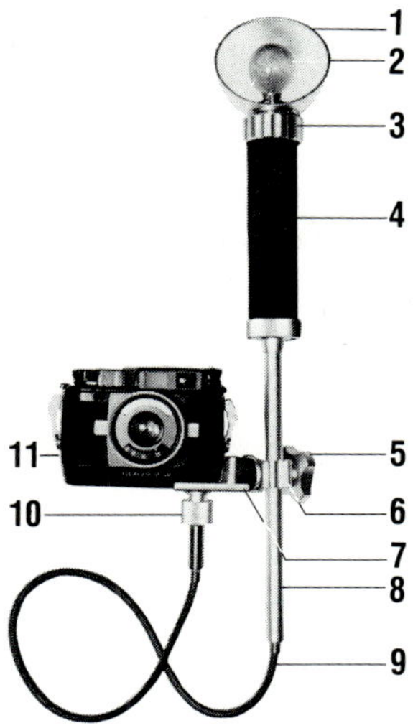

Nikonos Flash Attachment
1. Reflector.
2. Bulb.
3. Collar.
4. Hand-grip tube.
5. Clamp knob.
6. Clamp.
7. Bracket.
8. Cable sleeve.
9. Cable.
10. Connector.
11. Nikonos III.

to restore the capacitor. With battery-only circuits, the battery is subjected to periodic high-current drains each time the flash is fired.

The Nikonos Flash Unit uses a 22.5V battery (Eveready 412, Mallory M-505, or equivalent) and a 200 MFD capacitor.

Installing the Battery

To open the flash unit to install the battery, turn the collar just below the reflector in a counterclockwise direction until it spins freely. When the collar is free, pull the battery holder out of the hand-grip tube. Place the battery in the chamber, checking to see that the positive (+) and negative (−) terminals are positioned correctly. Before installing the battery, wrap a piece of tape around it and form a tab with the excess tape. This will facilitate removal of the battery from the battery compartment's tight-fitting terminals.

The capacitor, in the chamber adjacent to the battery, is permanently installed on Nikonos Flash Units designed for use with the Nikonos III. The earlier-model flash units have replaceable capacitors, but these do not have to be replaced as often as do the batteries. Capacitors do deteriorate with age, though, and the ones in the earlier models should be replaced every couple of years.

Though flashbulbs can be fired with only a fraction of the voltage a 22.5V battery delivers, it is a good idea to begin any extensive amount of photography with fresh batteries. Of course, on any extended diving trip, you should have a spare. More information on spares and back-up systems and traveling with your equipment is given in Chapter 9.

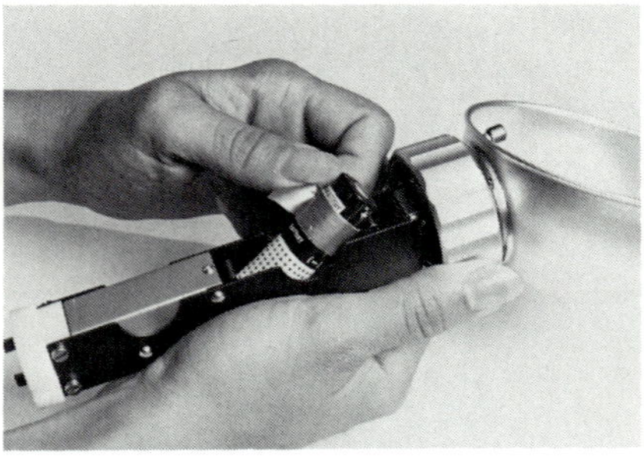

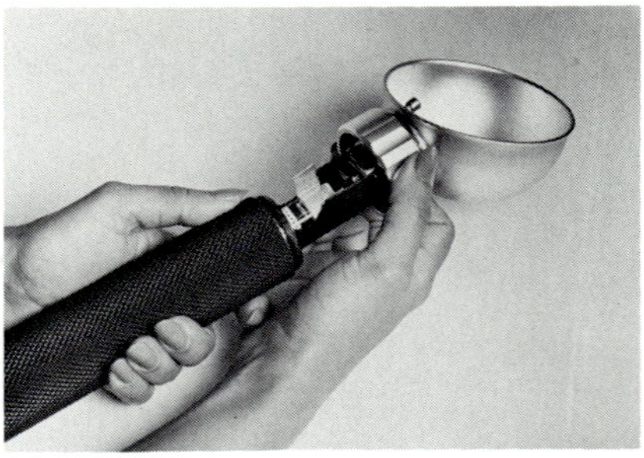

Insert 22.5V battery into battery chamber (left). Insert battery holder into hand-grip tube (right).

As with all battery-operated equipment, never leave the battery in place if the unit will be out of service for an extended period of time.

Replacing the Battery Holder

To replace the battery holder, slide it into the hand-grip tube and rotate it until the guide pin at the base of the tube slips into the opening at the bottom of the holder. When the pin is in position, press the holder inward and tighten the collar. Avoid applying pressure to the reflector; this could possibly damage the electrical connections in the flash head.

Mounting the Flash Unit

The first step when mounting the flash unit to the camera is to open the synch socket on the base of the camera. On the Nikonos II, the tripod socket doubles as the cover for the synch socket; on the Nikonos III, the cover is a single-function piece. In either case, use a coin in the slot provided and unscrew the synch cover counterclockwise. Immediately take the cover and screw it into the place provided on the clamp knob of the attaching bracket. Doing so immediately after removal from the camera will lessen the chance of losing this very important piece of the camera.

Attaching the Connector

To attach the flash bracket to the camera, position it on the camera base so that the white dot on the base of the camera appears in the notch on the bracket's attaching hole. Attaching the connector will vary slightly, depending on which model flash unit and camera you're using.

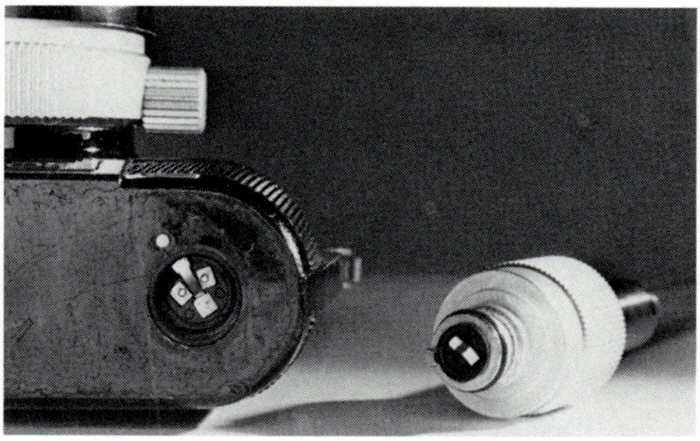

Earlier model Nikonos connector. The key on the connector makes contact with central (common) terminal. Left contact, FP synch; right contact, X synch.

Earlier models. One difference between the earlier Nikonos cameras and the Nikonos III is the connector socket in the base of the camera. Because of this design change, only the earlier flash units can be used with the earlier cameras. When using the Nikonos III, the current flash units with the newer three-pin connectors must be used.

To attach the earlier connectors, align the key on the connector with the recessed area in the body socket—the white dot is positioned over the recessed area as a guide. Next, push the connector into the socket. When firmly seated and square, begin screwing the connector collar into the camera.

Nikonos III. With the Nikonos III, align the groove on the connector with the projection in the socket—the white dot on the base of the camera is positioned over the projection as a guide. Next, push the connector into the socket. As with the earlier models, be sure the connector goes into the socket straight and that it is firmly seated before you begin screwing the connector collar into the camera.

If you encounter resistance when turning the collar, STOP. It is easy to cross-thread these two parts, so take your time while making this connection. Remove the connector and begin again if you have the slightest doubt about whether or not you've linked the two parts properly. When a Nikonos is flooded, the chances are 90 in 100 that carelessness in making the flash- (or strobe-) to-camera connection is the reason.

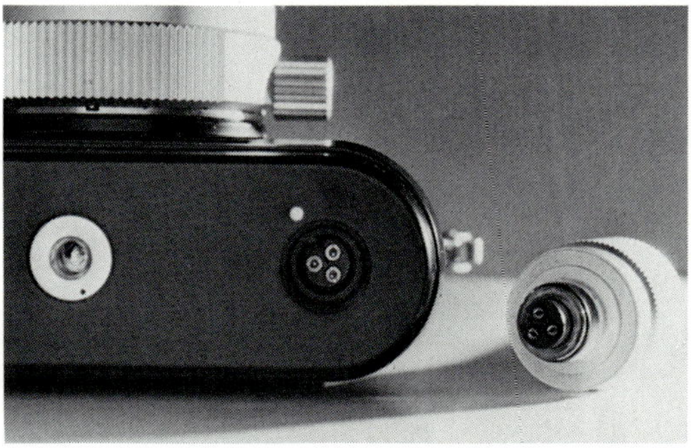

Nikonos III connector. The pin farthest from the index dot is the common terminal. Left pin, FP synch; right pin, X synch.

With the connector holding the bracket in place, screw the cable sleeve into the base of the hand-grip tube. The cable sleeve can now be slipped into the bracket's clamp and the flash unit placed in the desired position and angle. Tightening the knob secures the position and angle of the flash unit.

When adjusting the angle of the flash unit, be sure the clamp is loose enough so that the cable sleeve can turn freely in it. If the cable sleeve is forcibly turned into the base of the hand-grip tube, it is possible to damage the inner parts of the tube. When rinsing the camera and flash unit after use in salt water, be sure to unscrew the cable sleeve from the hand-grip tube to avoid salt deposits from forming in this area. Be sure to thoroughly rinse the flashbulb socket too.

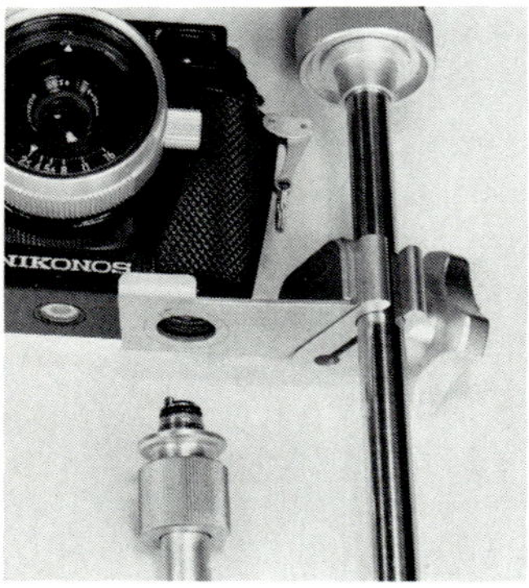

Align the connector carefully when inserting it into the camera socket. Screw the connector collar into the body of the camera slowly. Stop if you encounter resistance to avoid cross-threading.

Testing the Unit

With the flash unit mounted on the camera, now test the system. Currently, the Nikonos Flash Units are supplied with an accessory test lamp for that purpose. If you don't have a test lamp, don't wait until you're underwater to discover that your unit is inoperable. Waste a flashbulb to be sure your unit is working, or, if you have already loaded film in the camera, take a picture on the surface with flash.

To test the unit, select the appropriate shutter speed, place the test lamp (or flashbulb) in the socket, and release the shutter. The test lamp (or flashbulb) should light immediately if the flash circuit, connector, and battery are all in order.

Separating the Units

Before separating the flash unit and camera, thoroughly rinse them in tap water and let them dry. Immediately upon removal of the flash connector from the camera, replace the synch cover in the body socket. The synch cover *must* be in place if the camera is to be taken in the water without a flash or strobe connector attached. The camera will flood without it.

Synchronization

Though your flashbulbs will fire no matter what shutter speed you select, your shutter will only be synchronized with the burst of light at certain speeds. This is because of the mechanical workings of the focal-plane shutter and the duration and peak of intensity of the flash of light. The focal-plane shutter in the Nikonos consists of two curtains that sweep the film plane from top to bottom, the size of the opening between the curtains permitting the light reflected from the subject to fall on all or part of the film. In most cases, proper synchronization is simply a matter of opening the shutter curtains wide enough to coincide with peak intensity of the usually "short-duration" flash.

Focal Plane (FP) Flashbulbs

FP flashbulbs are made specifically for use with cameras with focal-plane shutters. FP bulbs have a "long-duration" flash (Note: The terms "long" and "short," when talking about the duration of a flashbulb's flash, are relative ones, the difference being only a matter of milliseconds.), which means they can be synchronized at shutter speeds from 1/60 sec. to 1/500 sec. with the Nikonos. Other class bulbs (M for medium-duration flash and MF for medium-fast) can only be synchronized at 1/30 sec. with the Nikonos because they reach their peak of illumination for a relatively short period of time. When these bulbs are used at speeds other than 1/30 sec., only part of the film frame will be exposed. Focal-plane bulbs are the preferred type of bulbs for use with the Nikonos, but they are more expensive than the other types, and they are sometimes difficult to obtain. M and MF class bulbs can be used, but using them will limit you to one shutter speed. Consult the accompanying chart to determine the shutter speed to use for proper synchronization with the class of bulb you're using.

The socket of the Nikonos Flash Unit accepts FP bulbs directly, but using other class bulbs will mean that an adapter will have to be

FLASHBULB SYNCHRONIZATION

Bulb Class	Typical Bulbs*	Shutter Speeds					
		500	250	125	60	30	B
M	M3, M3B, 25, 25B					●	
FP	6, 6B, 26, 26B	●	●	●	●		
MF	AG-1, AG-1B, M2, M2B					●	

* "B" following a bulb designation indicates "blue-coated."

used with them. Keep a supply of different kinds of adapters in case you find yourself in a situation where FP bulbs are unavailable. Any bulb will work for you, provided you're aware of the bulb's limitations and work within those limitations.

Blue Versus Clear

Once you've selected the type of flashbulb you plan to use, you must next decide whether to use clear or blue bulbs. In air, blue-coated bulbs are intended for use with daylight-type film because the light they yield is similar to daylight. In air, clear flashbulbs are balanced for use with indoor film, and since indoor lighting is generally "redder" than daylight, clear flashbulbs emit light that is redder than the light from blue flashbulbs. Underwater, the extra red of the clear bulbs tends to "warm" shots on daylight film taken at distances of 4 ft. to 8 ft. When used closer, the extra redness adds an overall cast that looks false—this is especially so in green water. For close shooting, blue bulbs will yield proper color balance with daylight film. At longer distances, it is generally agreed that the clear flashbulbs produce more pleasing results, though this might be considered improper color balance.

EXPOSURE

The universally accepted method of determining accurate flash exposure in air is by using the guide-number method. A guide number is simply a number assigned to a particular combination of film and light source. This number, when divided by the flash-to-subject distance, yields an *f*/number that will yield an acceptable exposure. For example, using ASA 64 film with 26B flashbulbs in air, synchronized at 1/125 sec., the recommended guide number is 75. At a flash-to-subject distance of 10 ft., the appropriate *f*/stop would be *f*/7.5—*f*/8 would be close enough.

$$\frac{\text{Guide Number}}{\text{Flash-to-Subject Distance}} = f/\text{stop} \qquad \frac{75}{10} = f/7.5 \qquad f/8$$

Remember, it is the flash-to-subject distance that is important. This distance is sometimes different for the camera-to-subject distance. Film speed (ASA) and light source are, of course, the most important factors that govern proper exposure, but other factors should be considered too—especially underwater. Some of these factors are:

Shutter-speed settings. When using focal-plane (FP) flashbulbs, guide numbers will change with the particular shutter speed you select.

With other bulbs, or with electronic flash, the shutter speed selected simply synchronizes the opening and closing of the shutter with the flash of light. But because FP bulbs have a "long" flash, the length of time the shutter is actually open determines (along with the *f*/stop) how much light will expose the film.

Equipment differences. All shutters vary in accuracy from camera to camera. On one camera, 1/125 sec. may actually expose the film for 1/125 sec., but on another, the actual exposure may be 1/100 sec. or 1/145 sec.

Reflector size. The size, shape, and finish of the reflector bowl of your unit will affect the quality of the light that falls on a subject. Highly polished bowls produce a harsher light than bowls with a satin finish. Large, shallow bowls diffuse light more than do small, deep ones.

Water clarity. From area to area, and from season to season, water clarity varies tremendously. Exposures during summers in the waters off New York City will be quite different from exposures off Bonaire at the same time of year.

With all these variables, some of which are completely beyond the control of the diver, it should be obvious that guide numbers derived under one set of conditions will not work universally. Published guide numbers and actual exposure settings supplied by equipment manufacturers can only give you a starting point from which to determine your own exposure information. You have to make a comprehensive test with your own camera and your own lighting unit in the water in which you'll be doing most of your work. Once you establish your own *personal* exposure information, you'll be on your way to consistently accurate exposures.

The Test Roll

With one roll of film, on one dive, you'll be able to make a test that will give you exposure information that should help you with all your future underwater photography. To make a meaningful test, though, you must keep an accurate record of exposures. Information such as surface light conditions, water clarity, film, and flashbulb type (or electronic flash unit) can be recorded in a notebook or log. It's a very good idea to keep a log of tests for ready reference when photographing under conditions similar to previous encounters. Information that will vary over the course of the test-roll dive should be recorded in the actual test frames. This can be accomplished by including in the frame a grease-pencil slate with flash-to-subject distance, *f*/stop, and depth. If you're using FP flashbulbs and varying shutter speeds, the shutter speeds should be noted too. If you're using an electronic flash unit with different power settings, the power setting should be noted.

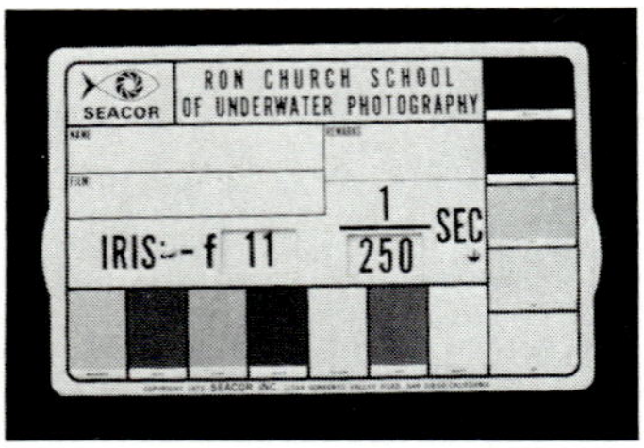

This test board by Seacor is ideal for testing film and equipment to establish your own personal guide numbers.

Ideally, the test frame will also include a color chart and a gray scale—both made by Kodak, but of cardboard. A test chart made by Seacor includes all of the above and provides an area in which to write variables, and it is large enough to include your constants if desired.

Including a diver in the test frames is a good idea too, to see how flesh tones are rendered. It is best to use transparency (slide) film for the test so there will be no darkroom "saves."

To begin your test, record your constants in your log, and then mark on your slate the depth, flash-to-subject distance, and your first *f*/stop (also record other variables if necessary). Begin with your widest aperture and make exposures at one *f*/stop intervals to your smallest aperture. Be sure to record the change in *f*/stops on your slate as you go. Make a series of exposures near the surface, a series at about 30 ft., and another series at about 60 ft. When your film is processed, evaluate the results carefully. (The ones that please *you* are accurately exposed unless you're thinking about doing professional shooting, in which case, you should seek professional advice.) Based on the results, establish your own *personal* guide number by working the previously mentioned formula backward, or simply make a chart that shows which *f*/stop to use at a particular distance.

Interpolation

Should you use a different film you should run a new test, but you'll be able to interpolate from your first test and get fairly accurate exposures. Doubling film speed (ASA) is equal to one *f*/stop more exposure. For example, if a test with ASA 25 film showed *f*/8 to yield a good exposure, changing to an ASA 50 would mean you would have to use *f*/11 for similar results (distance constant, of course). If your original test was on ASA 400 film, and *f*/16 gave a good exposure, going to an ASA 200 film would mean using *f*/11 for similar results. Going to an ASA 100 film would mean using *f*/8 (again, distance constant).

Bracketing

Even when you establish your own personal underwater guide numbers or exposure tables, bracketing your exposure is a way to ensure *perfect* exposure. Bracketing, as mentioned, is simply taking an extra shot that is one *f*/stop over your calculated *f*/stop and then taking another that is one *f*/stop under. Bracketing will help you compensate for the difference in reflectivity of a subject. Obviously, a black sea urchin on a dark rock will require more exposure than a light-colored fish on a sand bottom. Bracketing will also ensure your getting a usable exposure should your film speed vary slightly from the one stated, or should your film be processed somewhat incorrectly. Bracketing exposures underwater is not easy, but try to do it when you can.

Backscatter

Backscatter is a problem frequently encountered in underwater flash photography—a problem encountered in air only when taking flash pictures in a snow storm. Backscatter is characterized by bright spots of light that cover a scene and obscure the subject. Underwater, the spotting is caused by your flash or light reflecting off suspended particles into your lens. Particles, be they suspended debris or living planktonic creatures, are always present in all bodies of water. The number of the particles will vary with season and surface conditions and also with the type of bottom and the number of divers in the area.

To avoid their presence on your film, it is necessary to keep your light source away from your camera and to light your subject at an angle. Usually a distance of 18 in. and an angle of 45 degrees are sufficient. The idea is to avoid direct frontal lighting because with the flash close to your camera, it will bounce light off the particles right back into your lens. Lighting your subject from above and at an angle

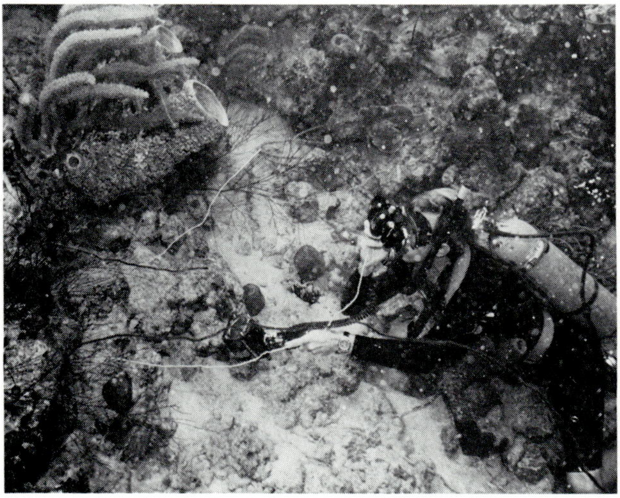

Backscatter degrades the quality of this photo. Note the light spots that cover it.

of 45 degrees to the side minimizes backscatter and creates natural-looking shadows.

You can further minimize backscatter by not disturbing bottom sediment in the area where you're taking pictures. If you know you will be working in an area where the bottom is easily roiled, you should move very slowly, and you might consider removing your fins.

Backscatter is more of a problem with flashbulbs than with electronic flash for two reasons: First, most electronic flash units have narrower angles of coverage than flashbulbs, therefore fewer particles are illuminated. Second, the duration of flash is much shorter from electronic flash units than from flashbulbs, therefore the particles are illuminated for a shorter period of time. If the particles are lit for a long period of time, they appear larger because of their movement during the exposure.

Carrying Flashbulbs Underwater

The problem of carrying around three dozen buoyant bulbs underwater can be solved in a number of ways. Keep in mind, though, that after you've used the bulbs, you'll want to be able to get them back into your holding device for later disposal. There is nothing more disconcerting than to be diving on a "virgin" reef and come across spent flashbulbs, or to walk "undiscovered" beaches littered with bulbs that have washed ashore.

Net bag. A net bag with a slotted, rubber top is a good solution to the problem of storing a large number of bulbs. The slot in the rubber top

Rubber strips (left) and net bags (right) can be used to carry flashbulbs underwater.

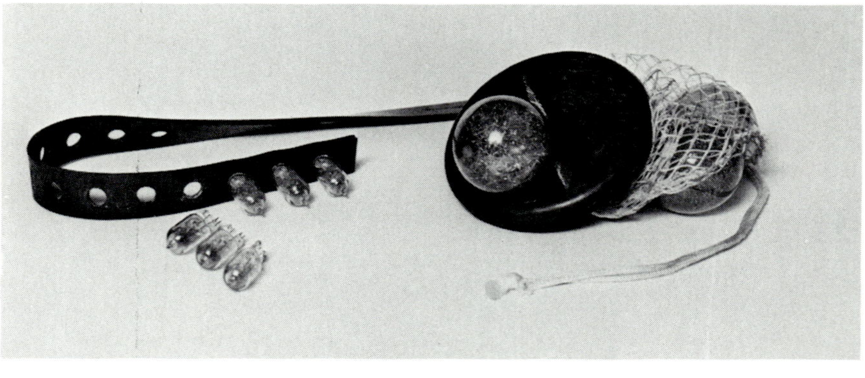

provides access to the bulbs but prevents them from floating away. Keeping track of the good bulbs versus the spent bulbs is a problem with this device, however, because most bulbs continue to float after they're fired—both good and bad bulbs will be around the access slot. AG bulbs are negatively buoyant, so they cannot be used in this type of carrier.

Rubber strips and panels. Another way to transport bulbs underwater is to make a strip or panel of neoprene or hard rubber and punch holes in it for the sockets of your flashbulbs. Just be sure not to make the holes too big, or the natural buoyancy of the bulbs will lift them from the holder as you dive. Compressed sheets of plastic foam (Styrofoam) can also be used in this manner. Strips, panels, and sleeves to fit around the Nikonos flash arm are available commercially.

Hints for Using Flashbulbs

1. Always wear gloves when handling flashbulbs underwater because bulbs break more often there than they do on the surface. Increased pressure causes them to implode. With flash units not equipped with a bulb ejector, it is difficult to remove the broken end of a bulb unless you're wearing gloves.

2. Whether you attach your bulb carrier to your wrist, belt, or on the flash arm of your unit, try to secure it in a way that will keep it from swinging in front of your reflector or lens while you're concentrating on your subject.

3. If, after a dive, you still have flashbulbs you have not used, wash them thoroughly, and just before your next dive, sandpaper or file the contacts clean to ensure a positive electrical connection.

4. Try not to be too startled the first time one of your flashbulbs implodes.

Flashcubes

Don't sell flashcubes short. They pack a great deal of light for their size and weight, and the fact that you can get four shots to one cube change is a great advantage. It means less bulk and less bulb changing. It also means you'll be able to take a sequence of four pictures (with artificial light) faster than by any other conventional method—even faster than electronic flash. No strobe unit on the market today can recycle as fast as a cube can turn for the next shot.

Flashcube holders for underwater use with the Nikonos are made by Sea Research and Development. Ikelite makes a flashcube holder and a BC flash unit, but they are both designed for use with housed cameras.

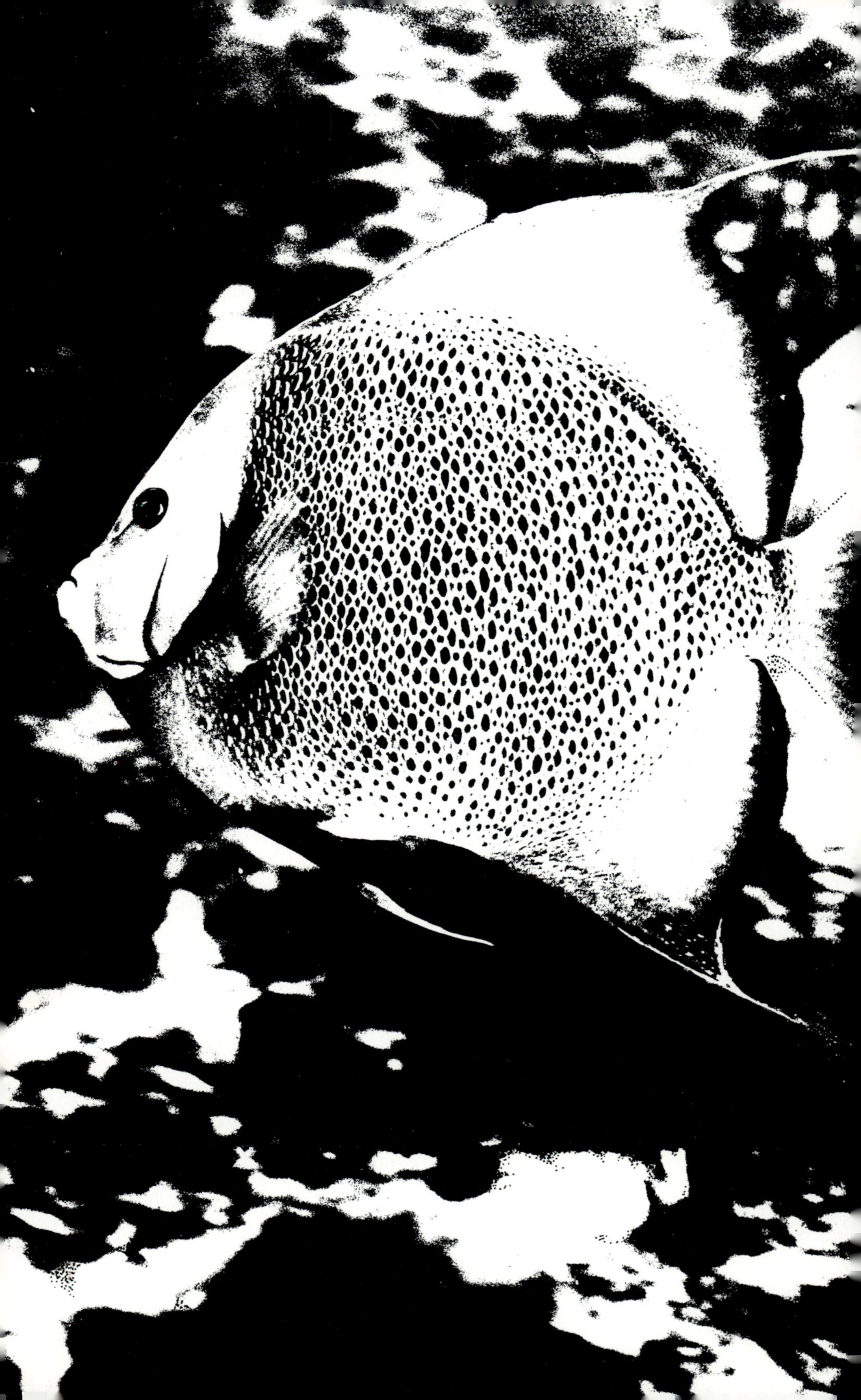

5

Electronic Flash Underwater

For the serious diving photographer, electronic flash units, also referred to as strobe units, are really the most practical solution for adding light to underwater photography. Two important reasons make this so: money and time.

Though the initial cost is high for most self-contained electronic flash units, the continuing expense for flashbulbs over a given period of time will eventually exceed that initial investment. What you must determine personally is how much flash photography you plan to do, and over what period of time, and then measure that against the specific pieces of equipment you're considering.

Time is an important factor because with electronic flash units you can take 36 exposures on a dive because of the fast recycling times of most units. It is important to realize that film is the least expensive part of a photo dive, so completing a dive with unexposed film left in the camera is not very economical. With flashbulbs, you simply cannot change flashbulbs, compose a picture, and make an exposure within a minute, and that is what you would be trying to do if you wanted to expose 36 frames on one average dive.

In addition to time and money, there are other reasons that will probably cause the serious diving photographer to choose electronic flash. Some advantages associated with using electronic flash are:

1. No flashbulbs to carry or change underwater.
2. No flashbulbs to dispose of.
3. More space when traveling—think about the space needed to transport enough FP bulbs for ten 36-exposure-roll dives.

The disadvantages associated with using electronic flash are:

1. Even when you know your costs will be cheaper over a couple of years, the initial cost of a large electronic flash unit can be high.
2. Only one, or at best two, shutter speeds can be used with electronic flash.
3. The more light you require, the bulkier the units become. The difference between AG-1 and FP6 flashbulbs is negligible, but the difference between moving through the water with a small strobe in a housing versus a large, self-contained unit is considerable.

Comparing Units

Electronic flash units for underwater use can be broken down into two general categories: self-contained units and housed units. Whether you decide on a unit designed and built exclusively for use underwater or choose to house a unit designed for use in air is again a matter of need for the kind of photography you intend to do. And whether or not you already own a strobe unit probably will influence your decision.

As with the different types of flashbulbs, all electronic flash units will do the job they are intended to do, but it is important to know the limitations of the unit you're using and to work within those limits.

Comparing electronic flash units, as far as their light output is concerned, is difficult because there is no consumer standard that is applied equally for rating light output. The closest thing to a consumer standard is a comparison of ASA 25 guide numbers. Most manufacturers state, as part of their unit's specifications, the guide number of the unit when used with ASA 25 film. This guide number is generally for in-air use only because, as was discussed in the previous chapter, establishing an underwater guide number that can be used universally is almost impossible.

In addition to light output, strobes can be compared on the basis of whether they use disposable or rechargeable batteries. With disposable-battery units, you're never out of service while your unit is on charge, but you do have a continuing cost of batteries. Again, the choice is a matter of personal needs.

The following information on the various self-contained units and housings is organized in a way that should make it possible for a diver to make intelligent decisions before investing in equipment. In the specifications section for each unit, the data is derived from manufacturer-supplied information. Connector information is given in the specifications sections too, but details about the various types of connectors available for use underwater are given in Chapter 6.

SELF-CONTAINED UNDERWATER STROBE UNITS

Subsea, Inc.

Subsea is the oldest manufacturer of self-contained underwater electronic flash units, and their line is the most extensive of all the manufacturers. All their units are constructed of rugged epoxy, and all have recessed domes so that it is possible to stand the units on their front end for easy access to the battery compartments. Two clips hold the whole rear portion of the unit to the front, and an o-ring makes the seal. Removing the rear portion provides access to the battery and the strobe mechanism.

Subsea Mark 25

Housed in a compact, black epoxy body, the Mark 25 is the smallest of the Subsea units. Rated at 18 watt-sec., the unit is excellent for close-up photography. It weighs 24 oz. in air and has slight negative buoyancy.

Mark 25 Specifications

Power/Modes:	2 alkaline "c" batteries
Nr. of Flashes:	300
Recycle Time:	6 sec.
ASA 25 GN (in air):	40
Coverage:	60° (diagonal)
Connectors:	EO
Operating Depth:	350 ft.

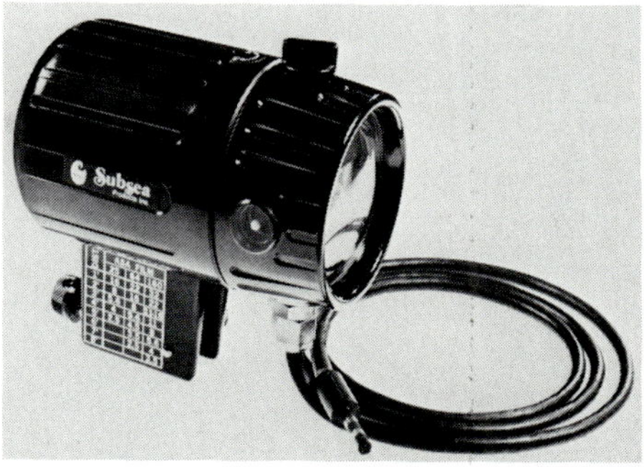

Subsea Mark 25.

Subsea Mark 50 (not illustrated)

The Mark 50 is slightly larger than the Mark 25. It too is constructed of rugged black epoxy. This unit can be operated at half power (36 watt-sec.) and full power (72 watt-sec.), offering the diver more control than with a single-mode unit.

Mark 50 Specifications

Power/Modes:	300v battery	
	half	full
Nr. of Flashes:	2000	1000
Recycle Time:	2 sec.	4 sec.
ASA 25 GN (in air):	18	28
Coverage:	90°	
Connector:	EO	
Operating Depth:	350 ft.	

AE 100 Specifications

Power/Modes:	Rechargeable nicad batteries
Nr. of Flashes:	135
Recycle Time:	2 sec.
ASA 25 GN (in air):	40
Coverage:	90°
Connector:	PC (in air) EO (in water)
Operating Depth:	160 ft.

Subsea AE 100 (not illustrated)

The AE 100 is Subsea's amphibious unit. Called the All-Environment Strobe, the unit was designed with versatility in mind. It can be recharged from standard 110V AC or 12V DC and can be used in air with standard PC synch cords or underwater with EO connectors. Rated at 100 watt-sec., the unit is comparable to many in-air-only units.

Subsea Mark 100

One of Subsea's most popular units, the Mark 100 has two power settings: 50 watt-sec. and 100 watt-sec. In air, the unit weighs a bit over 5 lbs.; underwater, the Mark 100 has slight negative buoyancy.

Subsea Mark 100.

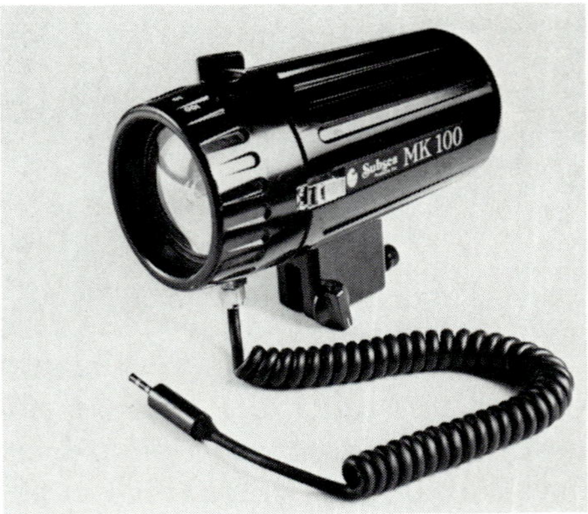

Mark 100 Specifications

Power/Modes:	300v battery	
	50 ws	100 ws
Nr. of Flashes:	1500	750
Recycle Time:	3 sec.	6 sec.
ASA 25 GN (in air):	25	35
Coverage:	90°	
Connector:	EO	
Operating Depth:	350 ft.	

Subsea Mark 150

Equally popular is the Mark 150. It has three power settings: 50 watt-sec., 100 watt-sec., and 150 watt-sec. It features a built-in slaving device and can be powered by a standard 510V battery or Subsea's Power Pack, which is rechargeable.

Mark 150 Specifications

Power/Modes:	510v battery		
	50 ws	100 ws	150 ws
Nr. of Flashes:	1500	750	500
Recycle Time:	2 sec.	4 sec.	6 sec.
ASA 25 GN (in air):	25	35	45
Coverage:	90°–150° (vertical)		
Connector:	EO		
Operating Depth:	350 ft.		

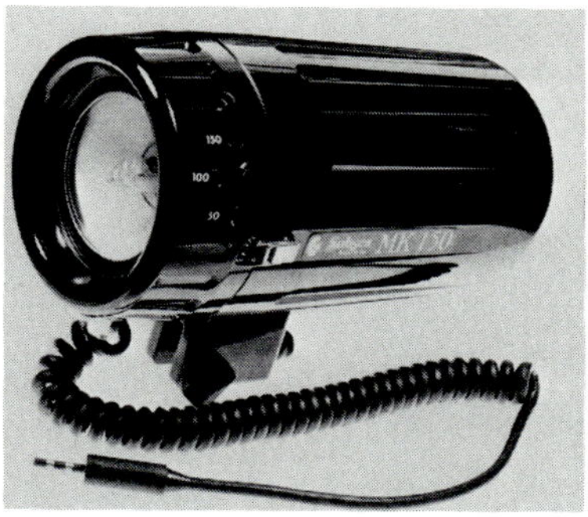

Subsea Mark 150.

Subsea Mark 225

The Mark 225 is a self-contained, rechargeable unit; it can be fully recharged in 7 hours with standard 110V AC. This unit features a built-in aiming/focusing light, necessary for pointing the strobe correctly and for focusing in dark water. The unit can be operated in three power modes: 75 watt-sec., 150 watt-sec., and 225 watt-sec.

Mark 225 Specifications

Power/Modes:	Rechargeable nicad batteries		
	75 ws	150 ws	225 ws
Nr. of Flashes:	300	200	100
Recycle Time:	2 sec.	4 sec.	6.5 sec.
ASA 25 GN (in air):	32	45	54
Coverage:	110°		
Connector:	EO		
Operating Depth:	350 ft.		

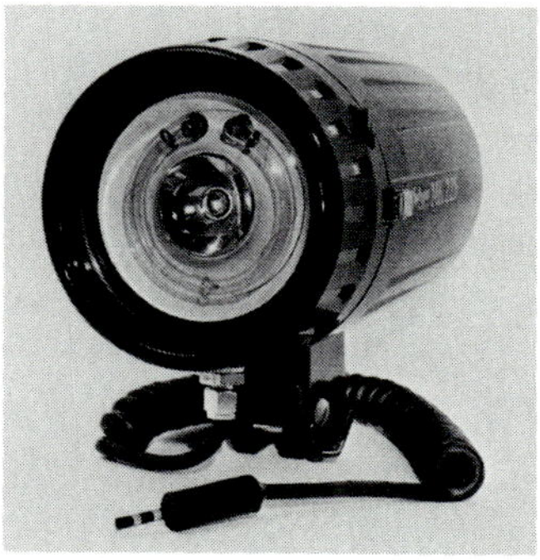

Subsea Mark 225.

Oceanic Products, Inc.

Oceanic Products manufactures a small, battery-operated strobe and three larger, rechargeable units. The larger units feature Honeywell electronics in a tough injection-molded housing. The chance of leakage has virtually been eliminated with these units because they are never opened except for a small recharging port.

Oceanic 2000

This compact and well-made unit is excellent for close-up work. It features an on-off switch and a ready light on its back end. The unit measures 6 in. in length and is less than 3 in. in diameter.

2000 Specifications

Power/Modes:	2 alkaline "c" batteries
Nr. of Flashes:	250
Recycle Time:	6 sec.
ASA 25 GN (in air):	35
Coverage:	50° (approx.)
Connector:	EO
Operating Depth:	200 ft.

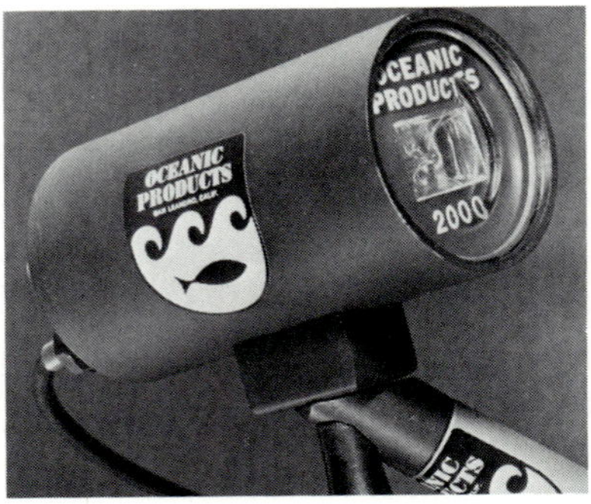

Oceanic 2000.

Oceanic 2001

Constructed of Cycolac, a high-impact plastic, this self-contained, rechargeable unit weighs 5 lbs. in air. In water, it is almost neutrally buoyant with a negative buoyancy of only half an ounce.

2001 Specifications

Power/Modes:	Rechargeable nicad batteries
Nr. of Flashes:	360
Recycle Time:	6 sec.
ASA 25 GN (in air):	55
Coverage:	95°
Connector:	EO, Ikelite, or Nikonos
Operating Depth:	350 ft.

2002 Specifications

Power/Modes:	Rechargeable nicad batteries
Nr. of Flashes:	360
Recycle Time:	6 sec.
ASA 25 GN (in air):	55
Coverage:	95°
Connector:	EO, Ikelite, or Nikonos
Operating Depth:	350 ft.

Oceanic 2002 (not illustrated)

The 2002 is an auto strobe that must be used in conjunction with the Honeywell Strobo-eye. If used with the Nikonos, the Strobo-eye must be contained in a small housing. Oceanic Products manufactures the Hydro-eye housing for that purpose. If the 2002 is used with a camera in a housing, the Strobo-eye can be used in the housing, provided, of course, that there is room for the unit and it can be placed with its sensor pointing in the same direction as the lens.

Oceanic 2003

This unit has all the features of the 2001 plus two power settings for added versatility. According to the manufacturer's specifications, three full *f*/stops separate the low and high power settings.

2003 Specifications

Power/Modes:	Rechargeable nicad batteries	
	partial	full
Nr. of Flashes:	430	280
Recycle Time:	4 sec.	6½ sec.
ASA 25 GN (in air):	40	65
Coverage:	95°	
Connector:	EO, Ikelite, or Nikonos	
Operating Depth:	350 ft.	

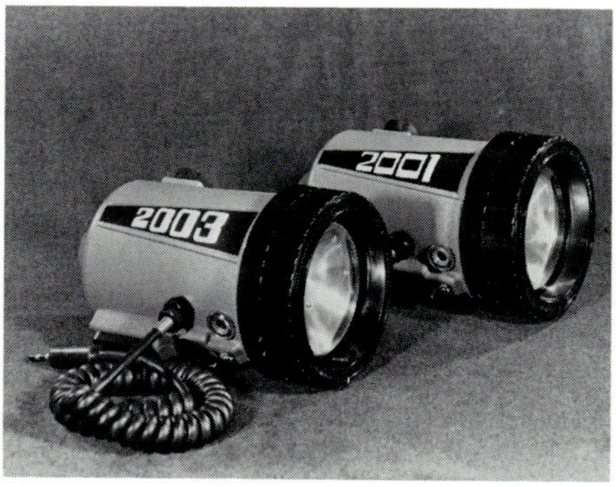

Oceanic 2003 (left). Oceanic 2001 (right).

Toshiba TM 1

The Toshiba TM 1 is a compact unit about the same size as the Nikonos flashbulb unit, and like that unit, it too comes with its own flash arm and attaching bracket. The connector supplied with the unit is the Nikonos type, and it can be adapted for use with either the earlier models or the Nikonos III. For its size and weight, the Toshiba TM 1 has a good light output that will more than adequately light the area covered by a 28mm lens underwater.

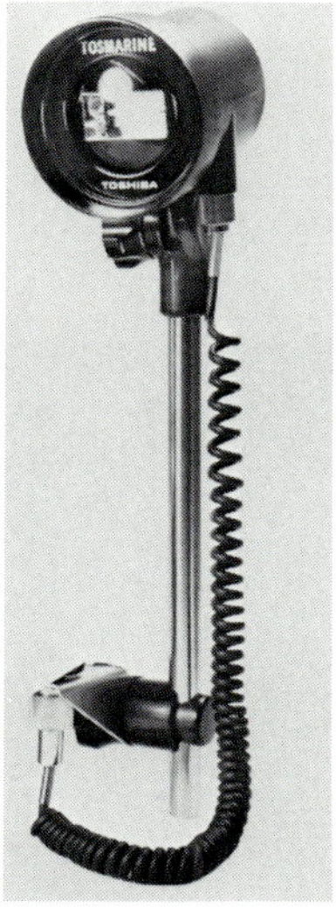

TM 1 Specifications

Power/Modes:	4 alkaline "AA" batteries
Nr. of Flashes:	250
Recycle Time:	5–7 sec.
ASA 25 GN (in air):	41
Coverage:	75° (horizontal)
Connector:	Nikonos (all models)
Operating Depth:	396 ft.

Toshiba TM1.

G/F Industries Twin Flash Model 250 (not illustrated)

This unit is actually two strobe units built into one cast aluminum housing. This configuration makes it possible to have very short intervals between flashes when operating in the "alternating" mode. When a big burst of light is needed, the two units can be fired simultaneously. The unit can be recharged from 12V DC or 110V AC. It is neutrally buoyant and features ready signals, a low-battery indicator, and a computer ring for exposure calculations.

Twin Flash 250 Specifications

Power/Modes:	Rechargeable single	double
Nr. of Flashes:	225	100
Recycle Time:	4–5 sec.	8–11 sec.
	(In alternate mode, virtually no recycle time)	
ASA 25 GN (in air):	40	60
Coverage:	35°–90°	
Connector:	EO	
Operating Depth:	600 ft.	

S-R2000 Specifications

Power/Modes:	Rechargeable nicad batteries
Nr. of Flashes:	150
Recycle Time:	3 sec.
ASA 25 GN (in air):	40
Coverage:	50°
Connector:	EO
Operating Depth:	220 ft.

Sonic Research S-R2000

The S-R2000 is one of the smallest self-contained underwater strobes on the market today. Sealed in a PVC tube 5 in. long and 2 in. in diameter, it is perfect for close-up work. It can be mounted in the Nikonos accessory shoe and aimed right in front of the lens. Four models of the S-R2000 are available: a standard synch model, a synch/slave model, and a slave-only version. The fourth version, a special-purpose cordless slave unit, can be ordered from the factory directly.

The Sonic Research System.

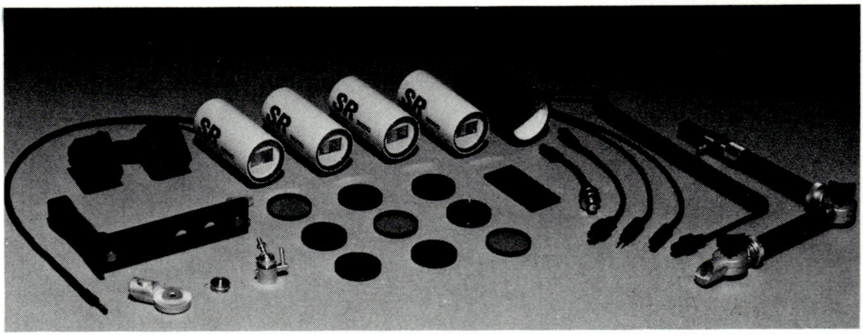

HOUSING IN-AIR ELECTRONIC FLASH UNITS

If you already own an in-air strobe, or if you want to use a strobe in air as well as underwater, housing a unit may be the best way to approach underwater lighting. One of the most popular lines of strobes housed for underwater use is the Honeywell 700 Series Strobonars. These units have been the mainstay of professional flash photography for years because they offer dependable operation and fast recycling times. All the units currently being produced have an in-air ASA 25 guide number of about 90, depending on the specific model. All the models use rechargeable ni-cad batteries that fit into the head of the unit. Some of the 700 Series Strobonars are manual units, others have manual/auto modes with light sensors in the flash head, and others are manual/auto units designed for use with the Strobo-eye accessory sensor. All the 700 Series Strobonars and the earlier versions (65 Series and 600 Series) will fit in the housings described below because although the inner workings of the units have been improved over the years, the familiar "potato-masher" configuration has changed little.

Hydro Strobe IV (for Honeywell 700 Series Strobonars)

The Hydro Strobe IV, made by Oceanic Products, accepts the Honeywell 700 Series Strobonars and the earlier versions of the same units. The housing is made entirely of heavy cast aluminum and coated with baked enamel to prevent salt-water corrosion. The strobe fires through a corrected dome on the front of the housing, and a ready-light port and on/off control are located on the back. Stainless steel clips secure the lid to the main portion of the housing, and a coil-type cord and EO connector are standard features. Brackets are available from Oceanic Products, which permit a 2- or 3-cell U.S. Divers flashlight to be attached to the top of the housing. A flashlight to help aim your strobe is a very useful accessory under most conditions and an absolute necessity on a photo dive at night.

Hydro Strobe IV Specifications

Units Accepted:	All 700 series Strobonars (and earlier versions)
Angle of Coverage:	70° (normal) 110° (with Sea-Wide Adapter behind port)
Connector:	EO
Operating Depth:	400 ft.

Note: See page 104 for an illustration of the Hydro Strobe IV.

Ikelite Housing (for Honeywell 700 Series Strobonars)

Ikelite encloses the Honeywell 700 Series Strobonars in a two-part housing. The base of the housing accepts the strobe handle and contains the plug to synch the strobe with the camera. The top of the housing is a clear plastic shell that contains the on/off control and through which the unit fires. Since the top of the unit is clear, the ready light and distance scale can be seen easily. The clear top also makes it easy to monitor the inside of the housing should you suspect leakage. The two halves of the housing are held together with quick-release clamps, and an o-ring ensures the unit's integrity. Within the top of the housing is room for filters, wide-angle diffusers, and a slaving device should you want to operate the unit as a secondary light source.

Ikelite Strobe Housing Specifications

Units Accepted:	Model 4171—710, 780, and 782 Model 4170—65C, 600, 660, 700, 770, and 772
Angle of Coverage:	60°
Connector:	Nikonos or EO
Operating Depth:	300 ft.

Ikelite housing with Honeywell 770 installed.

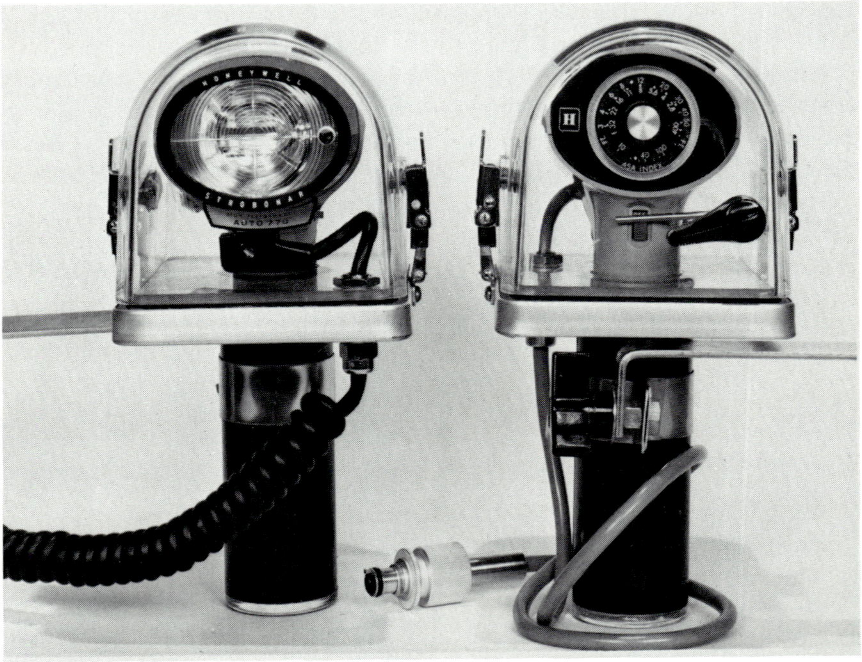

Housings for Smaller Units

Housings for all the popular, smaller electronic flash units on the market today are made by many different manufacturers of underwater equipment. Ikelite makes housings for almost 50 different units, and they will custom-build a housing for any other. Oceanic Products, U.S. Divers, Sea Research and Development, and other manufacturers also produce small strobe housings. Most are made of clear plastic, but some are of cast aluminum. Whether battery-operated or rechargeable, you can find a housing for almost any strobe.

With all small housings, you should be able to view the enclosed strobe's ready light and easily attach the housing to the camera or camera housing you're using. You also should be able to turn your unit on and off underwater to conserve batteries. Many small strobe units tend to drain batteries quickly underwater, so it is important to turn your unit off between shots.

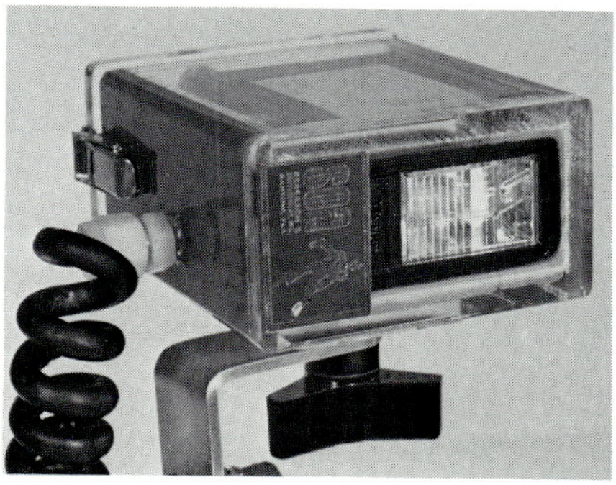

Many manufacturers make housings for small electronic flash units. At the left is one by Sea Research and Development. Below is one by Ikelite in use with a Nikonos II.

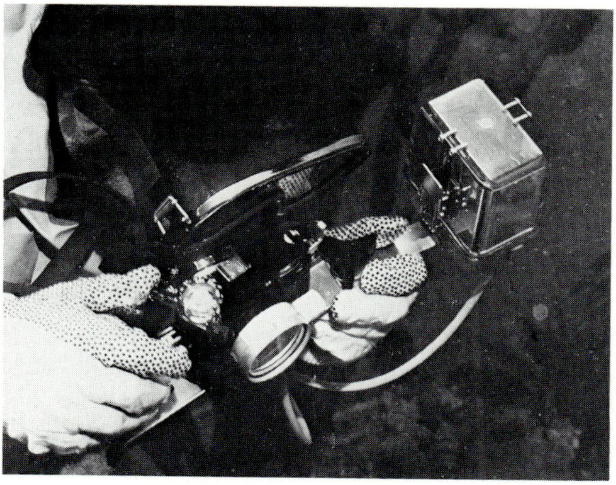

EXPOSURE

Exposure with strobe units is calculated in much the same manner as with flashbulbs. (See the section on exposure in Chapter 4 and make a test similar to the one described.) Once exposure is established, you will become aware of some special problems that occur when using strobe, one of which is "ghosting."

Double Images (Ghosting)

You should know that when using electronic flash, it is the instantaneous flash of light (in combination with the selected *f*/stop) that determines the amount of light that will expose the film. It is this instant flash of light, usually at least 1/1000 sec. and sometimes much faster with automatic strobes, that makes the exposure and freezes the fastest action. With FP bulbs, the light of the flash, the *f*/stop, *and* the shutter speed all play a role in determining exposure. The shutter speed you use with electronic flash, though, simply opens the shutter at the appropriate time to admit the light.

The highest shutter speed that synchronizes with electronic flash is most often 1/60 sec. with cameras that have focal-plane shutters. With the Nikonos cameras and the Nikon F, it is 1/60 sec.; with the Nikkormats, it is 1/125 sec.; and with the F2-Series cameras, it is 1/80 sec. ("X" setting).

Being locked into one comparatively slow shutter speed can be a problem. On bright days in clear water, it is possible for your flash exposure to match your exposure for available light. This can easily be the case when working near the surface. When this happens, you can get a double image, or "ghost." This is because your film is actually recording two images: the flash-exposed image and the available-light-exposed image. This is most noticeable only with a subject that is moving too fast for the 1/60 sec. shutter speed to stop. The accompanying photo illustrates ghosting. Note that the subject's hand was moving too fast for the 1/60 sec. synch speed to stop.

Fill-In Flash

The accompanying photo also illustrates the technique of fill-in flash. Fill-in flash is used when you want your pictures to have an available-light quality but without harsh shadows. You "fill-in" the shadows with light. The key is filling-in with just enough light to brighten dark areas, but not enough to match the daylight exposure. To determine your fill-in flash exposure, first find your daylight expo-

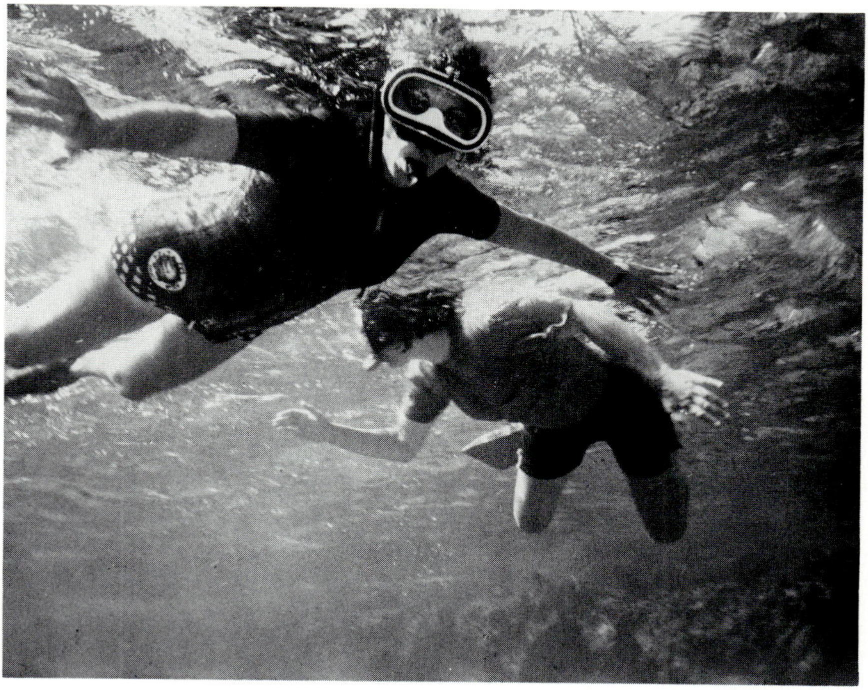

Fill-in flash should supply just enough light to "open up" shadows, as shown above. The photo also illustrates "ghosting." Note the subject's hands, they were moving too fast for the 1/60 sec. shutter speed to stop. See the explanation on the opposite page. This photo is a conversion from an Ektachrome-X transparency shown in color on page C6.

sure and set that on your camera. Next, calculate your standard flash exposure for the distance you're using. If your calculated lens aperture is smaller than or equal to the required daylight aperture, it means your strobe is supplying more or the same amount of light as the natural light. For a better balance, you will have to reduce the amount of light your unit will put on the subject. You can reduce your strobe output by:

1. increasing your flash-to-subject distance;
2. selecting a lower power setting if available; or
3. diffusing or blocking some of the strobe's light.

The idea is to have your flash exposure less than the daylight exposure by about one full *f*/stop.

Multiple Flash

At times, you may want to use more than one light source for a particular scene or effect. A second light can soften hard shadows created by a single light, and using two lights can be very helpful when working with extremely wide-angle lenses. Using more than one electronic flash unit at a time is much easier than trying to use more than one flashbulb because unlike bulbs, which are generally wired together and flashed electrically, multiple strobe units are usually triggered by light-sensing devices. When strobes are operated by such a device, they are known as slaves. Slaving units can be plugged into conventional strobe units to create a slave, or wired into a unit's circuitry as an added feature.

To take a photo with a slave, you simply use your main strobe in the conventional manner, position your slave to illuminate the area you want, and fire your main strobe. Light from it will trigger the second unit, and both will light the subject. The light sensor of the slave must, of course, receive some of the light from the prime strobe. Even underwater, light travels fast enough for both units to illuminate the scene within the time it takes for the shutter to open and close.

Proper exposure with multiple units is much simpler than you would at first imagine, provided that the units are of the same power and at equal distance from the subject. In cases where the two units do not overlap an area of the subject, just ignore the second unit and calculate exposure based on the first light. When the lights do overlap a significant portion of the subject, the additional light from the secondary source adds, at most, one-half *f*/stop of light. Even if the two lights were in the same position, the increase of light would be only one *f*/stop.

With multiple lighting, simply determine which light is your

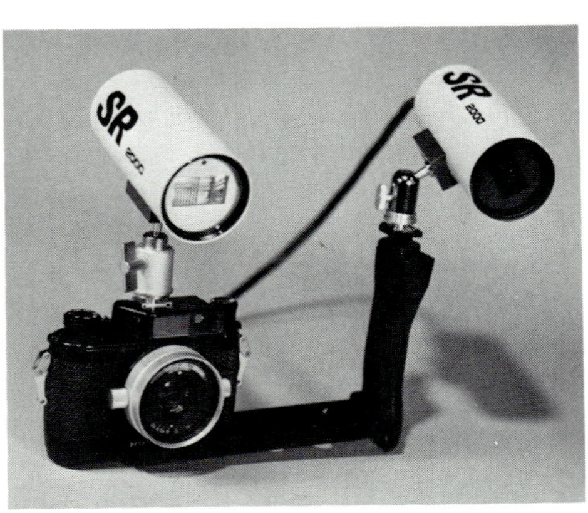

When using two equal-power strobes to light a subject, soften the light of one to avoid unnatural shadows. Here one strobe's output is reduced with a neutral density filter.

main light, calculate exposure for it, then make a minor adjustment, rarely more than one-half *f*/stop, for the additional light.

A bigger problem than exposure with multiple lighting is shadow control. Lighting that equally illuminates two sides of a subject creates unnatural, ugly shadows. Rather than place equally powered lights at equal distance from your subject, place your second light farther away, or diffuse it so it just brightens the shadows with a bit of light.

Photographing a Flash

Underwater photographs that show a diver's strobe going off at the instant the picture was taken are made with the help of slave units. To make a photo that shows a fellow diver's flash firing, you need the cooperation of a diver with a strobe unit that can act as a slave. Of course, you'll need your own camera and strobe to take the picture. Pose your cooperative diver and position the strobe (slave) to be photographed so that its light sensor will be triggered when your strobe goes off as you take the picture. The light from your unit will fire the one you're photographing, and its flash will be recorded on your film.

Backscatter

As mentioned in the previous chapter, backscatter is less of a problem with electronic flash than with flashbulbs because most strobes have narrower angles of coverage and shorter flash durations. Though lessened with strobe, the problem is not eliminated. The same methods outlined to control backscatter with flashbulbs should be employed with electronic flash. Backscatter does create a problem when using certain types of auto strobes.

Auto Strobes

Because of backscatter, the use of auto strobes with light sensors near the flashtube will not always work properly. In clear water, the units tend to function as intended—the light bounces off the subject and back to the sensor, the sensor reads the light and limits output when proper exposure is obtained, all in a matter of milliseconds. In water that is not clear, or in areas where the bottom sediment has been disturbed, light bouncing back to the sensor will be bouncing back from suspended particles in the water and not the subject. The result will be improper exposure.

The problem can be solved by using a system that has a separate limiting sensor placed *near* the camera. This way, light from the strobe will bounce off the subject and be measured and limited at the camera—the sensor will be reading the light that the camera will be recording. Honeywell's Strobo-eye is such a sensor, and remote sensors are available for Vivitar and Rollei flash units too. Both Oceanic Products and Ikelite make housings for the Honeywell remote sensor. Housings for the Vivitar and Rollei remote sensors are made by Ikelite.

In a separate housing, a remote sensor can be mounted near the Nikonos and used with the appropriate auto strobe. When used with a housed camera, remote sensors can sometimes be mounted within the camera housing, provided that there is room for the unit and the sensor can read light reflecting off the subject.

Strobe Care

Underwater electronic flash units, like units for use in air, require special treatment to keep them at peak operating efficiency. The special treatment is simply regular use. You should turn on your unit weekly and operate it for at least 15 minutes. If a unit is out of service for long periods of time, it will be necessary to "reform the capacitor." It is the capacitor in your strobe that stores the charge which creates the light. The capacitor's ability to store that charge deteriorates when it is not in use. Reforming the capacitor is done by recharging the unit and firing it a number of times during the recharging.

It is important to note that recharging and reforming should be done the night before a dive, and if your unit is operated with disposable batteries, the reforming of the capacitor should be done with an old battery. Reforming the capacitor puts excessive drain on a battery. Once your capacitor is reformed, a fresh battery should be used for shooting.

When doing an extensive amount of photography, use your batteries more efficiently by working with two sets and alternating their use. When you buy batteries, date and code them; a simple "A" and "B" will do. Use the "A" batteries one day and the "B's" the next. Letting the batteries "rest" will extend their lives—especially if they are stored cool. High-voltage batteries for electronic flash units should be stored at temperatures of about 40 F. (the vegetable bin of your refrigerator is perfect). Storing batteries at that temperature slows the chemical reaction that creates the electrical energy.

6

Accessories and Connectors

If you decide to use electronic flash, in addition to deciding which unit you're going to use, you also will have to decide how you're going to attach it to your camera. Choosing the arm, brackets, and connectors that will link your strobe and camera can be as trying as choosing the strobe itself.

It is possible to do without extension arms and camera brackets, but this means you will always have both hands full—a camera in one hand and a strobe in the other. Even though some of your shooting will be done just that way, there are times when you will want one hand free, even if it's only to equalize pressure as you descend. And being able to hold your camera and strobe together securely will be very helpful, especially during difficult entries and exits.

Most of the manufacturers of electronic flash units also make the attaching devices necessary for holding their units to Nikonos cameras and housings. You can choose a system that is completely Subsea, Oceanic Products, or any of the other manufacturers, or you can mix components. Versatility and adaptability should always be kept in mind, with particular attention to the kind of photography you plan to do.

Brackets

The first piece of equipment you will need to start "hanging" things will be a bracket (also referred to as a bar or tray) that attaches to the Nikonos. This bracket is most often attached to the camera by the

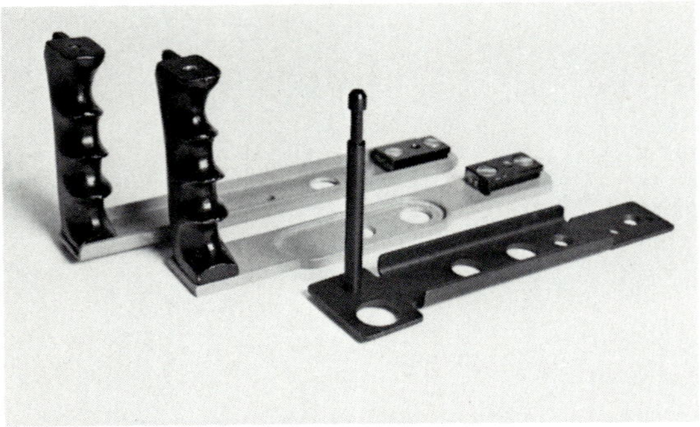

Brackets: (L. to R.) Oceanic Products for Nikonos III, Oceanic Products for II, Subsea for II.

nut on the connector that links the camera to the strobe. Some brackets, designed for use with the Nikonos III, take advantage of the central location of the tripod socket and use it as an extra attachment point.

Handles are usually a part of the brackets, and selecting the type that best suits your needs is a matter of personal preference. Some are simple shafts; some are angled for more comfortable handling; and others are contoured to fit your grip. When the brackets are correctly mounted, the handle is located near the film-advance/shutter-release lever. But operating the lever in the conventional manner is near impossible while holding the handle. Adding another piece of equipment to your camera solves the problem.

Thumb-Advance Levers

Adding a thumb-advance lever to your Nikonos puts the film-advance/shutter-release lever within reach and makes it possible to

Brackets, thumb-advance levers, and viewfinders—all available from Ikelite.

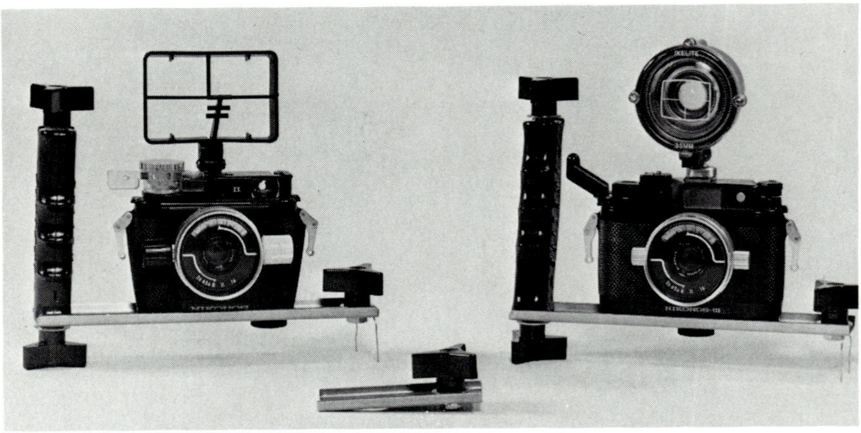

release the shutter without having to reach in front of the camera. Using a handle and thumb-advance lever makes it possible to operate the camera with the right hand and position your strobe with the left.

Because of the construction differences of the film-advance/shutter-release levers between the earlier Nikonos cameras and the Nikonos III, many accessory manufacturers produce two types of thumb-advance levers. All the levers are similar and are attached to the camera with simple screws or allen-head screws. Some thumb-advance levers are so constructed that when attached to the camera, only one shutter speed can be used. Others permit the selection of all shutter speeds. Using the type that locks one shutter speed in position can be a help when shooting with electronic flash. If you lock

Flash arms: (L. to R.) Subsea Flexarm with MK225 strobe unit, Hydro Photo Cobra Flash Arm, and Aqua-Craft S-41 Strobe Arm with Oceanic Products 2001 strobe unit.

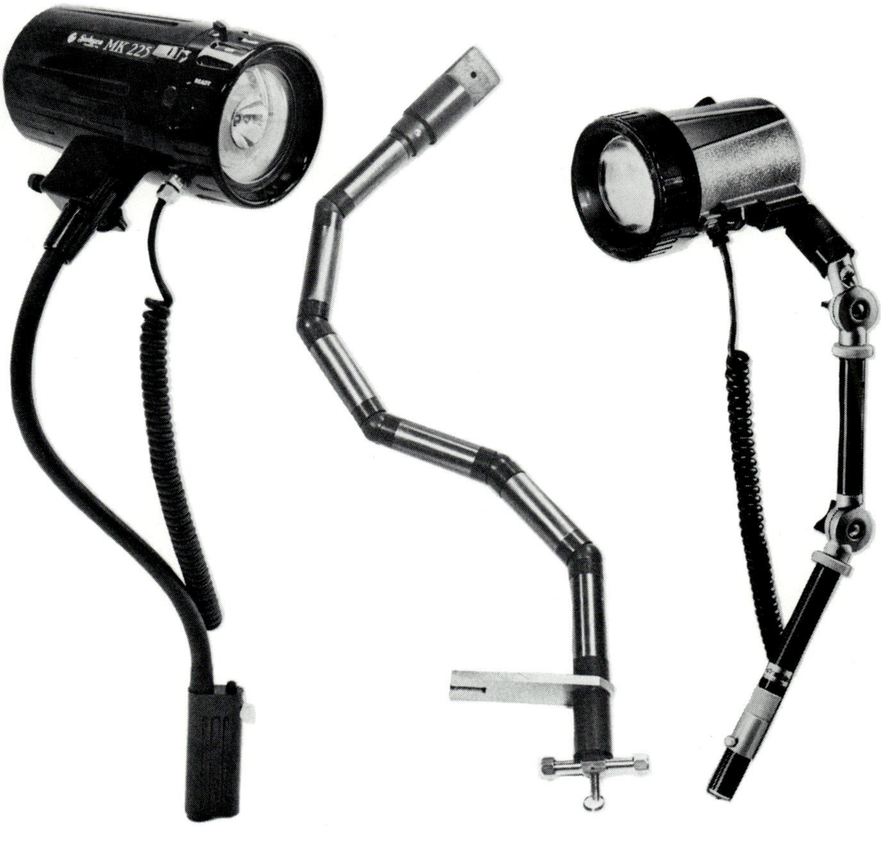

in 1/60 sec., you will never miss a shot because of an incorrect synchronization.

Flash Arms

The item that attaches to your strobe and keeps it a specific distance from the camera can be as simple as a straight metal bar or as complex as a multi-sectioned ball-jointed arm. To serve its principal purpose, and to be versatile, it should be long enough to avoid backscatter for normal shooting and flexible enough to be able to bring the strobe near the camera for close-up work. It should also be flexible enough to be angled in any direction and strong enough to support the weight of both the strobe and camera in air as well as in water. Finally, the arm should have a provision for easy separation from the bracket for the times you will want to operate the strobe "off camera."

When selecting the length you will need, keep in mind that there is little point in buying a flash arm 36 in. long and then trying to use it for close-up photography. In fact, long arms will be a hindrance when you're trying to illuminate an area less than a foot in front of the camera.

Subsea bracket, arm, and other accessories with a Nikonos II (left). Oceanic Products arm, Hydro Strobe IV housing, and Hydro 35 camera housing (right).

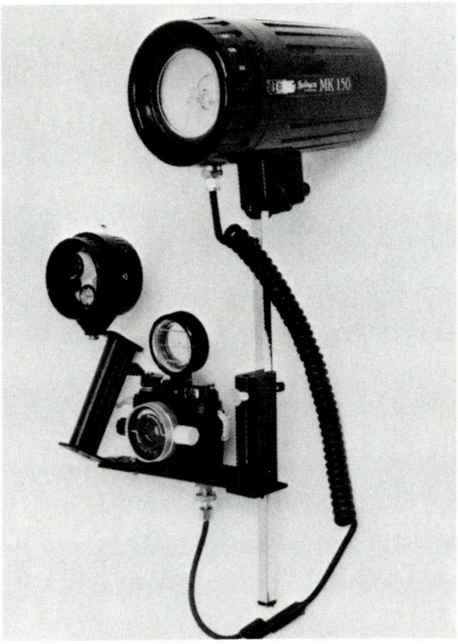

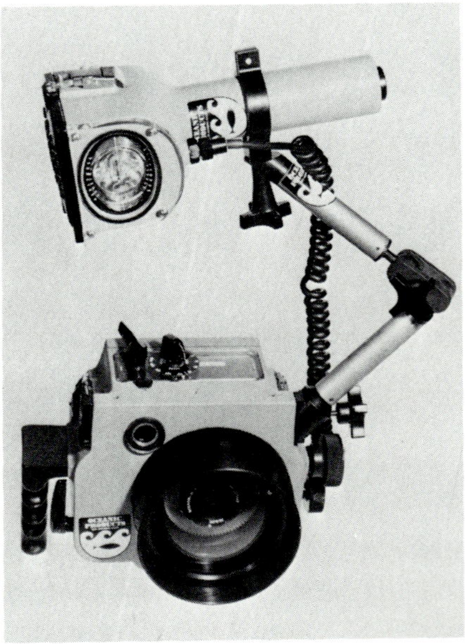

WET CONNECTORS

Another decision you must make when you expand your system to include electronic flash is the kind of connector you will use to electrically link your components together. You should give it considerable thought before you decide, and once you've chosen a type of connector, stick with it. Every flash or strobe unit you own should be adaptable to every camera you own. The more options available to you, the less likely that you will be "washed out" on an expensive trip because one part of your system fails. A back-up system is especially important in remote diving areas.

The type of connector you will want is the type that can be easily connected and disconnected underwater. With this type, you can take two cameras and one strobe on a dive (not an impossible task, especially with a cooperative buddy). After exposing the film in one camera, you'll be able to switch the strobe to the camera with unexposed film and return from the dive with 72 pictures. Keep in mind that film is the cheapest part of any dive vacation. After the money invested in diving and photo equipment, and in getting to and staying at the dive location, film cost is almost inconsequential.

There are three principal types of wet connectors that are currently on the market and widely used. They are made by Electro Oceanics, Ikelite, and Sea Research and Development.

EO Connectors

The EO connector is manufactured by Electro Oceanics and sold by almost all the underwater photo equipment manufacturers in different forms. The EO system is used by the government and private industry for a variety of underwater electrical applications. Simple in design and almost all rubber, the connectors are easy to use. The male end (generally wired to the strobe) consists of a shaft around which are two bands of copper—the terminals. For connection, the male end is inserted into the female end where the contact bands join the internal contacts. Silicone grease should always be used with these contacts to facilitate joining them and to reduce wear. Friction holds the two parts together.

To use EO connectors with Nikonos cameras, an adapter must be used. An EO-to-Nikonos adapter is simply a standard Nikonos connector (with terminals rigged for electronic flash) wired and sealed to a female EO connector. The adapter is mounted to the camera in the same way the Nikonos Flash Units are attached. When in place, the EO portions can be connected and disconnected underwater at will.

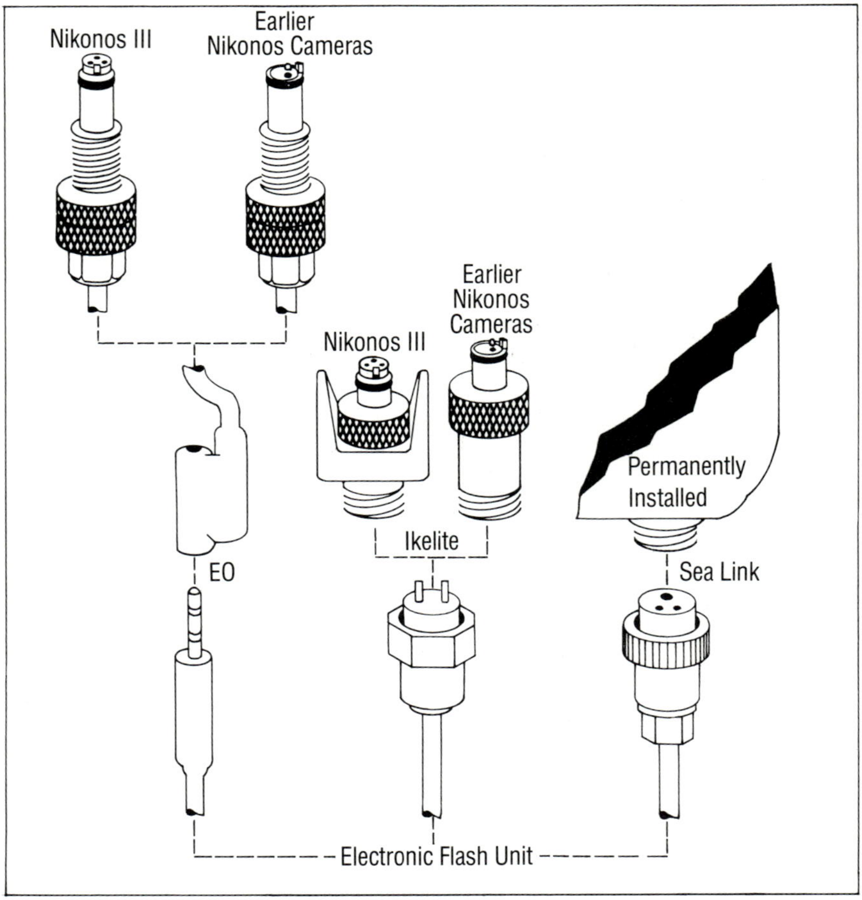

The three principal wet connector systems in use today are illustrated above. To use EO connectors with the Nikonos system, an adapter like the one below must be used. Adapters are available for use with the earlier models or the III.

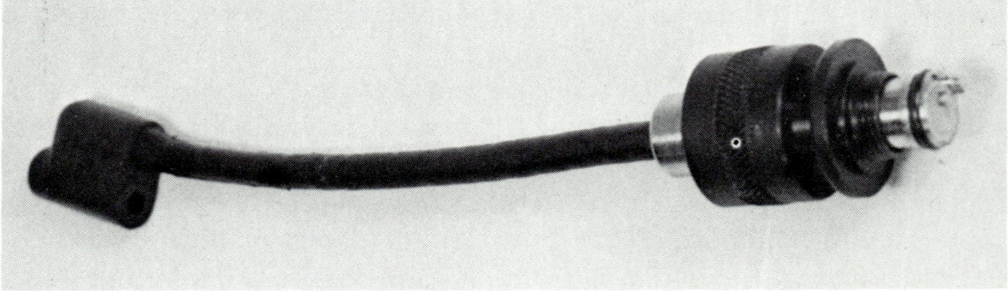

Ikelite Connector System

The Ikelite system consists of a plastic female module that mounts directly on the Nikonos (versions exist for the earlier Nikonos cameras and the III) and a male module that links with the strobe. When the connectors are joined, the two units are held together by an attaching collar on the male module.

The female modules that screw into the Nikonos hold the Ikelite trays in place for the attachment of strobe units and other accessories. The male modules can be attached to any ¼-in. diameter cable with only a wrench and a screwdriver. Silicone grease should always be packed around the terminals of the connectors to prevent corrosion.

Sea-Link Connectors

Sea Research and Development make the Sea-Link connector system. When used with the Nikonos, the male module is permanently installed on the base of the camera's outer shell. The female module is wired to the strobe, and when the two units are joined, they are held together by a threaded collar on the female end. The connectors are made of Cycolac, a completely corrosion-resistant material. Sea Research and Development can permanently install a male module on your Nikonos the same day they receive the outer shell, and installing the female module on any ¼-in. diameter cable is easy—instructions are supplied with the connectors.

Silicone grease should always cover the connector terminals to preclude the possibility of corrosion occurring and creating poor electrical connections.

Sea-Link connector system on a Nikonos III (left) and Ikelite connector system on a housing (right).

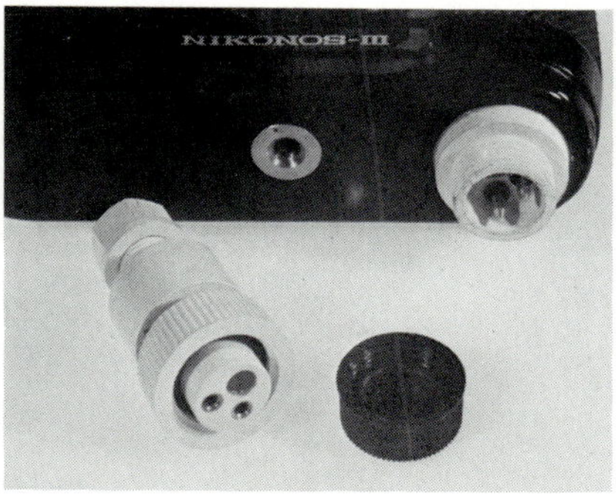

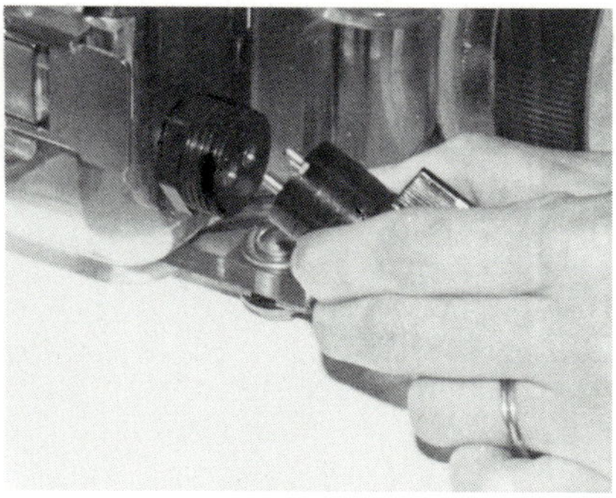

Connectors with Housed Cameras

All the wet connectors described above can, of course, be used with housed cameras. The end of the connector affixed to the housing wall would simply require an internal connection to join with the camera's PC terminal. Externally, the connections would be used as described. Chapter 7 has more information on housings and internal connections.

IN-AIR FLASH UNIT ADAPTER

You can use underwater flash equipment to take flash pictures in air, but you will find it somewhat cumbersome. A useful accessory that will enable you to use in-air flashbulb units and electronic flash units is the Nikonos Flash Unit Adapter. There are two types: one for use with the Nikonos III, and another for use with the earlier models. Both adapters screw into the synchronization socket in the base of the cameras and provide standard PC sockets for in-air flash and strobe units. Care should be exercised when screwing the units into the camera to avoid the possibility of cross-threading.

When the Nikonos III adapter is in place, two PC sockets are available for use. One is marked "X," for use with electronic flash, and the other is marked "FP," for use with flashbulbs. Simply use the terminal desired after consulting the table on page 77 for proper synchronization.

When the earlier-model adapter is in place, only one PC socket is visible. To synchronize the camera with electronic flash, turn the base plate of the adapter clockwise until a black dot appears in the hole on the base plate. The black dot matches the black "X" engraved on the base plate. To synchronize the camera with flashbulbs, turn the base plate counterclockwise until the red dot appears in the hole on the base plate. The red dot matches the red "FP" engraved on the base plate. When the desired synchronization setting is selected, plug your unit into the PC socket.

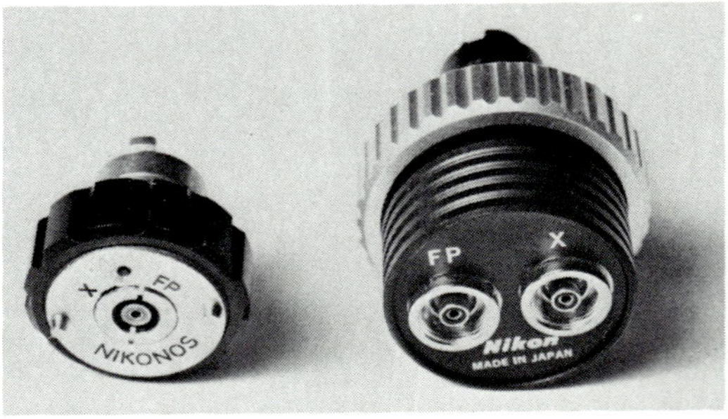

In-air adapter for use with the Nikonos I and II (left). In-air adapter for III (right).

7

Housings

Incredible as the Nikonos System is, there will be times when only a housed camera will do a particular job. Cameras in housings can use a wider variety of lenses than are available for the Nikonos, and cameras in housings can also be equipped with motor drives. But the biggest advantage gained by housing a camera is that the camera housed can be a single-lens reflex. In fact, it makes little sense to house anything but an SLR.

The advantages of using a single-lens reflex camera underwater are the same ones gained by using that type camera in air, the two most important being that you view and focus your subject through the camera lens. This is true no matter what lens you have on the camera. Seeing exactly what will be recorded on your film is most useful because pictures that are perfectly exposed but poorly composed are disappointing. Visual focusing eliminates doubts and produces crisp pictures every time. Being able to focus visually becomes increasingly important the closer you get to your subjects, and for close-up photography, proper focusing is critical.

The Nikon family of cameras is ideal for use underwater for all the same reasons that make them the popular choice on land: precision optics, construction of the finest quality, system flexibility, and ruggedness. Another big factor that makes Nikon the ideal system to take underwater is that more housings are made for Nikon cameras than for any other SLR on the market.

By sealing a Nikon camera in a modern housing, you will have at your disposal a system that is unequaled. In a modern housing, almost

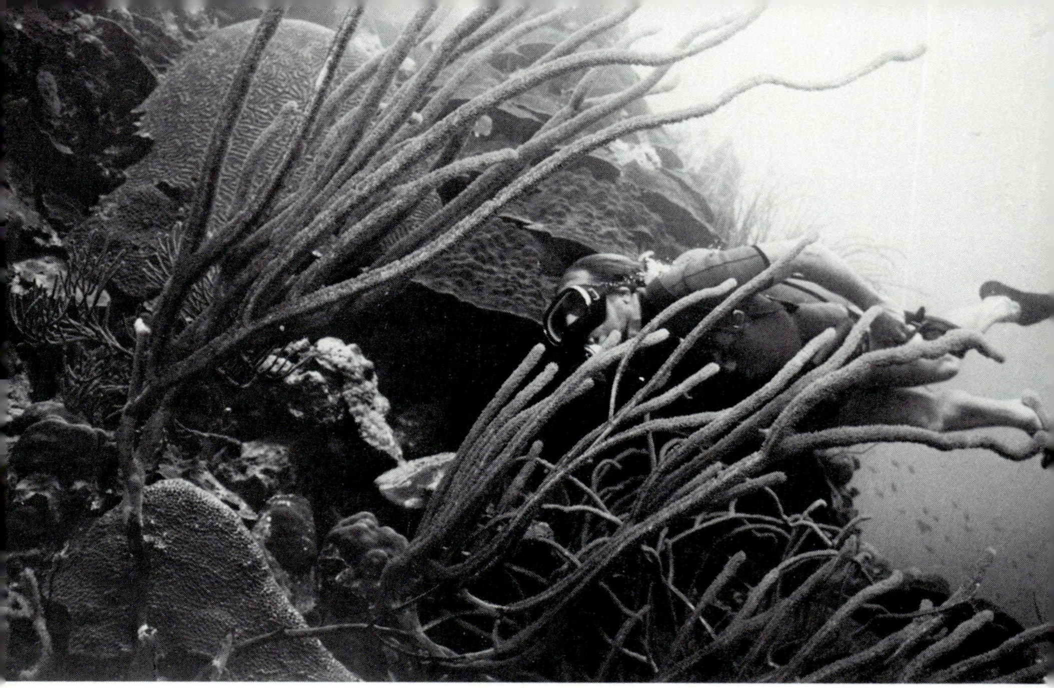

With an SLR in a housing it is easy to align picture elements because what you see is what the lens will record.

all the system's features that can be used in air can be used underwater, and the array of lenses available makes it possible to photograph just about anything. Most modern housings are equipped with interchangeable ports; standard ports make it possible to use normal and wide-angle lenses, and with special-purpose ports, macro lenses, fisheyes, and telephotos can be used.

Finally, most modern housings are designed to permit the use of the DA-1 Action Finder. Using this special-purpose viewfinder, for use with the F and F2 cameras, gives the diving photographer a bright image that measures a full 1¼″ × 1″. The image the viewfinder provides is erect and unreversed, and the whole image can be seen when the eye is positioned 2½ in. from the screen—about the distance your eye will be from the screen when the camera is in a housing and you're wearing a face mask. In the overall dimness generally encountered underwater, focusing is difficult at best; the advantage of being able to easily view a big bright image cannot be overstated.

SELECTING A HOUSING

The first function of a housing is, of course, to protect the camera within. Once the quality of a housing is determined, and the camera's protection assured, next consider how many features of your in-air camera are lost when it is enclosed in the housing. The housing should limit the camera's normal functions as little as possible, and all the controls should be as easy to operate underwater as on land.

Whether you decide on an all-metal housing or a plastic one will probably be a matter of how much money you have to spend. Metal housings can be four times as expensive as plastic ones, but metal housings have some advantages over plastic ones.

Metal Versus Plastic

Metal housings for Nikon cameras are generally made of anodized cast aluminum and protected against salt-water corrosion with an impervious coating of paint or epoxy. Modern plastic housings are generally made of injected-molded high-impact plastic. They have a toughness thought impossible to achieve in plastics a few years ago, but they do not have the strength of metal housings.

Metal housings are finely machined and precision-fitted with controls that are smooth and easy to operate even at great depths. Controls in metal housings tend to be either gear-driven or operated directly through mechanical linkages. Polycarbonate plastics, the type of plastic most often used in modern plastic housings, can also be machined, but the controls in plastic housings do not operate as smoothly as metal-housing controls, and they sometimes function sluggishly in deep water.

Metal housings are usually well balanced and negatively buoyant, making them easy to handle underwater. Plastic housings are generally lighter than metal housings in air, but this means they are buoyant and therefore difficult to control underwater unless weighted.

One advantage clear plastic housings have over metal housings is that they can be continually monitored for signs of leakage. Should a leak develop, it might be possible to keep water away from the camera and get the unit to the surface before serious damage resulted. Should a leak develop in a metal housing, it could easily go unnoticed during a dive.

Both metal and plastic housings are widely used by amateur and professional photographers, and both types more than adequately serve the first function of a housing: to keep dry the camera within. Most of the advantages of metal housings over plastic ones are matters of strength and convenience. Whether those advantages are worth the extra cost (approximately $600 versus $150) is for you to decide.

After you've decided on the type housing that is best for you, you'll next have to pick the port through which you will be taking your pictures. Flat ports and dome ports are the types available.

Refraction and Flat Ports

Flat ports are the type that have been used in housings since cameras were first taken underwater, and many fine underwater housings employ glass or optical plastic flat ports today. Flat ports *do* have a place in modern underwater photography, but they do produce refraction.

Refraction is the bending of light rays as they pass from one medium to another. As light rays pass from water to air, as they do when light rays from a subject underwater pass through a housing port and into the air in the housing, the rays are bent. (The rays are actually bent twice, once as they leave the water and enter the glass, and a second time when they leave the glass and enter the air. In this discussion, the double bending is discounted for simplification as its effect is negligible.)

At the port, rays entering from the water are bent away from the "norm"—the norm simply being a line perpendicular to the flat port. The reason for the bending has to do with the fact that light travels faster in air than in water, but the important thing to keep in mind is that this bending of light rays produces a number of different effects:

1. Objects appear closer (larger) to the human eye/brain viewing the object through a flat port. Objects appear to be about 3/4 the distance they actually are from the observer.
2. Angles of coverage of lenses behind flat ports change; the angle of coverage of a lens behind a flat port will be about 3/4 its angle of coverage in air.
3. Peripheral distortion begins to take place. Around the edges of pictures taken through flat ports, blurring and color shifts are sometimes visible. They become more apparent as wider-angle lenses are used.

It is this last effect of refraction that gives flat ports a bad name, but it is only with extremely wide-angle lenses that the distortion produces unacceptable pictures. Flat ports *can* be used successfully underwater—the first elements in both the 35mm and 80mm Nikonos lenses are flat ports.

Most flat-port distortion occurs when wider-angle lenses are used because the light ray bending at the periphery of the port is greatest, as the accompanying illustration shows. This causes the white-light rays to break up into their component colors, causing the distortion (technically referred to as chromatic aberration).

The least amount of distortion occurs when lenses longer than 35mm are used behind a flat port because the least amount of severe light ray bending takes place. With telephoto lenses, the distortion is not noticeable, and the apparent shortening of distance and reduced angle of acceptance is advantageous. In the accompanying illustration, note that the ray entering the port at a 90-degree angle is not bent. No distortion is produced there.

Dome Ports

Dome ports are also called corrected ports because they correct (actually eliminate) the distortion associated with flat ports. Because dome ports are spherical, all light rays entering the port do so at a (theoretical) 90-degree angle. None of the distortion associated with flat ports occurs because of light ray bending. Even at the periphery of the port, when super-wide-angle and fisheye lenses are used, no light rays are bent. Dome ports make it possible to use these lenses underwater and to get sharpness and color fidelity impossible with flat ports.

There are some things you should be aware of when using dome ports. In water, a dome acts as a lens and produces an apparent, or virtual, image that is much closer to the dome than the actual distance to the object. When focusing your camera lens, you actually focus on the virtual image. This will not confuse you because you will not be aware it is happening—you will be focusing visually, and normally will not be consulting the distance scale on your camera lens. If you could see the camera's distance scale (in most housings you can't), it might confuse you because the scale would give you a distance much closer than what you would estimate the actual subject distance to be. Because the virtual image is formed close to the dome, the particular lens you're using must be capable of focusing that close. With some dome housings, it will be necessary to attach close-up lenses to certain camera lenses to permit you to focus on the close, virtual image. The manufacturers of housings always include specific information concerning any close-up lenses needed to get good results.

Light rays through a flat port (left); dome port (right).

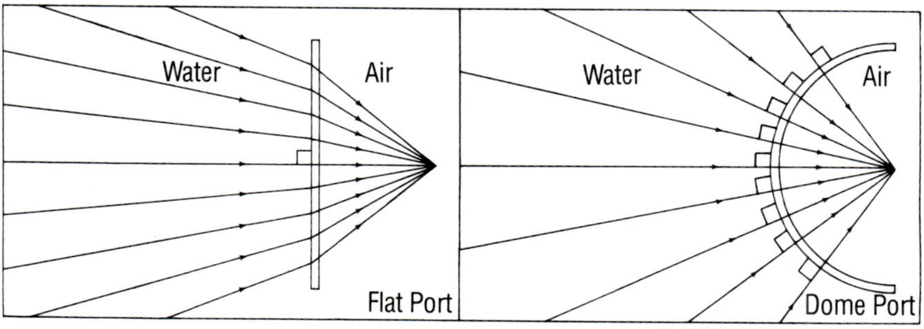

Hydro 35

The Hydro 35, made by Oceanic Products, is a rugged cast aluminum housing that can be used with the Nikon F and F2 cameras. The housing is anodized and coated with a heavy enamel to protect it against salt-water corrosion. The dome rings are made of aluminum, and the interchangeable domes themselves are made of an optical-quality acrylic plastic. The camera mounts on the rear half of the housing, and it must be completely removed when film is changed. A large o-ring seals the two halves of the housing together when the four stainless steel latches are properly closed. Smaller o-rings seal the control shafts. With a camera installed, the housing has slight negative buoyancy.

The specifications below and the accompanying illustration provide detailed information on the various parts of the housing.

Hydro 35 Specifications

Cameras:	Nikon F and F2 series.
Ports and Lenses:	Fisheye port used with most fisheye and extreme wide-angle Nikkor lenses.
	Standard dome port used with 24mm through normal lenses, including 55mm Macro (without M-ring and without filters). Note: 28mm *f*/3.5, 50mm *f*/1.4, and 50mm *f*/2 require a No. 2 close-up lens.
	Flat port and extension ring used with 85mm through 135mm lenses.
Viewfinder Recommended:	DA-1 Action Finder.
Controls:	Shutter speed—direct mechanical linkage.
	Film advance—direct mechanical linkage.
	Focus control—gears.
	Shutter release—direct mechanical linkage.
	Aperture—direct mechanical linkage.
Motor Drive:	Housing requires factory modification for battery pack installation.
Connector:	EO
Internal Accessories:	Platform and port for auto-strobe sensor.
External Accessories:	Threaded holes for meter brackets and tripod.
	Accessory shoes for flash arms.
	50-ft. cord with EO connector for remote control with motor-drive cameras.
	Manual override kit for motor-drive cameras in case motor fails.
	Motor-drive reset button—factory-installed modification to prevent accidental triggering of motor-driven Nikon F cameras only.
Operating Depth:	300 ft.

Hydro 35 ports: Fisheye (left), Standard dome (on housing), and Flat (right).

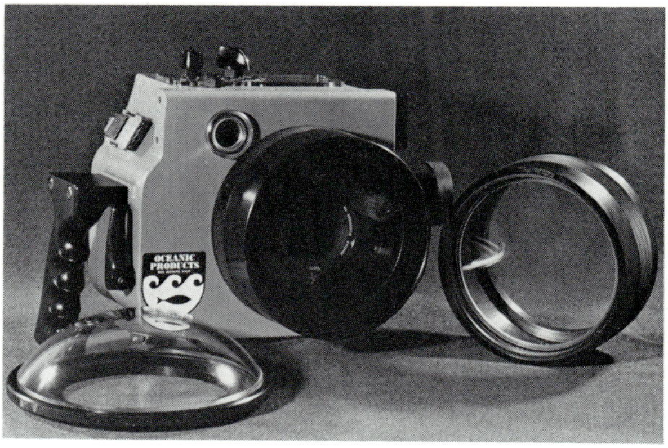

Hydro 35 with Nikon F, 24mm lens and AD-1 finder.

1. Shutter-release control.
2. Latch (4).
3. Accessory shoe.
4. Film-advance control.
5. Shutter-speed control.
6. Auto-strobe-sensor port.
7. Aperture-control shaft (knob on back).
8. Focus control.
9. Viewing port.
10. Aperture-control linkage.
11. Focus-control gear.

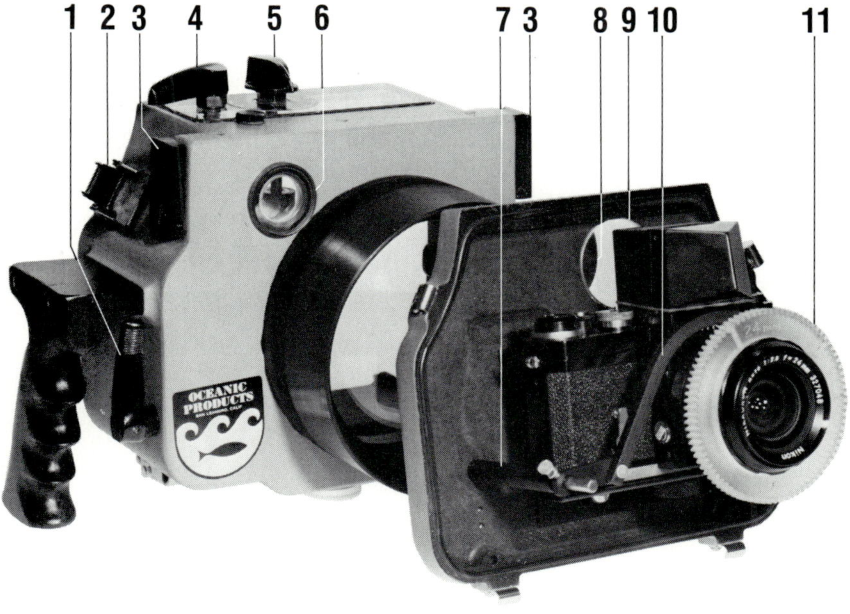

Ikelite Housings

The Ikelite housings for the Nikon F and F2 cameras are made of a clear molded plastic called Lexan. Totally impervious to salt-water corrosion, the housings are extremely tough and capable of taking a lot of abuse—the housings should not be compared to the glued acrylic boxes of the past. The ports used with the housing are made of Plexiglas, a material not as tough as Lexan, but its optical qualities are much better. The camera is attached to the back of the housing with a tripod screw, so before film can be changed, the camera must be removed completely. Four stainless steel latches hold the two halves of the housing together, and a large o-ring ensures the housing's waterproof integrity. All the controls are sealed with patented Quad-X rings—a type of o-ring with four lobes for greater sealing efficiency.

See the following specifications and illustration for detailed information on the different parts of the housing.

Ikelite Housing Specifications

Cameras:	Nikon F and F2 series.
Ports and Lenses:	Standard flat port used with normal through 35mm wide-angle lenses.
	Macro port used with 105mm lens through 55mm Macro (without M-ring).
	Dome port used with 35mm through 20mm lenses. Note: Lenses that cannot focus to 12 in. require a close-up lens.
	Extension port used with 135mm lens through 55mm Macro with M-ring (no focus control).
	Extension port with focus knob used with 135mm lens through 55mm Macro (with M-ring) to provide full focus control.
Viewfinder Recommended:	DA-1 Action Finder.
Controls:	Shutter speed—gear.
	Film advance—direct mechanical linkage.
	Focus control—gears.
	Shutter release—direct mechanical linkage.
	Aperture—friction.
Motor Drive:	See Ikelite SLR-MD-250.
Connector:	Ikelite.
External Accessories:	Hardware and mounting holes for brackets and flash arms.
Operating Depth:	300 ft.

Ikelite ports: (L. to R.) Macro, Extension, Dome, Extension with focus control, and Standard flat.

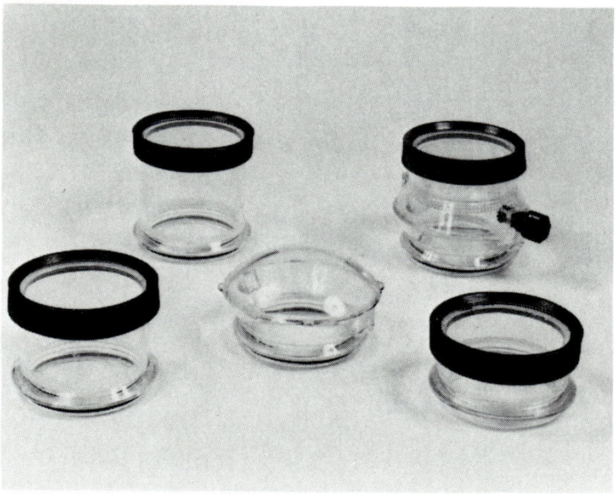

Ikelite housing wired for use with flashbulbs.

1. Shutter release.
2. Connector.
3. Accessory hardware.
4. Film-advance control.
5. Port latch.
6. Latch (4).
7. Shutter-speed control.
8. Aperture control.
9. Focus control.
10. Camera tray.
11. Synch cord.
12. Battery.
13. Flash terminals.

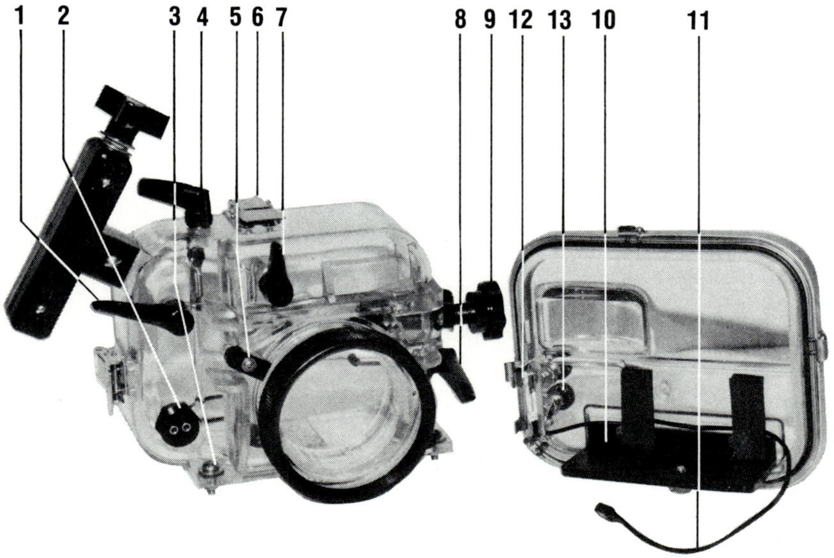

Ikelite MD 250 Housing

This Ikelite housing is designed specifically for use with the F2-Series cameras equipped with motor drive and 250-exposure magazine back. The housing is made of the same materials used in the standard Ikelite housings for the F and F2 cameras and is as rugged and well constructed.

The 250-exposure magazine provides the equivalent of seven 36-exposure rolls of film in one 100-ft. bulk-loaded roll. Without opening the housing or camera, 250 pictures can be taken. Perfect for the professional photographer on assignment or the scientist making a detailed study, the large film capacity this housing affords may also give the diver who makes infrequent trips to clear water the perfect opportunity to get the most out of a diving vacation.

With the motor drive, film can be exposed one frame at a time or at a continuously variable rate of 1 to 5 frames per second. At maximum frame-exposure rates, slow shutter speeds cannot be used, and the use of electronic flash is limited to special units with fast recycling times. In the one-frame-at-a-time mode, motor-driven cameras can be used with standard underwater strobe units.

The housing—with camera, motor drive, and 250-exposure magazine—weighs slightly less than 15 lbs. in air, but underwater, it has neutral buoyancy when the detachable 3-lb. handle is in place. The handle is centrally located, making the housing well balanced and fairly easy to use, considering its bulk.

SLR-MD-250 Housing Specifications

Cameras:	Nikon F and F2 series.
Ports and Lenses:	Standard flat port used with normal through 35mm wide-angle lenses.
	Macro port (flat) used with 105mm lens through 55mm Macro (without M-ring).
	Extension port (flat) used with 135mm lens through 55mm Macro (with M-ring).
	Dome port used with 35mm through 20mm lenses. Note: Lenses that cannot focus to 12 in. require a close-up lens.
Viewfinder Recommended:	DA-1 Action Finder.
Controls:	Focus control—gears.
	Shutter release—direct mechanical linkage.
	Aperture—gears.
Motor Drive:	Designed to accept motor drive and 250-exposure magazine. Can be used with motor drive and 36-exposure back.
Connector:	Ikelite.
External Accessories:	Hardware and mounting holes for brackets and flash arms.
Operating Depth:	300 ft.

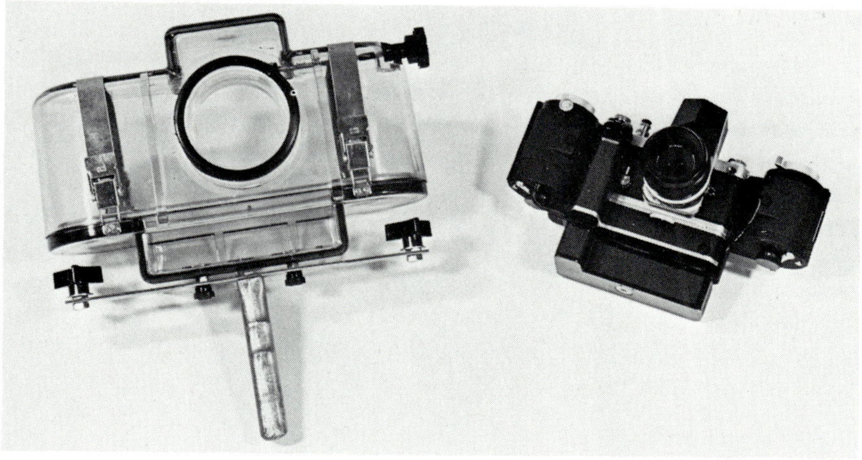

Ikelite SLR-MD-250 housing (left) and Nikon F with motor drive, 250-exposure magazine and AD-1 finder (right).

The housings on this page are early models of the SLR-MD-250. Exact control locations differ on models now in production.

1. Accessory tray.
2. Latch and strap.
3. Handle.
4. Port.
5. Accessory hardware.
6. Focus control.

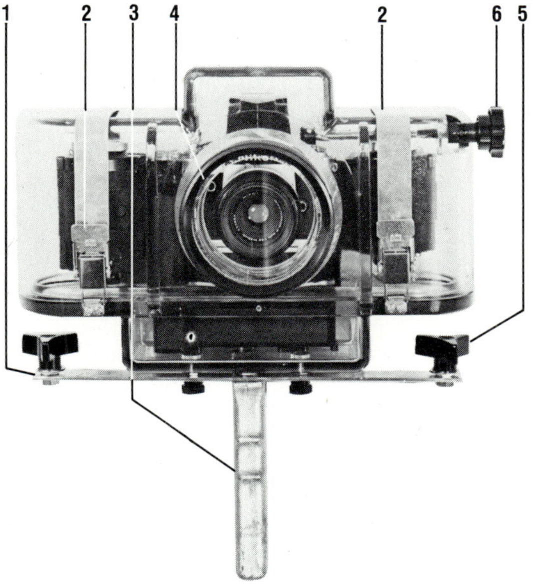

Housing the Nikkormats

Off-the-shelf housings for the Nikkormats are presently available only from Ikelite. Lexan housings similar to the ones described for the Nikon F and F2 cameras are available for the Nikkormat FTn, FT2, and EL. The lens- and port-acceptance specifications are exactly the same; the housings differ only with respect to control location and other minor aspects. The housings for the FT and FT2 do not have a shutter-speed control, but shutter-speed control is provided on the EL housing. Nikkormats are good cameras to use underwater because they can synchronize with electronic flash at a high shutter speed (1/125 sec.) and because they retain their light-metering capabilities when housed.

Discontinued Housings

Over the years, many housings have been made for the Nikon cameras. Many of the companies that made these housings are no longer in business, but their housings continue to be popular with those who have them, and many old housings are sought after when they appear on the used-equipment market. Many of these housings

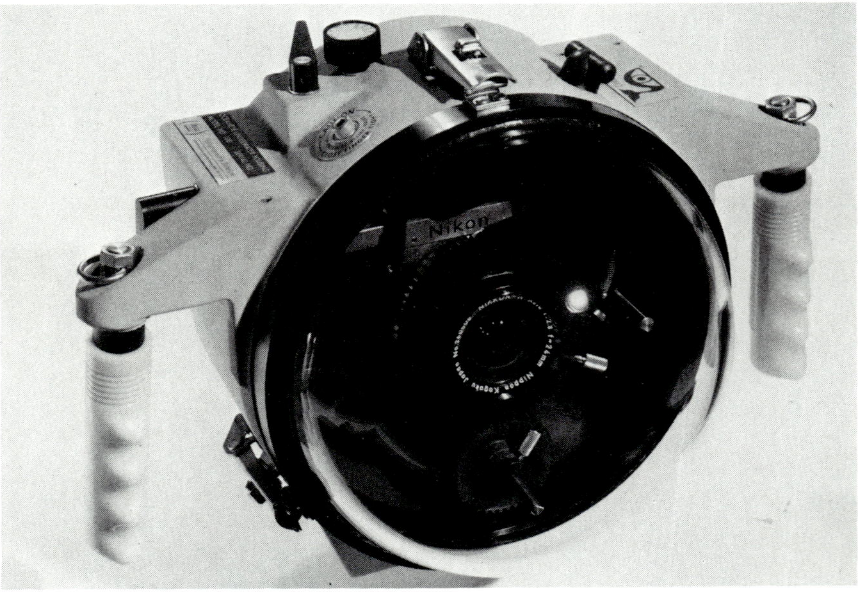

Ocean Eye 100. Though this housing has not been made for a number of years, it continues to be sought after. The principal housing used by National Geographic photographers, it accepts almost all the Nikkor lenses up to 135mm without changing domes. A new housing similar to the Ocean Eye 100 may soon be on the market.

were excellent, and the demise of the manufacturers had little to do with the quality of their products. Quite the contrary. Many of the housings were sold for less money than it cost to produce them. Some of the more popular housings, no longer available from the manufacturer, are illustrated here.

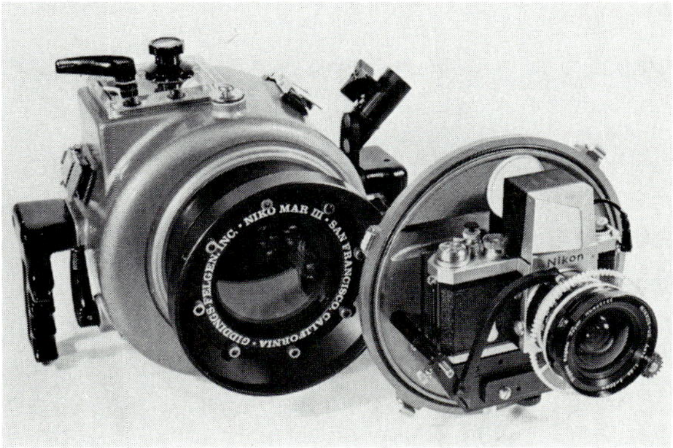

Niko-Mar III. This housing is no longer made, but it is available on the used-equipment market and it is still popular. Originally made by Giddings-Felgen, Inc. (no longer in business), the housing and other products made by the company are being serviced and repaired by G/F Industries, Inc.

Sub 35. French Underwater Industries produced this housing for a short time during the early 1970's, but it is no longer available.

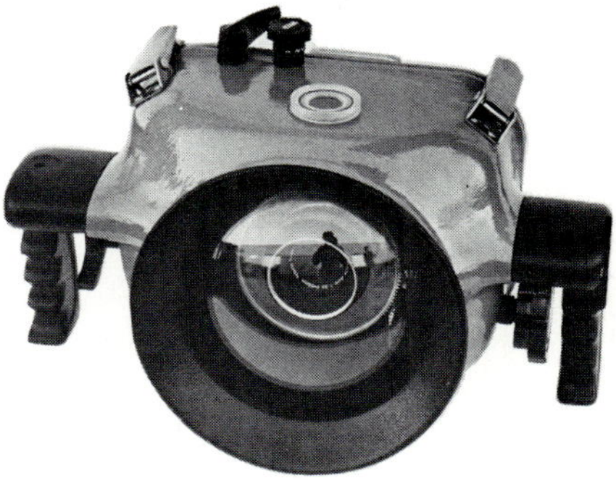

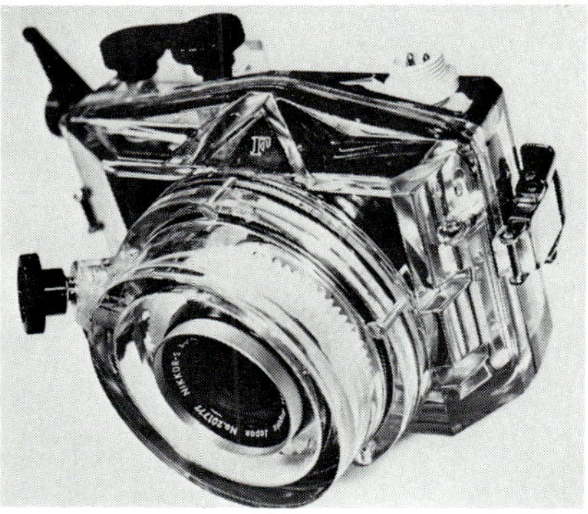

Sea Glove. This housing literally fits the Nikon F like a glove. The compact housing has interchangeable ports and is equipped with Sea Link connectors. Produced for a short time by Sea Research and Development, the housings are now discontinued, but the company will build custom housings for any Nikon camera.

CAMERA INSTALLATION

When installing your camera in any of the previously described housings, follow the manufacturer's instructions to the letter. The manufacturers want you to get the most from your housings, and the last thing they want you to do is to flood one of their housings with your camera in it. Follow their instructions.

In addition, with any housing you use, consider the general procedures and precautions below to avoid spoiling a dive by losing pictures or, worse yet, a camera.

Synchronization

One of the easiest ways to return from a dive with no pictures is to incorrectly synch the camera. Before attaching your camera to the housing, check to be sure that the camera is set to the proper synchronization mode and shutter speed for the type of lighting you're using. On the Nikon F cameras, you must lift the shutter ring and turn it until the required synchronization-mode symbol appears in the window in front of the shutter-speed dial. On the Nikon F2 cameras, proper synch modes are automatically selected when the appropriate shutter speeds are used.

Once the camera is mounted on the open housing, you can attach

Inside the housing (left) the PC connector is inserted in the PC terminal on the camera body linking the camera to female EO connector on the outside of the housing (right). The male EO connector links the camera and housing to the strobe.

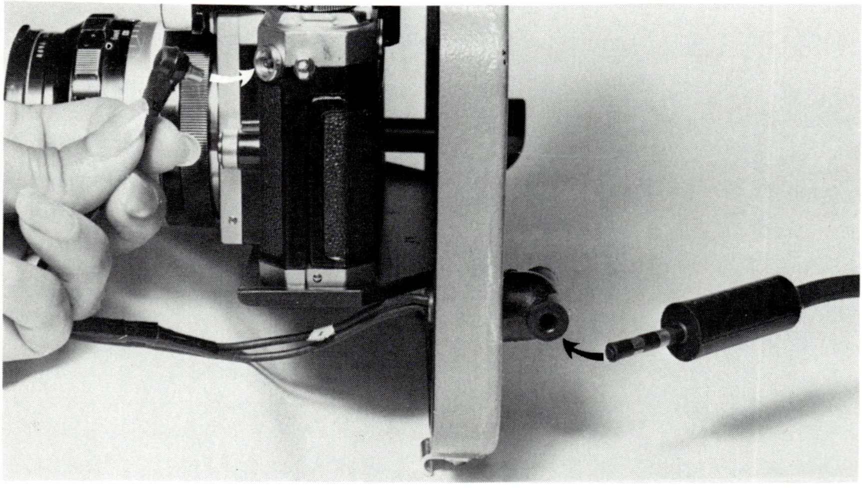

the PC connector that will link the strobe to the camera. When selecting a housing, check to see that the PC plug on the housing matches the PC terminal on your camera. PC terminals on the Nikon F are the simple push-in type. On the F2 cameras, the PC terminals and connector are held together by a screw-in collar on the male connection. Nikkormat FTn and FT2 cameras have push-in-type PC terminals, and EL and ELW cameras have the screw-in type. You can easily adapt your housing PC cord to accept either or both types if there's a chance you'll be using cameras with different PC terminals in the same housing.

When the PC terminal and connector are joined, position the PC cord so that it does not interfere with any of the housing controls. Tape it in position if there is a chance it could.

Final Assembly

Avoid condensation. Condensation tends to be more of a problem with metal housings than with plastic ones, but to avoid the problem entirely, a fresh desiccant (silica gel) packet should be enclosed in the housing with the camera before a dive. Secure the packet to the housing or camera, with tape or a rubber band, so that it does not interfere with any of the controls and so it will not break free during the dive. A free-floating packet of desiccant can block controls and your view if it works its way in front of the lens.

Protect ports. When doing *anything* around the housing, protect the port as you would your camera lens. Construct an outside port cover of some kind and cover the inside of the port when working in the housing. Most ports are made of plastic and can be scratched easily.

Align camera. When mounting the camera to the housing, be sure the camera is square and properly aligned. After tightening the tripod nut, tape the nut in position. This will prevent it from backing off and will eliminate the chance of the camera becoming loose and shifting its position during a dive.

Check controls. Before you seal the housing, visually inspect and check the operation of all the controls you have connected. After sealing, link and check the remaining controls.

Seal carefully. Immediately before sealing the housing, carefully inspect the main o-ring for foreign matter and nicks; clean and change the o-ring if required. As you join the two halves of the housing, check the PC cord to be sure it is not in the way. When closing the housing, do so by securing the snap clamps diagonally opposite each other at the same time. In clear plastic housings, you should be able to see the actual forming of the o-ring seal as the snap clamps are closed. Open the housing by releasing diagonally opposite clamps at the same time.

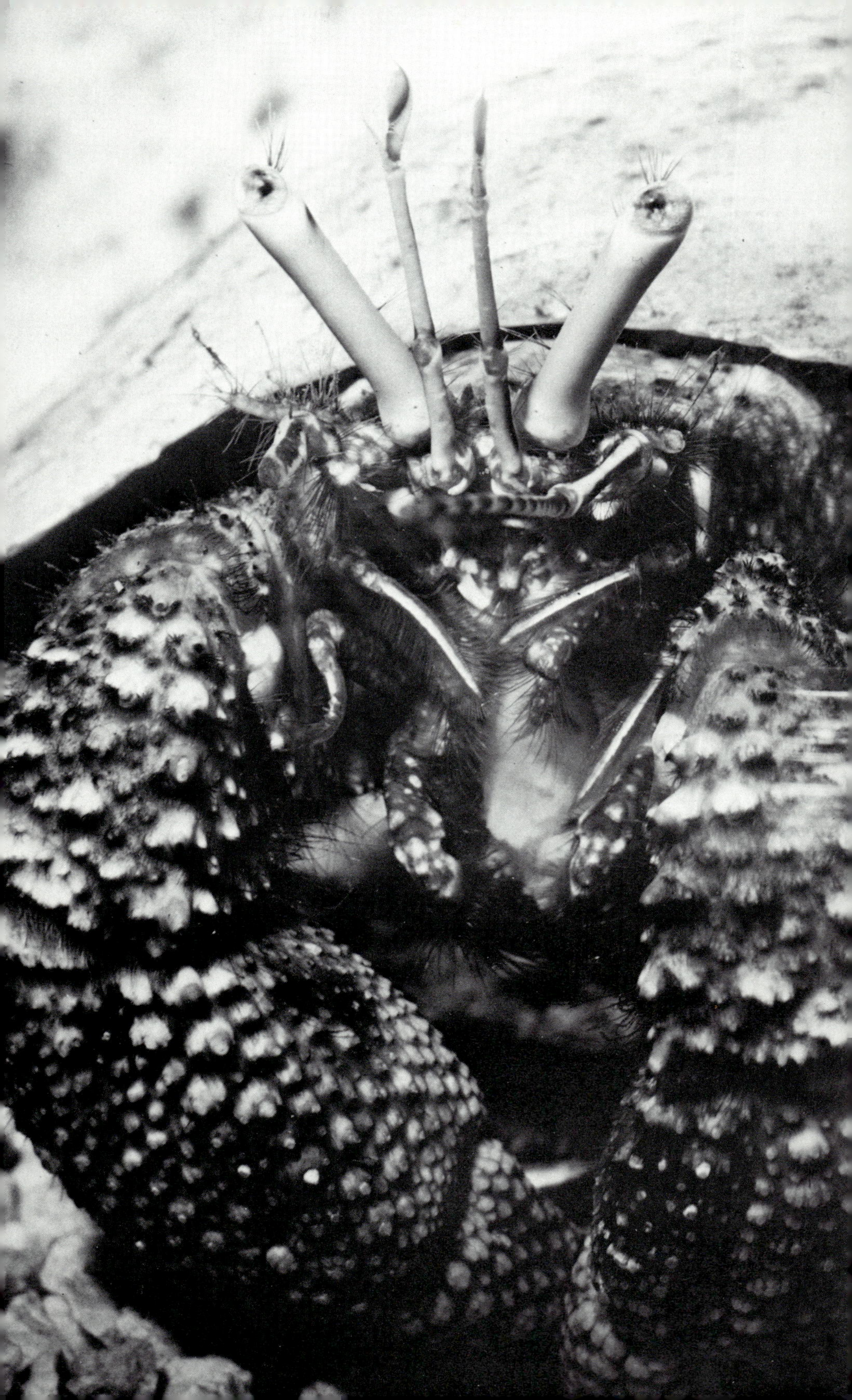

8

Close-Up Photography

After you have been diving awhile, you become aware of the tiny creatures that often go unnoticed by novice divers. Whether in the cold waters off northern California, or in the tropical seas off Bonaire, one square foot of rocky bottom or coral reef can reveal, to the diver willing to look, myriad beautiful creatures. Almost all of them are easy to photograph because they are slow-moving or actually live attached to the bottom.

Close-up photography and macrophotography (also called extreme close-up photography) are the recording of images at distances closer than the normal shortest focusing distance of the camera lens you're using. For the Nikonos user, there are essentially two ways to form images on film of subjects that are close to the lens. One way is to attach an optical element to the front of the camera's lens, which acts much like a magnifying glass. The second way is to reposition the camera lens a greater-than-normal distance from the film plane.

Close-Up Lenses

Close-up lenses (also called supplementary, or auxiliary, lenses), which attach to the front of a lens, make it possible to focus the lens closer than normal. Exactly how close depends on the optical strength

Results like this closeup of a hermit crab (left) can be attained with the equipment described in this chapter.

of the particular close-up lens and the particular lens being used on the camera.

With all supplementary lenses, though, if the camera lens with which it is being used can focus at a certain distance, the combination will yield a specific area of coverage and a specific depth of field. This is true of all close-up lenses because of strict optical laws. No matter who the manufacturer, if a close-up lens in combination with a camera lens can be focused at X distance, it will yield Y area of coverage and have Z depth of field. Using focusing distance is a good way to compare underwater close-up lenses by different manufacturers because they all designate the optical strength of their lenses in different ways. Most close-up lenses available to Nikonos photographers can focus between 6 in. and 20 in. when used with the 35mm lens. The table below may be helpful in selecting a lens for your particular needs.

CLOSE-UP LENSES USED WITH THE NIKONOS 35mm LENS
(Measured Underwater Distances)

FOCUSED DISTANCE (in.)	AREA COVERAGE (in.)
6	3 × 4
8	4 × 6
10	5 × 8
12	6 × 9
14	7 × 11
16	8 × 12
18	13.5 × 20
20	15 × 22

Note: Depth of field varies with the aperture selected.

To select a close-up lens, simply determine if the area covered by the field of the lens is appropriate for the kind of subjects you're interested in photographing.

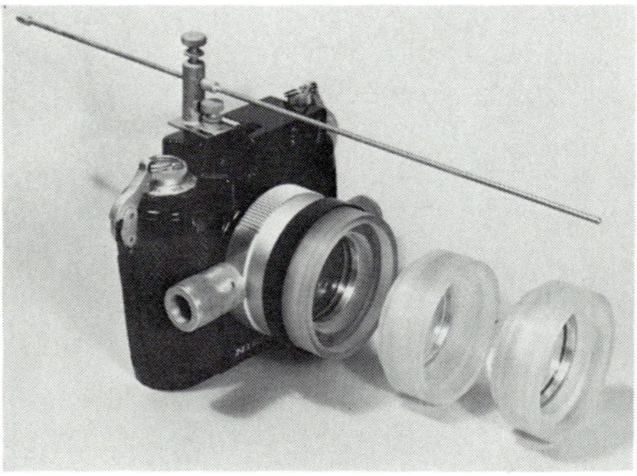

Close-up lenses, like these made by Hydro Photo, are placed in front of the camera lens. They can be installed and removed underwater.

Since close-up lenses attach to the front of the camera lens, they can be attached and removed underwater. This is an advantage over the next type of close-up device.

Extension Tubes

Using extension tubes (also called macro tubes, or extension rings) is the second method available to Nikonos users for close-up work. An extension tube is simply a tube that is inserted between the camera body and the camera lens. The tube, equipped with its own o-ring seals, physically locates the lens at a precise distance from the film plane. This makes it possible to focus the lens at closer-than-normal distances. Exactly how close depends on the length of the extension: The longer the tube, the closer the lens can be focused, and, therefore, the higher the magnification. Most Nikonos extension tubes on the market make it possible to focus the 35mm lens closer than with the close-up lenses in common use. With extension tubes, Nikonos photographers can record on film images that are life size and larger. Close-up lenses at these magnifications simply can't match the quality that a tube can produce.

Extension tubes are generally discussed in terms of their reproduction ratio. Reproduction ratio is simply the size of the image on film compared to the actual subject photographed. A reproduction ratio of 1:1 is life size, meaning that if an object's image is 1 in. long on film, the object *is* 1 in. long. A reproduction ratio of 1:2 means the image on film will be half the actual size of the object. And a reproduction ratio of 2:1 means that the film image is twice the size of the real object. Remember, the first number of ratio indicates the image size.

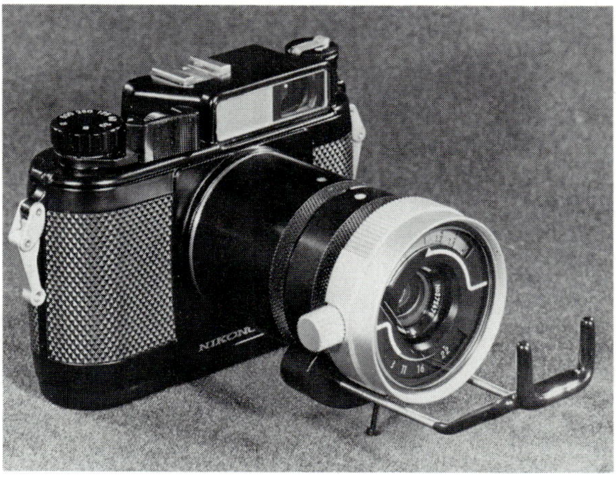

Extension tubes, like these two by Oceanic Products, are placed between the lens and the camera body. They cannot be removed underwater. Tubes by OP can be used stacked or singly.

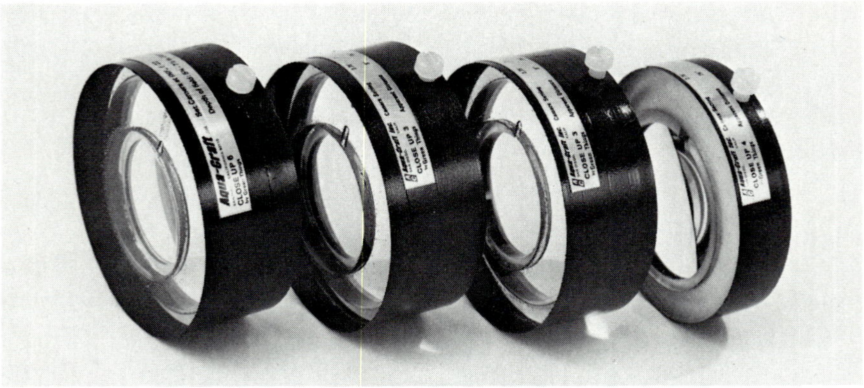

Close-up lenses by Aqua-Craft (above). Extension tubes by Subsea (below).

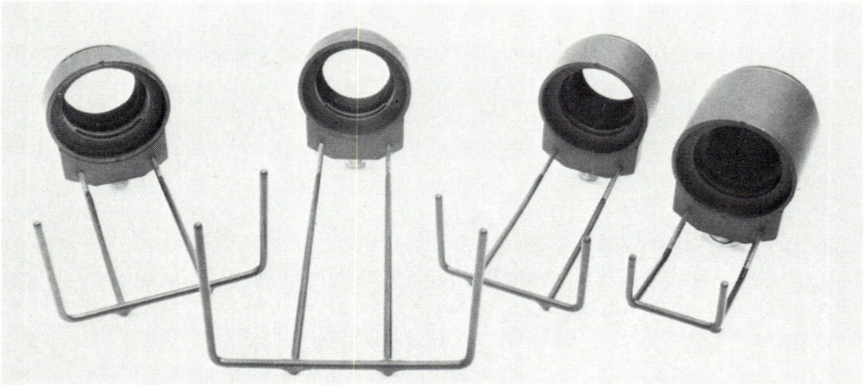

Framing and Focusing Devices

Almost all the close-up devices designed for use with the Nikonos are equipped with some kind of aid to assist photographers in framing and focusing their subjects. As you saw in Chapter 1, looking through the Nikonos viewfinder at a subject at close range will not show you what the lens will record on film. This is because of parallax. Working close-up with the Nikonos therefore makes it absolutely necessary to use a framing aid.

A framing aid is also necessary for another reason: It is an optical fact of life that the closer you focus a lens, the shallower its depth of field becomes. As with normal photography, depth of field is determined by film-to-subject distance and aperture, for any given lens. At very close distances, depth of field decreases drastically; it can often

With this lens focuser by Aqua-Craft you can visually focus your Nikonos lenses to ensure that your framer is correctly positioned. To use, it must stand in a tray of water deep enough to cover the front element of the lens.

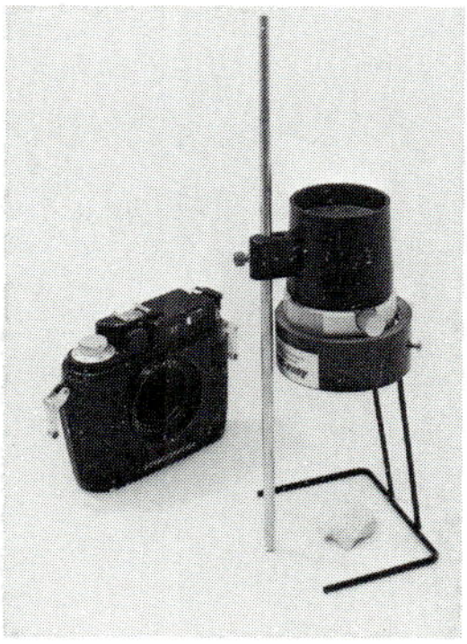

be as shallow as $^1/_{16}$ in. Estimating the distance to a field of focus that thin is virtually impossible; the need for a framing and focusing aid is apparent.

Framing and focusing devices are simply wire guides that project in front of the lens and end at the point where the camera lens (with the close-up device) focuses. At this plane of focus, the wire guides form a frame slightly larger than the field covered by the lens and close-up device. To use these devices properly, simply move the frame until the subject is positioned within it. Bear in mind that depth of field is not split equally in front of and behind the frame; the zone of sharpness is greater behind the frame than in front of it.

Whatever device you use, be sure to follow the manufacturer's instructions to the letter, especially with regard to the recommended

Using a framing device will frighten some marine creatures. Here a photographer works with a close-up lens but no framer. For good results without a framer you must know the depth of field your close-up equipment will yield.

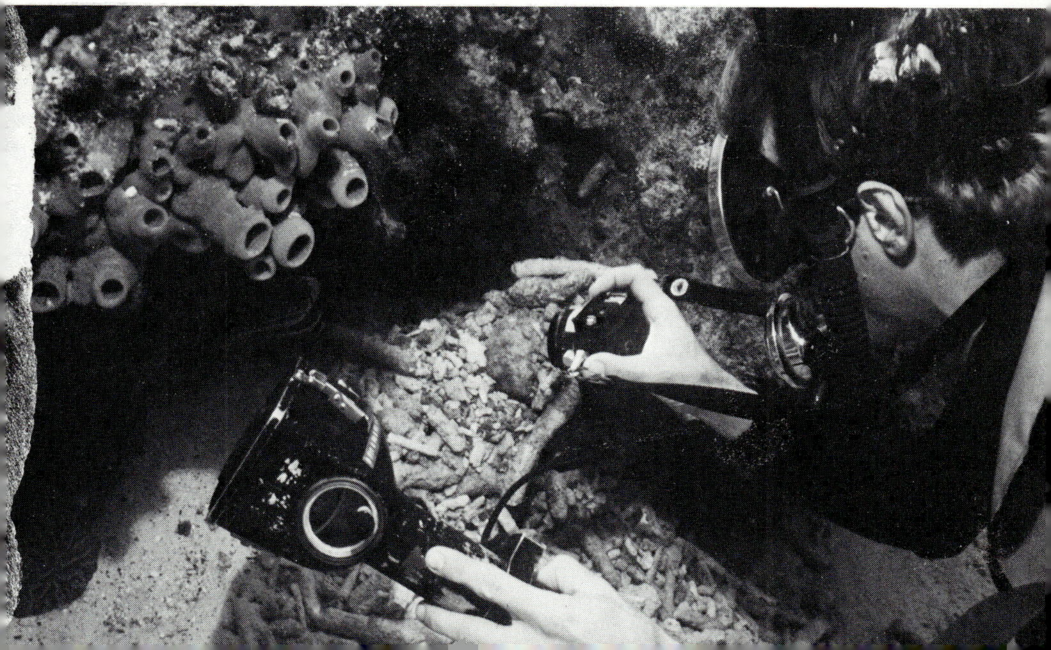

distance setting of your camera lens. Some close-up devices require the camera lens to be set at infinity; others function properly when the camera lens is focused at its closest focusing distance. Using the wrong settings can mean unsharp pictures. Any close-up device (lens or tube) and camera lens can operate together over the entire focusing range of the camera lens—from its closest focusing distance to infinity. But to change the position of the framer/focuser requires a specialized piece of equipment: a lens focuser. With a lens focuser, you can visually focus a Nikonos lens and set the framer/focuser to any plane of focus you desire. If you do not have a lens focuser, follow the instructions with your close-up device, and do not change the position of your framer/focuser.

NIKONOS CLOSE-UP OUTFIT

The Nikonos Close-Up Outfit is an auxiliary lens system, but the lens used is not a simple close-up lens. It is a two-element, two-group precision lens computed to maintain the high quality of the optics of the Nikonos lenses. The auxiliary lens, in combination with the appropriate frame, can be used to produce crisp close-ups with the 28mm, 35mm, or 80mm lenses. In addition to the auxiliary lens and three frames, the outfit consists of the distance-determining bracket, supporting rod, special flash bracket, and carrying case.

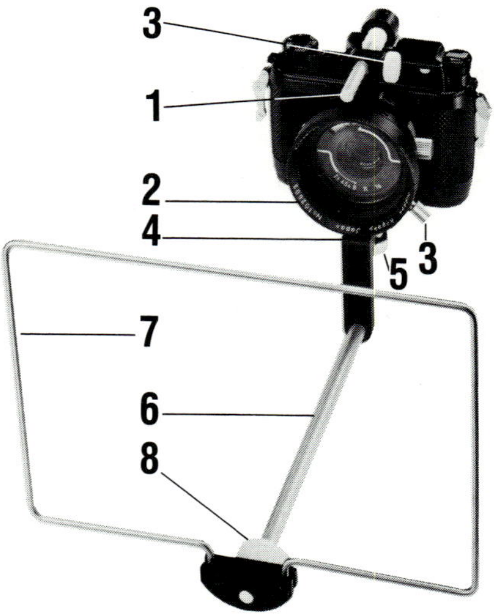

Nikonos Close-Up Outfit

1. Supporting rod.
2. Auxiliary lens.
3. Lens-attachment knobs.
4. Accessory shoe (not visible).
5. Bracket-attachment knob.
6. Distance-determining bracket.
7. W28 framer.
8. Collar.

Assembling the Close-Up Outfit

To rig your Nikonos for close-up work, first slide the supporting rod into the accessory shoe on top of the camera. Holding it in place, slip the auxiliary lens over the camera lens so the supporting rod goes into the hole on the auxiliary lens mount. Push the auxiliary lens toward the camera body until it comes to rest evenly. Tighten the two knobs on the auxiliary lens mount.

Next, slide the distance-determining bracket into the accessory shoe on the auxiliary lens and secure it by tightening the knob on the bracket. Finally, select the field frame that matches the camera lens. Use the W28 frame with the 28mm lens, the W35 with the 35mm lens, and the W80 with the 80mm lens. Insert the open end of the frame into the holes at the end of the distance-determining bracket. Tightening the collar at the end of the bracket will complete the assembly.

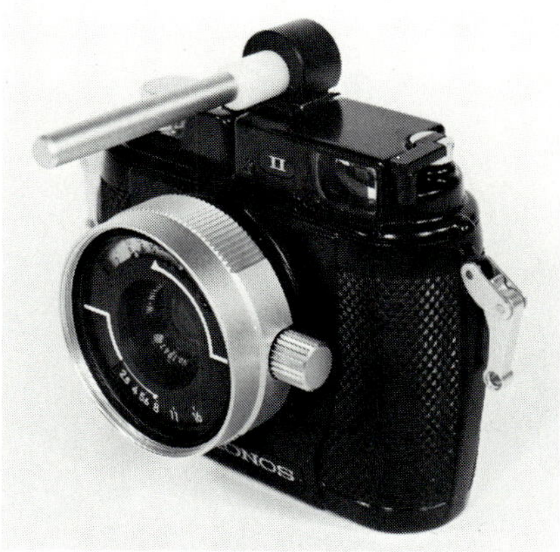

Insert supporting rod in camera accessory shoe.

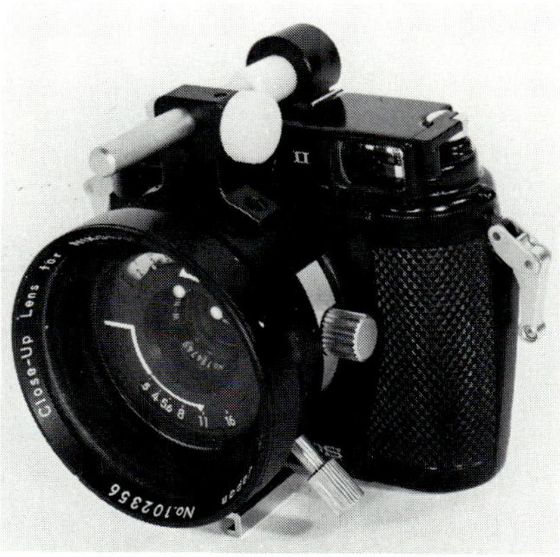

Slip close-up lens over supporting rod and tighten knobs.

Slide bracket into lens accessory shoe and tighten knob.

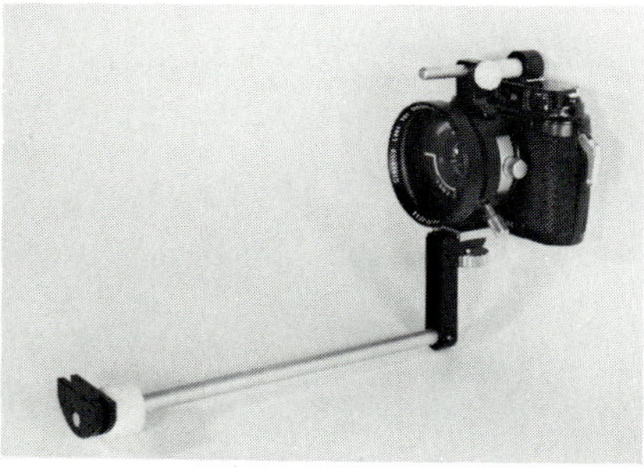

Insert frame into end of bracket and tighten the collar.

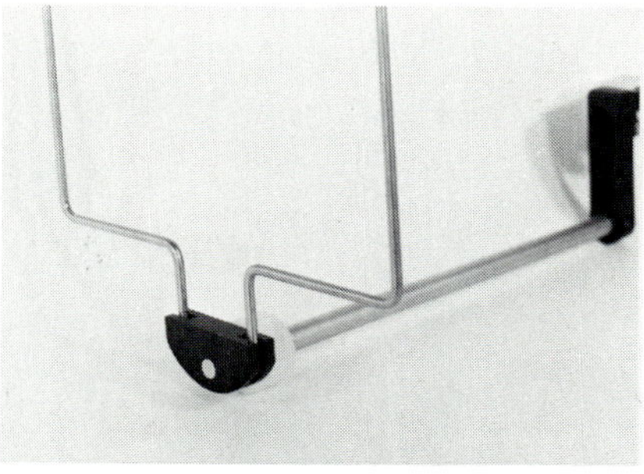

Attaching the Flash Unit

To fix the Nikonos Flash Unit on the camera for close-up photography, it is necessary to use the special-purpose holder supplied with the Nikonos Close-Up Outfit. First, attach the standard Nikonos flash bracket to the camera (see page 74 for detailed instructions). Next, attach the special-purpose holder to it by inserting the locating rod into the clamp of the bracket on the camera. Be sure the locating pin on the rod goes into the groove on the clamp. Tighten the clamp's knob to secure the rod.

Next, open the special-purpose holder and place the hand-grip tube in it. Shut the holder and adjust the reflector so that it is level with the camera lens and pointing toward the frame. There is also an engraved black line on the special-purpose bracket to help you point the reflector in the correct direction. Finally, tighten the unit in place.

It is best not to attach the cable sleeve to the hand-grip tube because it may interfere with aiming and handling the camera.

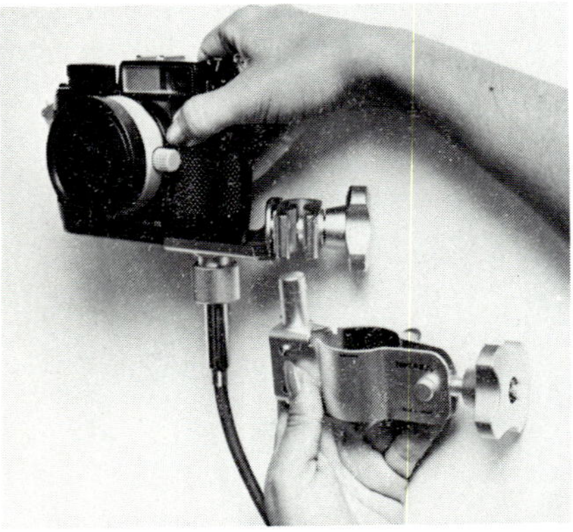

Insert close-up flash bracket into standard flash bracket.

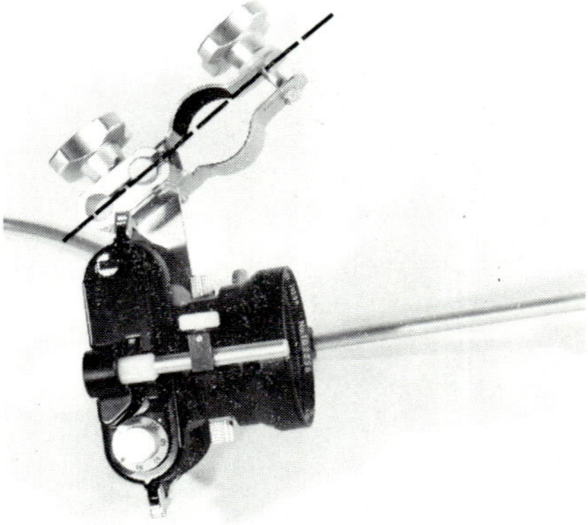

Align bracket as shown and tighten.

Place flash unit in bracket.

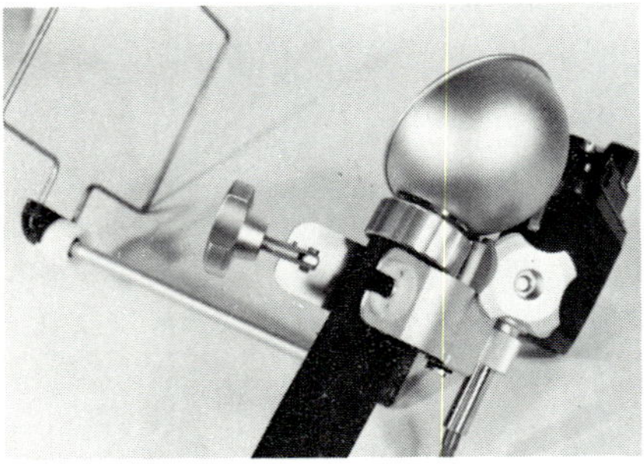

Position flash to illuminate field and tighten.

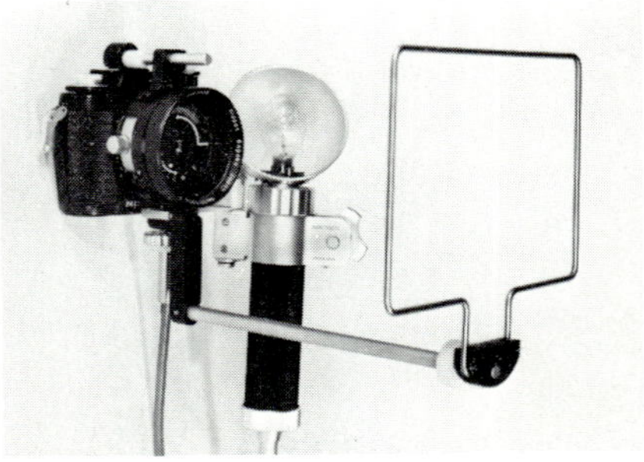

Using the Nikonos Close-Up Outfit Underwater

Before you take your first picture, be sure that the distance scale of your camera is set at infinity. This is an important step. Your pictures will be out of focus if the lens is not set at infinity. Next, check the aperture to be sure it is adjusted for proper exposure with the kind of film and flashbulb you're using. Also check your shutter-speed dial for proper synchronization of your flash. Finally, check to make sure there are no air bubbles trapped between the camera lens and the auxiliary lens. If bubbles are trapped, simply reposition the camera to let them escape.

Move the camera toward the subject until it is positioned within the field frame. The image recorded on the film will be bounded by an imaginary line approximately ⅜ in. within the frame. You can make your exposure when your subject is within that area.

Subject Field with Nikonos Close-Up Outfit

Lens	Application	Subject field
28mm	Underwater	144 x 216mm (5.68 x 8.51in.)
35mm	On land	155 x 233mm (6.11 x 9.18in.)
	Underwater	109 x 164mm (4.30 x 6.38in.)
80mm	On land	71 x 106mm (2.80 x 4.18in.)
	Underwater	53 x 79mm (2.09 x 3.11in.)

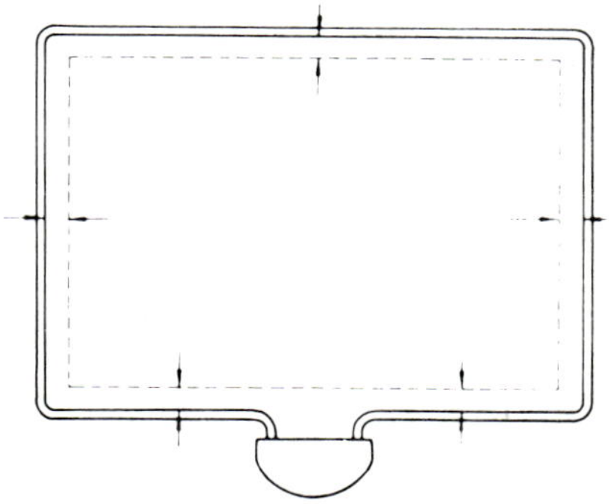

The image you will record is the area approximately 3/8 in. within the frame.

Depth of Field Underwater

With the 28mm lens in place, and using an aperture of *f*/22, depth of field will be approximately 3 in. (about 2/5 the DOF in front of the frame and about 3/5 beyond it). With the 80mm lens in place and the aperture at *f*/4, depth of field will be less than 1/16 in. When using the 80mm lens, it is best to avoid apertures wider than *f*/11. At *f*/11, you will have depth of field of approximately 3/16 in. When working with a shallow depth of field, you will have good results if you concentrate on subjects that are virtually two-dimensional, such as the surface of various corals, sponges, sea fans, and the other animals that cover pilings and rocks. Page C7 in the color section illustrates some of these creatures.

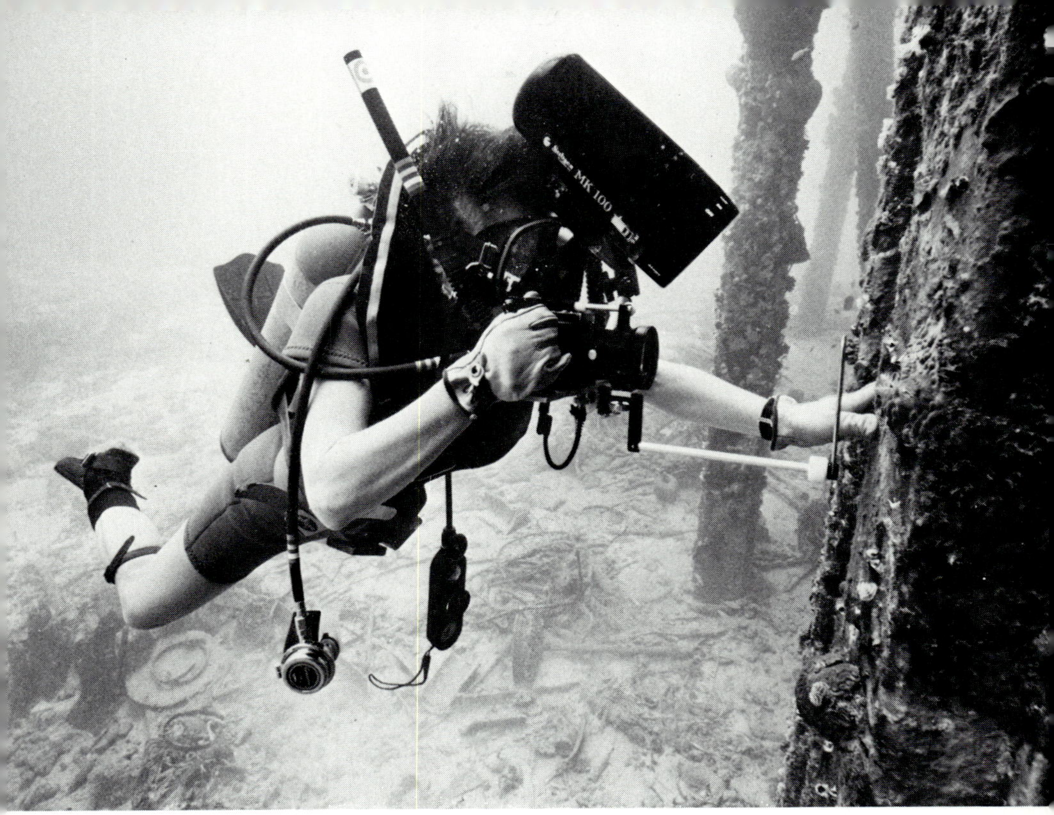

Depth of Field with Nikonos Close-Up Outfit

Lens	Application	Depth of Field						
		Open	f/4	f/5.6	f/8	f/11	f/16	f/22
28mm f/3.5	Underwater	+6.3mm (+0.252 in.) −5.9mm (−0.233 in.)	+7.2mm (+0.284 in.) −6.7mm (−0.268 in.)	+10.2mm (+0.402 in.) −9.3mm (−0.368 in.)	+14.8mm (+0.583 in.) −13.2mm (−0.520 in.)	+21.5mm (+0.847 in.) −17.8mm (−0.706 in.)	+31.3mm (+1.233 in.) −25.1mm (−0.989 in.)	+45.1m (+1.776 i −33.3m (−1.311
35mm f/2.5	On land	+3.7mm (+0.146 in.) −3.6mm (−0.142 in.)	+6.0mm (+0.236 in.) −5.6mm (−0.221 in.)	+8.5mm (+0.335 in.) −7.8mm (−0.308 in.)	+12.3mm (+0.485 in.) −11.1mm (−0.438 in.)	+17.3mm (+0.682 in.) −14.9mm (−0.587 in.)	+26.1mm (+1.035 in.) −21.1mm (−0.832 in.)	+37.4m (+1.474 i −27.8m (−1.095
	Underwater	+2.8mm (+0.110 in.) −2.7mm (−0.106 in.)	+4.5mm (+0.177 in.) −4.2mm (−0.166 in.)	+6.4mm (+0.252 in.) −5.9mm (−0.232 in.)	+9.2mm (+0.362 in.) −8.4mm (−0.331 in.)	+12.8mm (+0.504 in.) −11.4mm (−0.449 in.)	+19.1mm (+0.753 in.) −16.2mm (−0.638 in.)	+27.0m (+1.063 i −21.7m (−0.855
80mm f/4	On land		+1.3mm (+0.051 in.) −1.1mm (−0.043 in.)	+1.8mm (+0.071 in.) −1.5mm (−0.059 in.)	+2.5mm (+0.099 in.) −2.2mm (−0.087 in.)	+3.4mm (+0.138 in.) −3.1mm (−0.124 in.)	+5.0mm (+0.197 in.) −4.5mm (−0.177 in.)	+6.9m (+0.272 i −6.2m (−0.244
	Underwater		+1.0mm (+0.039 in.) −0.8mm (−0.032 in.)	+1.3mm (+0.051 in.) −1.2mm (−0.047 in.)	+1.9mm (+0.075 in.) −1.7mm (−0.067 in.)	+2.6mm (+0.102 in.) −2.3mm (−0.091 in.)	+3.7mm (+0.149 in.) −3.4mm (−0.138 in.)	+5.1m (+0.201 i −4.7m (−0.185

The (+) sign indicates rear depth, i.e., the distance beyond the field frame.
The (−) sign indicates front depth, i.e., the distance from the field frame in the direction towards the camera.

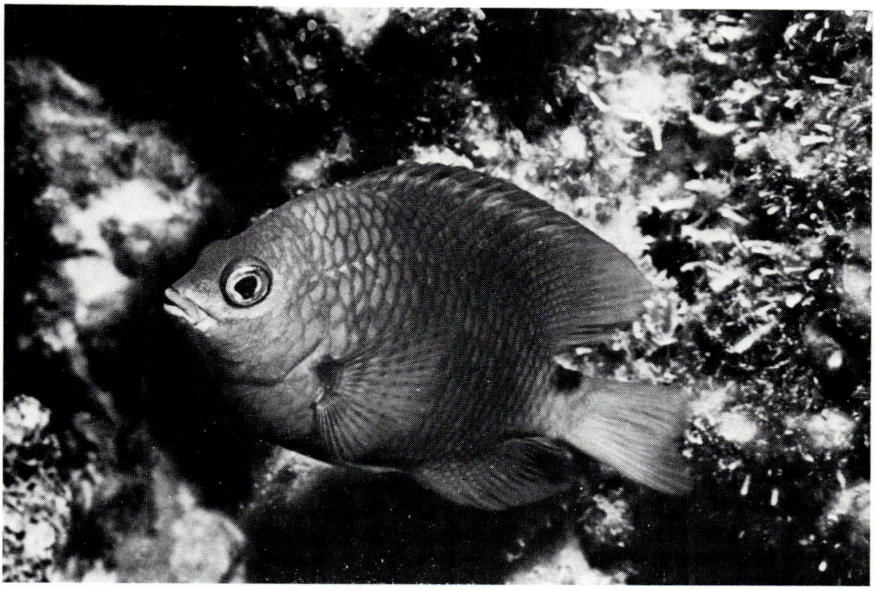

Pilings in tropical waters are excellent places to find close-up subjects(left). Here a photographer uses the Nikonos Close-Up Outfit with the 80mm lens. (above) A juvenile damselfish reproduced here life size.

Using the Nikonos Close-Up Outfit in Air

The Nikonos Close-Up Outfit can be used successfully in air, but it is necessary to use the W28 framer with the 35mm lens and the W35 framer with the 80mm lens. If the normal underwater frames are used, they will be recorded on film because in air the angles of coverage of the lenses are greater than underwater. For specific details on the areas covered when the system is used in air, see the table on page 133. Also remember that in-air depth of field will be less than a comparable lens–aperture combination will produce underwater. See the accompanying depth-of-field table for exact figures.

CLOSE-UPS WITH HOUSED CAMERAS

The advantages of using an SLR in a housing becomes especially apparent when doing close-up photography. There is nothing better than visually focusing on your subject and composing through the lens that will take the picture. You will know without a doubt that your picture will be sharp and that no extraneous elements you failed to notice will spoil your composition.

Certain species of fish and invertebrates are almost impossible to photograph when you have to use framing and focusing devices because the animals shy away as the framer approaches. With a housed SLR and the lenses described below, you will be able to focus, compose, and shoot, yet still keep the camera far enough away from your subjects to avoid frightening them.

To do SLR close-up photography underwater, you can use auxiliary lenses and extension tubes within the housing, but one of the Nikkor special-purpose lenses would make the task much easier and much more enjoyable. Either the 55mm *f*/3.5 Micro-Nikkor or the 105mm *f*/4 Micro-Nikkor is an excellent choice. With either one, you take "normal" pictures and extreme close-ups. Each can give a reproduction ratio of 1:2 at its closest focusing distance. With the 55mm *f*/3.5, the closest focusing distance is 9½ in.; with the 105mm *f*/4, it is 18 in. Greater reproduction ratios and closer focusing distances are attained when the lenses are used with their respective extension rings.

To use either of the above lenses in a housing, you will have to be sure there is enough room behind the lens port to permit the full extension of the lens when the housing is sealed. Most of the housings discussed previously can be equipped with special extension ports to accommodate lenses with long extensions.

EXPOSURE

For most of your close-up photography, you will probably work with flashbulbs or strobe lighting to show the brilliant colors and minute details of the subjects you'll be focusing on most often. Auxiliary lighting too makes it possible to use small *f*/stops and therefore attain maximum depth of field. As with normal-distance flash photography, making a test is the best way to ensure accurate exposures. Follow a procedure similar to the one outlined on page 79, keeping in mind that your flash-to-subject distances will be much smaller and that conducting the test at various depths will not be necessary because ambient light should have little effect on your exposures.

If you have already established exposure information and are trying to make adjustments for close-up photography, you will find that with a supplementary lens on the front of the camera lens, you won't have to make an exposure adjustment. Supplementary lenses do not affect the amount of light that will fall on your film. Your normal exposures will remain unchanged even with the higher magnification lenses. With extension tubes, this is not the case.

Extension tubes physically locate the lens a longer distance from the film plane than when the lens is mounted directly on the camera. This means that the light going to the film must travel a longer-than-normal distance. Because of this, there is a resultant falloff of light. The longer the extension tube, the more light lost.

With a 35mm lens and an extension tube that gives a reproduction ratio of 1:2, the light lost would require a compensation of one full *f*/stop; with a 1:1 tube, the exposure increase would be about two full *f*/stops; with a 2:1 tube, three full *f*/stops; and with a 3:1 tube, four full *f*/stops. (Because of the minimal amount of water between the subject and the lens at these magnifications, you'll find that the exposure compensations for extension tubes underwater are virtually the same for the corresponding tubes in air.)

Exposure compensation with extension tubes can be made by selecting wider apertures, but then depth of field will become more shallow. Moving your light source closer to your subject is the preferred method of increasing exposure because you'll be able to maintain depth of field. If your light is as close as it can be to your subject, and if you're using the largest flashbulb available or the highest power setting on your strobe and your exposure is still not adequate, you can change to a film of higher light sensitivity (higher ASA number). Again, conducting a test is the best way to establish accurate exposures.

Once you've established correct exposures for your particular equipment and film, you'll find that your flash-to-subject distance will change little. You should be able to lock your camera and light source in position and not have to move either through the course of a dive concentrating on close-up photography. Generally, you will make only minor aperture adjustments to compensate for a subject's reflectivity—opening one or two *f*/stops for a dark subject on a dark background, or stopping down one or two *f*/stops for a light-colored subject on a bright background.

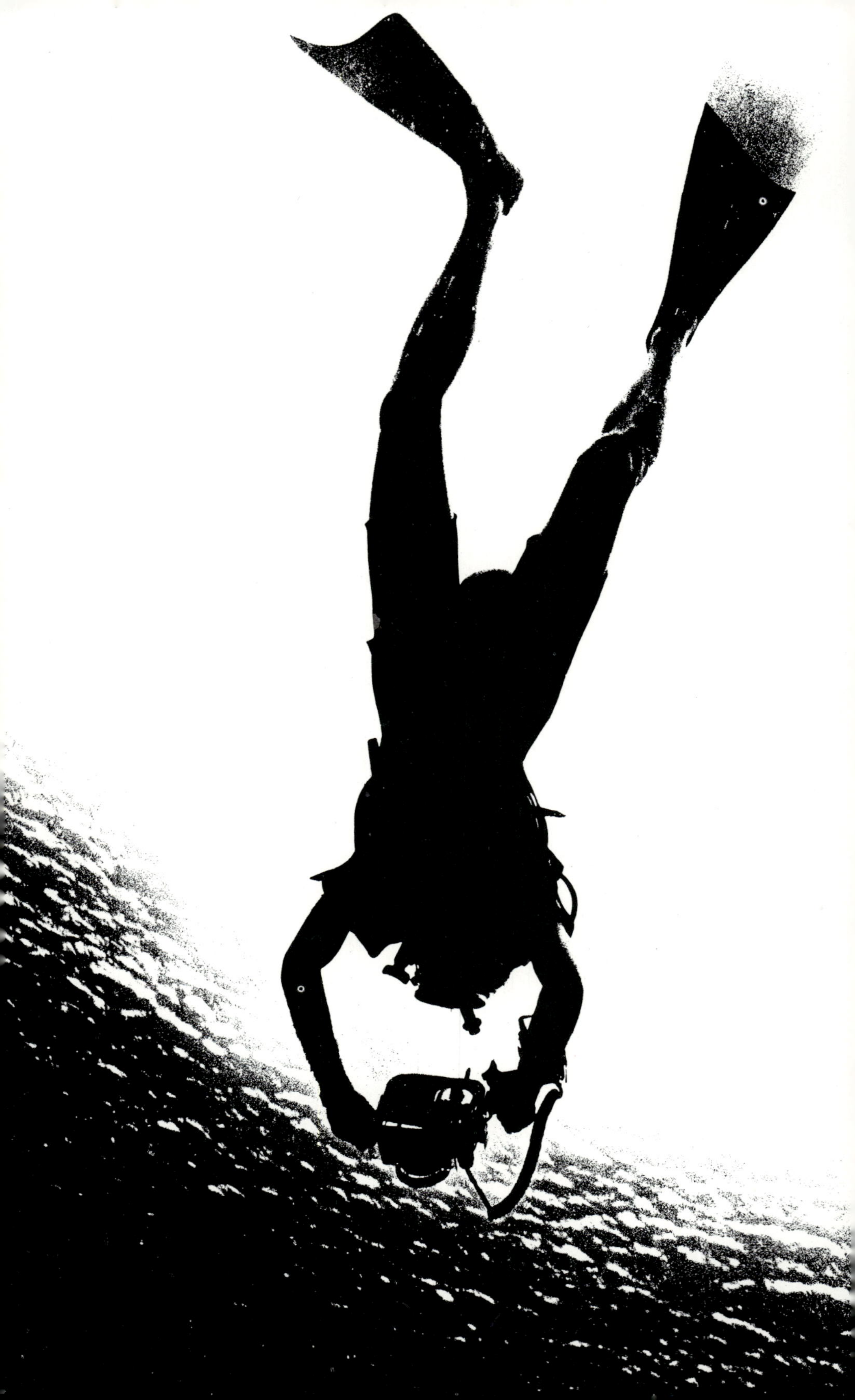

9

Practical Tips

Once you've gathered together the equipment you intend to use, and understand what it can do, the information in this chapter will help you with some of the practical aspects of underwater photography. Knowing how to properly maintain and safely transport your equipment is almost as important as knowing how to dive with it.

DIVING WITH CAMERAS

Before You Dive

"Don't leave your camera in the sun" is something that should go without saying, but on a dive boat, or on a beach, it takes a determined effort to follow that warning. You should make the effort, though, because the heat build-up in a camera or housing in hot sun can be enough to do serious harm to your equipment. And should an uncovered lens catch the sun's rays directly, the result could be damage to the shutter and film.

High temperatures can also break down o-ring grease, and leaving a Nikonos in the sun can cause the air inside to expand (remember the camera is sealed). The combined effect of these two points can cause a serious problem. The o-ring that seals the glass plate over the frame counter on the Nikonos I and Nikonos II can actually be "popped"

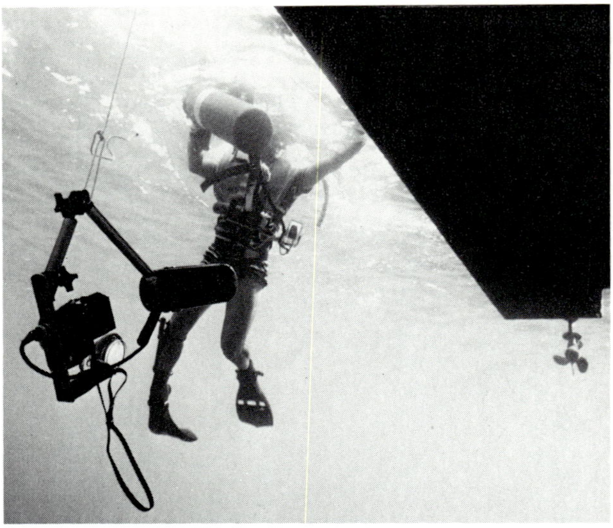

Using a line to suspend your equipment below the surface is a good way to keep it safe as you enter and leave the water.

because of internal pressure build-up caused by heat. Should you discover that your camera has been in the sun for a long period, check that o-ring; the camera will flood without it.

If you're on a beach, preparing to enter the water, try to find some shade for your equipment, or at least cover it with a light-colored towel. If you're on a dive boat, leave your gear below deck until you're ready to go in the water. Or better yet, while preparing to enter from an anchored boat, keep your camera out of the sun and also out of harm's way by hanging it over the side on a line.

Aqua-Craft makes a line specifically for that purpose. It is 18 ft. long and comes with a shock cord and snap clips. Hanging your photo gear on a line beneath the surface is an especially good idea if you're on a crowded dive boat. This will keep your equipment away from the scene of a potential disaster—many divers trying to enter the water at the same time. Of course, you will have to make sure no one makes an entry onto your camera.

Leave the line over the side when you dive so that when you return you can hang your equipment again while you board the boat. This avoids having to pass your equipment to someone who might not know how to handle it. As soon as you are on deck again, haul your equipment aboard immediately. Hanging under the boat, it is easy to forget, and should the boat get underway with your equipment underneath it, you would have a real disaster on your hands.

Difficult exits and entries can be made easier if you've got a good diving buddy. It is a comfortable feeling to be able to pass valuable equipment to someone you know. The last thing you want to do is make jump entries with cameras in your hands. Underwater photo gear is tough, but there is no reason to subject it to undue shock—it receives enough in the normal course of events.

Before you leave the surface with your cameras, check your equipment carefully—your personal gear and your photo gear. Make sure everything is tight and in place. Inspect your equipment thoroughly, looking for leaks or anything out of the ordinary. Turn your electronic flash unit on. Should it begin to flash without your having activated it, the unit is probably taking water. If so, remove it from the water and determine the problem. Information on handling flooded equipment appears further in this chapter.

During the Dive

Diving with someone you know and trust is important on any dive, but on a photo dive, a good dive buddy is invaluable. Taking pictures underwater can be a real joy if you've got an insightful partner who becomes, in addition to a dive buddy, an assistant photographer and model.

As a dive buddy, your partner will keep track of position and air supplies to avoid a tiring surface swim after the dive. A good partner, too, will be aware of potential dangers to keep you from settling into fire coral or sea urchins while focusing on something else.

As an assistant photographer, your partner will know what kind of pictures you're after before the dive, to be able to help you find what you want or herd fish your way. In addition to carrying your extra camera, a good partner will help you transfer your strobe to it when you've finished the film in your first camera—a maneuver that always requires extra hands.

As a model, your partner will pose patiently in the coldest of waters and will feed anything that swims or crawls to help you get a picture. You can make your partner a better model by providing brightly colored gloves, hood and suit stripes, and by explaining that better pictures can be had if gauges, octopus regulators, and straps aren't dangling.

Diving at night for pictures is almost impossible without a good assistant. You simply do not have enough hands to operate a camera, strobe, and flashlight easily. A good partner will know when to point a light at a potential subject to help you focus, and when to point it at your camera to help you make adjustments. A good partner, too, will know enough to keep their light out of your eyes.

During any dive, if you move slowly and easily, you won't miss pictures, you won't scare away potential subjects, and you *will* conserve energy and air. Also, moving slowly, you avoid disturbing bottom sediment, which could reduce visibility and cause backscatter problems.

Diving in a wetsuit that covers your arms and legs is useful for the diving photographer, even in the tropics; you'll be able to forget about the minor annoyances encountered while diving. Abrasions, stinging corals, and jellyfish will be less of a problem for the protected diver. Thus attired, you can settle into the bottom (after looking for major annoyances like moray eels, stingrays, and stonefish) and concentrate on photography.

A good buoyance-compensating device will aid a diver carrying a lot of equipment. During a dive, a BC (Buoyance Compensator) can help you maintain good position control, and after a dive, it will make a long surface swim easy.

Safety

Diving itself is a strenuous activity, and you must be in peak physical condition to dive. Pushing a camera before you as you swim underwater makes diving even more strenuous. Because the hydrodynamics of most underwater camera housings and strobes is bad, moving through the water with them is difficult. Since the water doesn't flow smoothly around the equipment, drag is created, and you consume more air and burn more energy than divers without cameras (all other factors that make good divers being equal).

Know your limits. Safe diving should always be first and foremost in your mind. Should you ever find yourself in a difficult or dangerous situation, don't hesitate for a second to abandon your photo gear if that would have any influence on improving the situation. Equipment can always be replaced.

MAINTENANCE

All equipment used underwater needs special care, especially if it is photographic equipment and is used in salt water. Salt water, when left to evaporate on cameras and housings, leaves mineral deposits around delicate controls and switches, which can play havoc with your equipment. Do all you can to prevent that from happening.

At the very first opportunity after a dive, thoroughly soak and then rinse all your gear in tap water. Be sure to flush any areas where salt water could accumulate, for instance, the flashbulb socket on the Nikonos Flash Unit, the areas around your synch connections, and the areas around the controls on your Nikonos or housings.

When thoroughly rinsed, let the equipment air dry, or blot it dry with a soft towel. Never use forced hot air to dry equipment, and never leave it to dry in the sun. The ports of your equipment should always be blotted dry to prevent the formation of waterspots. When drying ports of acrylic plastic (most dome ports are), be especially careful not to scratch the port's surface. Scratches are extremely difficult to remove, and although small ones probably will not affect the quality of your photos, large ones can.

When thoroughly dry, begin disassembly (do this in an area where you have plenty of room to spread your equipment). When you begin this phase, you should have within reach all the tools and accessories you will need to break down your equipment for thorough cleaning and lubrication. You should also have handy the film you will use for your next dive. This will save you the trouble and extra work of opening and loading film at the dive site.

When you open your equipment, you should have within reach:

paper towels
cotton swabs (Q-tips)
silicone grease
desiccant packets
(silica gel)
WD-40 spray
dust blower (ear syringe)
small brush
photographic lens tissue
lens cleaning fluid
screwdrivers (if required)
open-end wrenches
(if required)
o-rings and other spares

Nikonos Care

After removing the film from your Nikonos, inspect the camera for signs of leakage. Look for moisture that may have worked its way past the main o-rings and inspect the synch socket on the bottom of the camera for signs of corrosion or seepage. Often, the "outside" of the two main o-rings will have droplets of moisture on them. If any wetness or salt deposits are detected "inside" the o-rings, replace them. If not, the o-rings can be wiped dry and relubricated. An annual change of o-rings is a good maintenance procedure. It is not necessary to remove the o-rings that surround the lens and inner body every time the camera is opened, but they should be removed, cleaned, and relubricated if they become dry or gritty.

To remove the o-rings, squeeze them with your fingertips and slide them away from their grooves. Don't use sharp or pointed tools to pick an o-ring out of its groove as that could cause damage. Wipe the o-rings clean with a paper towel to remove accumulated grease and grit. If necessary, wash them in cool tap water and blot dry.

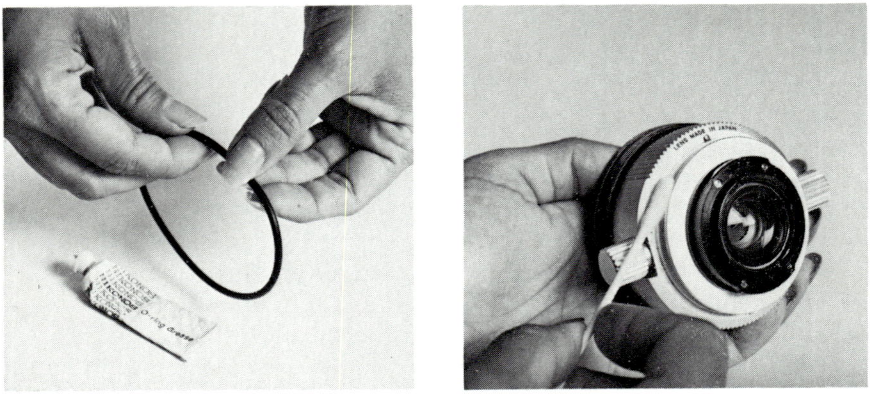

Lubricate all o-rings lightly (left) and clean the o-ring grooves thoroughly (right).

Clean the o-ring grooves around the lens, the top of the inner body, and the synch-socket plug with cotton swabs to remove all traces of sand, dirt, and old grease.

Next, relubricate the o-rings with silicone grease. Apply a dab of grease between your fingertips and draw the o-ring through it. The o-ring should be lightly coated; too much grease can cause as many problems as too little.

When replacing the o-ring on the lens, take special care to avoid getting silicone grease, from the o-ring or your fingertips, onto the lens elements. Silicone lubricants are extremely difficult to remove from glass and plastic surfaces.

Always keep your fingers away from your lenses and ports. The acid from your fingers can actually etch itself into glass or plastic and can damage lens coatings. If the lens needs cleaning (the rear element rarely should), use a photographic lens tissue (not the type intended for cleaning eyeglasses) and a lens cleaning fluid. Apply a drop of the fluid to the tissue and then gently wipe the lens. Do not apply pressure when wiping the lens. Never apply drops of fluid to the rear element of the lens as they can seep between the elements.

After cleaning the lens, put it aside and blow or brush out the camera's inner body and outer shell. Use a small brush for this purpose, but do not use the same brush on your lenses because it may pick up silicone or other lubricants from inside the camera.

Now load the camera with the film for your next shooting, but before assembling the camera, inspect the o-rings for lint or traces of any other foreign matter that could interfere with the sealing. Remove any material detected and reassemble the camera.

Housings Care

Housings should be treated with the same care as the Nikonos. They too require thorough rinsing, drying, and o-ring maintenance. The o-ring that seals the two halves of the housing and the one that seals the ports (if the ports are interchangeable) are the two you will have easy access to. To lubricate the o-rings not easily accessible, you can apply small amounts of silicone grease to control shafts and then move them in and out. Regular maintenance should include packing of silicone grease in the threaded accessory-mounting holes on metal housings to prevent salt deposits from forming and corrosion from attacking the threads.

When the housing is opened, and the camera removed, carefully inspect the points inside the housing where the controls enter the housing wall. Should signs of moisture or salt deposits be detected near a control shaft, it will be necessary to remove that shaft to determine the reason for the leakage. Whether you decide to remove the defective control yourself or send the whole unit to the manufacturer will depend on the tools required and the faith you have in yourself to accomplish the task. Some housing manufacturers ask that their housings be returned to them annually for maintenance.

Electronic Flash Unit Care

Like the Nikonos and housings for cameras, in-air strobes, or meters, self-contained electronic flash units should be rinsed, disassembled, cleaned, and lubricated. When reassembling self-contained strobe units that employ o-ring seals, be sure the o-rings are sealing when the two parts of the housing come together. In clear plastic housings, you can actually see the forming of the seal as the housing is joined; with self-contained strobes, you can't. To be sure the o-ring is squarely seated, hold the unit at eye-level and look around the circumference, checking to see if the unit is assembled properly. Squarely seating the o-ring may require more pressure than retaining clips can apply. The two halves of these type units may have to be pushed together for a better seal.

Connector Care

All connectors should be inspected carefully for loose terminals, broken contacts, worn threads, or damaged o-rings. All connectors that are capable of being connected and disconnected underwater should be packed with silicone grease; EO connectors must be regularly packed with silicone grease for easy connecting and disconnecting. The terminals within the Nikonos synch socket can be lightly sprayed with a lubricant, such as WD-40, to inhibit corrosion.

TROUBLESHOOTING

After cleaning and reassembly, next test your electrical connections to be sure your flash and camera are functioning properly. Don't wait until you're at the dive site or, worse, underwater to discover your unit is malfunctioning. If your flash does not fire when you release the shutter, check to see if it has been turned on. If it was turned on and didn't fire, the problem is either with the camera, the flash, or the connecting wires. Try to logically isolate the area of the problem.

First, check to see if the flash fires when you short-circuit the flash terminals on the end of the connector. If it does not fire, check the battery strength (use a voltmeter) and check the flash terminals for corrosion (sandpaper or file the terminals clean if necessary). If the batteries are good and the terminals are clean, next carefully check the flash cable and the points where it joins your connector and the unit itself. If PC connections are involved, check them to be sure they are tight enough for good electrical contact. If your units have the push-in type PC connector, investigate the possibility of changing to the screw-in type; they make a more positive connection. Inspect for corrosion, breaks in the line, and breaks in soldered connections.

If you've checked all of the above, and the flash is still not firing, bring the unit to a professional repair facility and have it bench-tested to determine the problem.

If the flash fires when you cross its terminals, focus your attention on the camera. Check its synch terminals for corrosion or broken contacts. If the camera is a Nikonos, check the synch socket for corrosion, broken contacts, or loose pins. Check also the contacts on the inside of the outer shell and the points where they meet the contacts on the inner body. If any of the contact points are loose, try to tighten them; if they are corroded, try to clean them; if they are broken, try to replace them.

If the camera is an in-air Nikon in a housing, check the PC connections, as described above, and the PC cord that joins the camera to the wall of the housing. Check, too, the connector outside the housing. If the problem is within the camera, bring it to a repair center for testing.

Storage

When your equipment will be out of service for a few months, there are a few precautions you should take to ensure that it will be in top shape when next you use it.

As mentioned before, never store any battery-operated equipment with the batteries in place. When batteries deteriorate, they can create an incredible mess and a costly repair bill if they break down in your camera, strobe, housing, or exposure meter.

All equipment that is o-ring-sealed should be stored without the o-rings in place or else stored disassembled so no pressure is on the o-rings. Long-term pressure on o-rings will create flat surfaces that will impair the sealing capacity of the unit. Store your equipment in plastic bags to prevent dust accumulation. Store packets of desiccant (silica gel) with the equipment to absorb any moisture present.

All lenses stored for any length of time should be set at their widest aperture; this will release the tension on the spring that operates the diaphragm. To keep tension off the spring that operates the shutter of your camera, do not keep the shutter cocked for storage. With the Nikonos, leave the film-advance/shutter-release lever "out." Do not return it to the cocked position after you release the shutter. On the Nikon in-air cameras, press the shutter-release button and do not advance the film-advance lever as this will cock the shutter.

Store all your equipment in a cool, dry, and dust-free place.

Flashbulbs left over from a dive should be rinsed in tap water before storage.

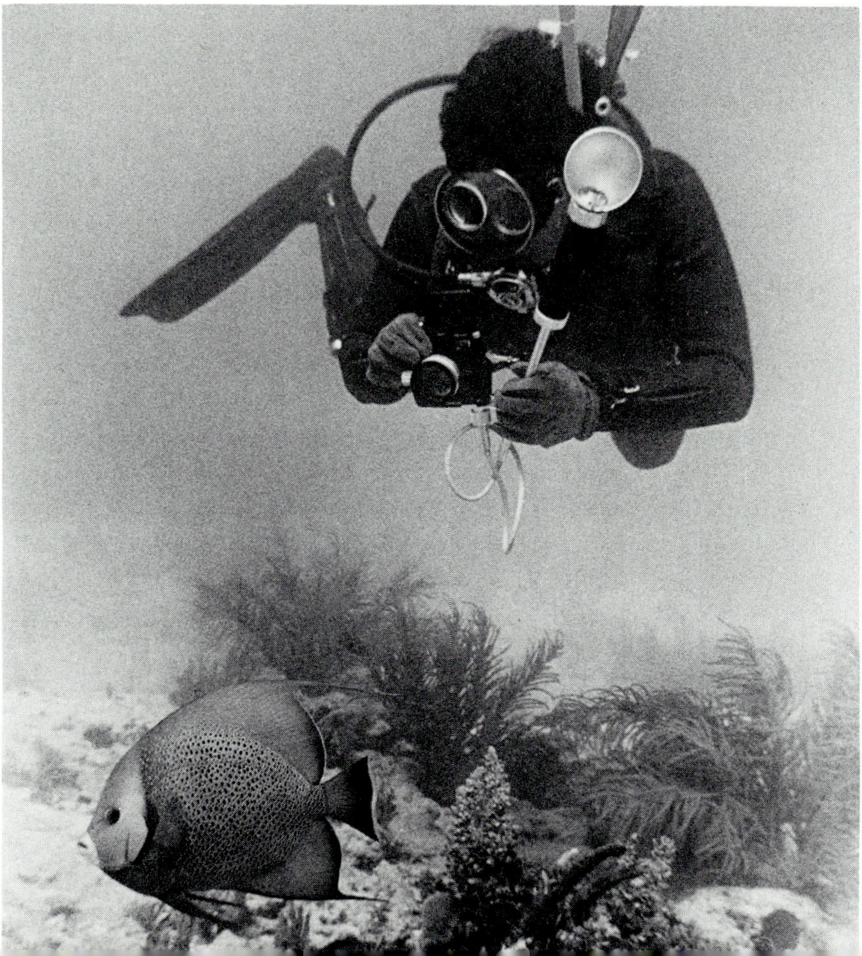

Flooding

Nothing can match the experience of having a very expensive piece of photographic equipment flood with seawater. It shouldn't happen, but it can. When it does, it is too late for the precautions and care that should have gone into preparing the equipment for the dive, and heaping abuse on yourself will do little good. You must *immediately* get to the business of trying to salvage what you can.

Step 1. If your camera floods, remove the film and any batteries that might be in it. If the flooded item is an electronic flash unit, turn it off, open it to let the water drain away from the batteries, and then carefully remove the batteries. Be especially careful with high-voltage batteries to avoid a shock. Whether your Nikonos, strobe, or equipment housing floods, the following procedures are the same.

Step 2. As quickly as you can, get the flooded item into tap water. Salt water begins its corrosive action in very short time—a few hours can make the difference between a relatively easy (major, but easy) repair job and a difficult and costly one. Soak the flooded item in a large container filled with tap water and then hold it under flowing tap water. The item should be immersed for at least half an hour. While the unit is in the tap water, operate the controls. Operate switches, levers, the shutter—all the controls. The idea is to drive away all the salt water from pockets where it might accumulate, and also to drive it away from the tiny gears and springs, which salt water attacks with amazing speed.

Step 3. Use a gentle stream of compressed air from your scuba tank to drive away as much moisture as possible from the workings of the equipment.

Step 4. Soak the item in alcohol, and again activate all the controls for at least half an hour. Now the idea is to drive away the moisture from the inside workings of the camera; this the alcohol does as it absorbs the water and evaporates quickly. As the alcohol removes the moisture, though, it also removes most of the camera's lubricating fluids.

Step 5. You can use more compressed air at this time to drive out the remaining moisture and help the alcohol evaporate.

Nikon recommends that you stop after Step 2 if the flooded item is a Nikonos or one of their in-air cameras. They recommend packing the wet-with-tap-water camera so that it will remain wet in transit, and then shipping it to their nearest repair center. Manufacturers of other equipment recommend that you stop after Step 5, pack the equipment with a desiccant, and then ship it to them. Whenever you return equipment to the manufacturer, be sure to include details about the flooding and the steps you took immediately afterward.

If you've spent a good deal of money getting somewhere to take pictures, and that amount of money is more than what the flooded item is worth, you may want to attempt to repair the item on the spot. Many diving resorts have knowledgeable personnel who encounter flooded equipment regularly, and you can generally rely on their advice regarding the probability of making a successful on-the-spot repair. You may be lucky enough to find someone who can help.

If you do decide to attempt an in-the-field salvage, you will need some special tools, lubricants, extra o-rings, and a detailed knowledge of your equipment. Nikonos cameras and most housings can be returned to service overnight, but you must know what you're doing. Any field repair you make should be looked upon as a stopgap emergency measure to permit you to get some film through the camera. When you return from the field, get your equipment into the hands of a professional repair person as quickly as possible, with details about the steps you took after the flooding.

Flooding a camera in a lake or river is not the worst thing that can happen to a camera, but flooding one in seawater really is. Nothing short of a complete stripping, cleaning, and reassembly of the camera—a virtual rebuilding—can ever get it back into anywhere near its original condition. Only a fully qualified repair technician can provide the care your equipment needs after exposure to salt water.

Flood Prevention

Most floodings occur because of carelessness, rushing to assemble your equipment, or a combination of the two. Most floodings of the earlier Nikonos cameras occur because of carelessness in making the connection at the synch socket or simply forgetting to replace the synch-socket plug. Nikon states that flooding through the synch socket of the Nikonos III cannot happen, but salt water in your synch terminals will do them no good. If you must change connectors, or open cameras and housings at dive sites, work slowly and carefully to make sure your connections are tight and your o-rings are seated properly.

Check your equipment as many times as you can before you dive with it. Check it the night before you dive (when it should be assembled and prepared to go); check it at the dive site before you enter the water; and check it one more time on the surface before you go down. If at all possible, avoid on-site equipment changes and loading and unloading of film. The last place you want to open your camera is on a crowded boat or a sandy shore—unless absolutely necessary.

If you must open your camera or housing to change film at the dive site, try to do it out of the sun's direct rays and away from salt spray. Also try to prevent moisture from wet hands and dripping hair from entering the camera. If possible, dip the camera in tap water and dry it thoroughly before you open it. Then, open it carefully and slowly to keep any moisture that accumulates around the o-rings from entering the camera. Try to keep paper towels handy to blot dry any water that does enter.

As soon as the lens comes out of the camera body, immediately place a rear lens cap on it; its front lens cap should always be in place when you're not taking pictures with the camera. The rear cap will protect the rear element from salt spray, and both caps will protect the lens even if it's dropped in sand. Should you drop an uncapped lens in sand, don't try to rub the sand off the lens; gently blow it away from the lens to avoid scratching the glass.

TRAVEL

Long-distance travel with large amounts of expensive equipment almost takes the fun out of underwater photography, but the following information may make preparing for a trip somewhat easier. Two basic rules are: (1) Pack your equipment as if it were eggs. (2) Bring more of everything than you think you'll need. In addition, when you travel by air with underwater photographic equipment, there are some points you should be aware of to prevent mishaps when you arrive at your destination.

Air-Travel Precautions

The Nikonos (and all o-ring-sealed underwater photo equipment) is designed to operate deep underwater. The camera suffers no ill effects when the pressure on the outside of the camera is greater than the pressure on the inside of the camera. But when it is subjected to pressure within the camera that is greater than the surrounding pressure, damage to the camera may result.

Such a situation may occur when a Nikonos is transported in an airplane. As every diver knows, atmospheric pressure at sea level is 14.7 psi., and pressure increases as you go underwater and decreases as you move away from the surface of the earth into the atmosphere. When a Nikonos, sealed at sea level, is exposed to the reduced pressure experienced on a commercial flight, a pressure differential is created. The pressure inside the camera is still 14.7 psi., but the surrounding pressure is less.

How great the differential depends on where the camera is within the aircraft and the altitude at which the craft is flying. If the Nikonos is in the unpressurized cargo hold of an airplane flying at an altitude of 37,000 ft. (typical altitude for a commercial flight) the pressure differential would be about 11 psi. (Internal camera pressure, 14.7 psi., minus atmospheric pressure at 37,000 ft., 3.7 psi., equals 11 psi.) A pressure differential that high is sufficient to "pop" the o-ring that seals the glass plate over the frame counter on the Nikonos I and II cameras, and these cameras will flood if taken underwater without that o-ring. This situation is similar to what can happen to the same cameras when left in the sun for a long period of time, as mentioned earlier.

If the Nikonos is in the pressurized cabin of the airplane, the pressure differential created would not be as great. On a typical 37,000 ft. flight, the cabin pressure would be about 11.7 psi. (the atmospheric pressure at about 6,000 ft.). This would create a differential of only about 3 psi.—probably not enough to "pop" that same o-ring.

The simplest way to avoid possible damage to your Nikonos when flying with it, and the subsequent possibility of flooding the camera should the damage go unnoticed, is to remove the o-rings or transport the camera unassembled. However, don't forget to replace the o-rings before you dive.

Another problem you might encounter when flying with a Nikonos concerns what would happen if you opened and sealed the camera, with all o-rings in place, during a flight. Sealing the camera *during* the flight would mean that the internal pressure would be less than the surrounding pressure once you returned to the ground. The external pressure would actually be pushing the camera together. That pressure could make disassembly of the camera very difficult. Disassembly would be almost impossible if the differential were great.

All of the above precautions pertaining to Nikonos cameras apply to other pieces of underwater equipment that use o-ring seals. Housings for cameras, strobes, and exposure meters would all best be air-transported without their principal o-rings in place. Again, remember to replace the o-rings before the equipment is taken in the water.

Spares

When you travel to out-of-the-way diving areas, it is best to assume that you will not be able to purchase any of the things you will need to do underwater photography. If you're paying a great deal of money to "get away from it all," you can't expect to find a corner store that will have odd-size batteries, any-size o-rings, or 36-exposure rolls of your favorite film.

With the above in mind, you should bring spare parts for all your equipment and extras of everything you will use.

Batteries. Put fresh batteries in your equipment before you leave and bring at least one spare for each type of battery you use. If you know your flash unit drains batteries quickly, bring more than you think you'll need.

O-rings. Bring spare o-rings to replace those which experience the greatest wear, such as the ones around the Nikonos lens, body, and synch-socket plug. If you have a housing, bring spare o-rings for the control shafts, in addition to the main ones, in case you have to remove a control.

Film and flashbulbs. Bring twice as much film and twice as many flashbulbs as you think you can use. Film can be very expensive in out-of-the-way places, and often you have to settle for film you don't really want. If you buy more than you need before you leave, you'll be better off. You'll use the film sooner or later anyway, and you may save some money by buying in large quantities.

Tools. Bring every tool you need to assemble, adjust, or work on your equipment. See the list in the maintenance section of this chapter.

Miscellaneous spares. If any piece of your equipment needs tiny screws or small, vital parts, bring a spare—anything small can be lost easily. If you're bringing a flashbulb unit, bring bulb adapters for different-size bulbs.

Back-up system. If at all possible, bring a complete and separate camera and lighting unit. Often, a dive trip can be salvaged should your new, self-contained strobe unit flood if you have a small, housed strobe or flashbulbs and a flash unit on which to fall back. If you're using a Nikon F2 in a housing as your principal camera, don't leave your Nikonos at home.

How much equipment, spare parts, supplies, and back-up equipment you'll want to carry with you when you travel depends on how involved you are in underwater photography and also how badly you want to return home with usable pictures. Obviously, a professional can't afford to get somewhere and not have what's needed, but with a casual hobbyist, it makes little difference. Sometimes what starts out as a "vacation" can become an expedition, with the participants working harder than they do all year just to be able to "get some pictures."

Carrying Cases

With all the equipment that's needed, if you're involved in underwater photography in a more than casual way, finding an easy way to transport it all safely is essential. After you've spent a great deal of money for equipment, you should really invest a little more and acquire a container that will adequately protect the items within.

The ideal container should fully protect everything in it from shocks, dust, moisture, and heat, and it should be lightweight. The ideal container should be big enough to hold all your gear, yet small enough to be moved easily when full. It also should provide easy access to all the equipment when it is opened. The ideal container doesn't exist, but there are many types that come close.

What you need to carry your equipment will depend, first of all, on how much equipment you own, or how much you plan to carry with you. If you've got a Nikonos, an extra lens, a flash attachment, an exposure meter, and a few rolls of film, you will probably be able to get everything into a fishing tackle box. If you're traveling with housings, cameras, strobes, and back-up systems, you'll probably need more than one large container for all your equipment.

Large, rugged, fiberglass or metal cases that seal shut and surround your equipment in a shock-absorbing mass of foam rubber are probably the safest containers you can buy. They can't be beat for

For local traveling with a limited amount of equipment, a fishing tackle box can be utilized to carry enough equipment for one or two photo dives.

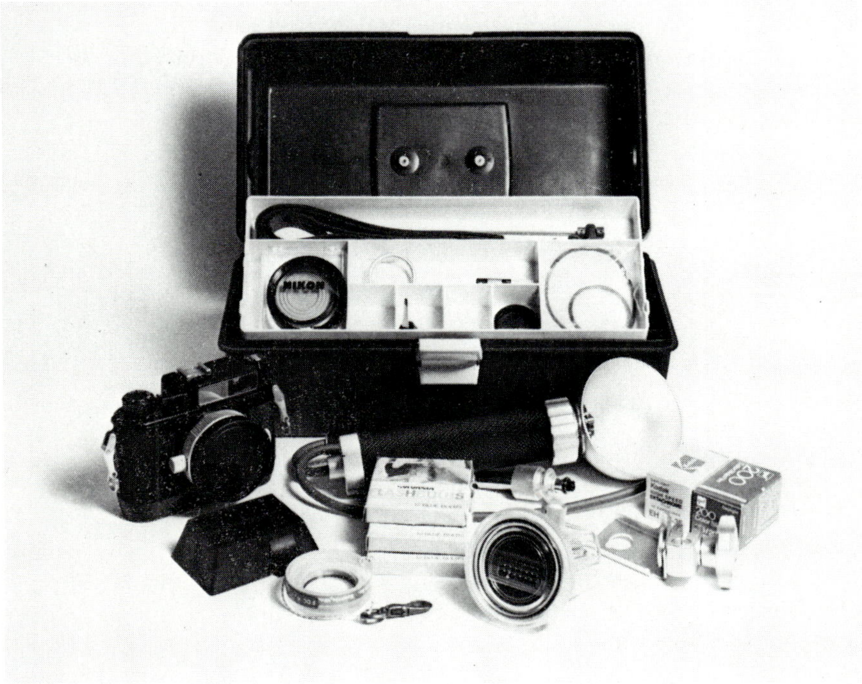

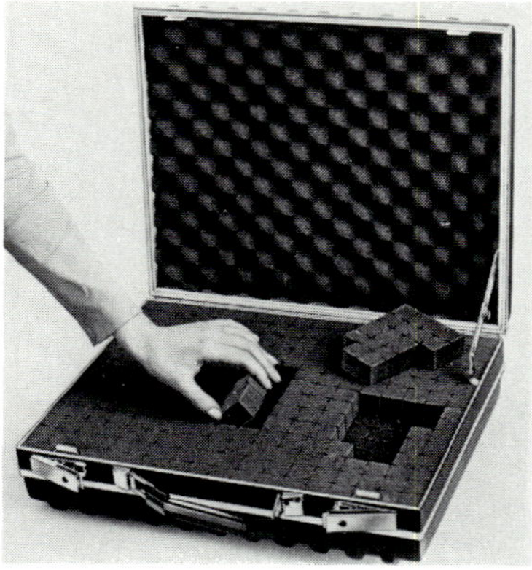

Cases that surround your equipment in a shock-absorbing material provide excellent protection. This case, with partially cut foam rubber, is made by Ikelheimer-Ernst.

protecting delicate and expensive equipment. They are expensive, but they are easy to care for, the foam padding can be custom cut to fit your needs, and they *do* keep your equipment safe. Subsea and Oceanic Products make containers of this type as does a company called Skydyne. Skydyne is one of the oldest manufacturers in the field of packaging for delicate instruments. They make a variety of containers in many different sizes and shapes.

If you can get all of your equipment into one luggage-like carrying case, try to get it into one that measures 21″ × 14″ × 9″ or smaller. That is about the maximum size for luggage that can fit under the seat of most commercial aircraft. If you need more than one bag to carry your equipment, one of them should be that size. You will able to pack your most delicate equipment in it for hand carrying when you travel. Cases made by Zero/Halliburton and Ikelheimer–Ernst are versatile and rugged, and most of them fulfill the above size requirement.

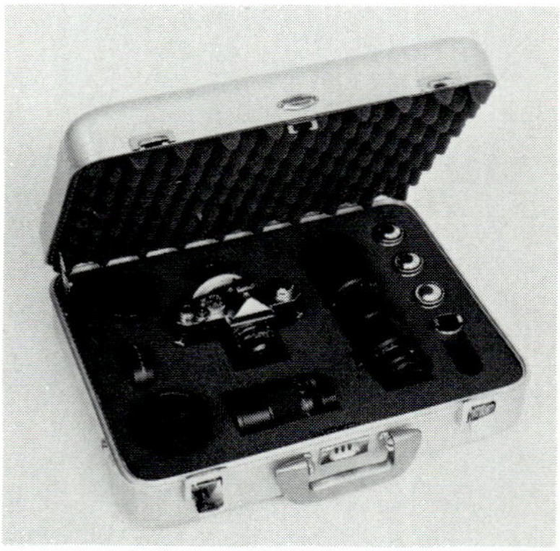

This aluminum luggage-type camera case is made by Zero/Halliburton.

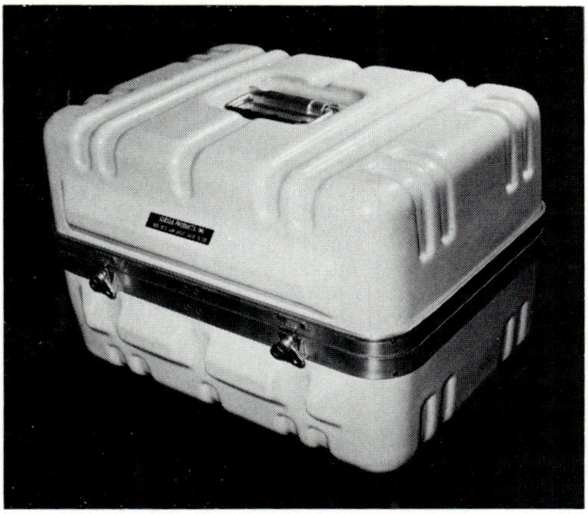

Large fiberglass cases that envelop equipment in shock-insulating foam are the safest types available. This one is made by Subsea.

Should you ever have to hike to a dive site with photo gear, Anzen Products makes a rigid backpack, perfect for hauling equipment into inaccessible areas. Called the Rec-Pac, the polyethylene box can be used to carry loads up to about 75 lbs.

Whatever the container, how you pack it is as important as its strength. Never let delicate items "float" about within the case. All cameras, lenses, and other pieces of equipment should be enveloped in shock-absorbing materials and snugly fitted together. When packed correctly, you should be able to turn your case on its side or upside down without any shifting of the equipment within.

Before any photo-dive trip, especially if you and your equipment have not been in the water for a long time, find a pool and get your body into physical condition and get your equipment functioning again. Build your personal endurance and refamiliarize yourself with the problems of underwater photography. A pool is the perfect place to conduct preliminary tests, to check out new equipment, and to check out yourself.

Good diving.

APPENDIX A: Metric Conversion Information

When You Know	Multiply by	To Find
inches (in.)	25.4	millimeters (mm)
feet (ft.)	0.3048	meters (m)
miles (mi.)	1.609	kilometers (km)
ounces (oz.)	28.349	grams (g)
pounds (lbs.)	0.453	kilograms (kg)
pounds per square inch (psi.)	0.0703	kilograms per square centimeter (kg/sqcm)
cubic feet (cu. ft.)	0.0283	cubic meters
Fahrenheit temperature (°F.)	1.8 after subtracting 32	Celsius temperature (°C)

APPENDIX B: Manufacturers and Distributors

Anzen Products
15314 E. Proctor Ave.
City of Industry, Calif. 91744

Aqua-Craft, Inc.
3280 Kurtz St.
San Diego, Calif. 92110

Beall Engineering, Inc.
887 South Route 21
Gurnee, Ill. 60031

Copal Corp. of America
56-01 Queens Blvd.
Woodside, N.Y. 11377

G/F Industries/ Oceanic Products
814 Castro St.
San Leandro, Calif. 94577

Hydro Photo
3909 13 Ave. South
Seattle, Wash. 98108

Honeywell Photographic Products
P.O. Box 22083
Littleton, Colorado 80120

Ikelheimer-Ernst, Inc.
601 West 26 St.
N.Y., N.Y. 10001

Ikelite Underwater Systems
3303 North Illinois St.
Indianapolis, Ind. 46208

Nikon, Inc.
Ehrenreich Photo-Optical Industries, Inc.
623 Stewart Ave.
Garden City, N.Y. 11530

Oceanic Products
814 Castro St.
San Leandro, Calif. 94577

Rollei of America
100 Lehigh Drive
Fairfield, N.J. 07006

Sea Research and Development, Inc.
P.O. Box 589
Bartow, Florida 33830

Seacor, Inc.
P.O. Box 22126
San Diego, Calif. 92122

Skydyne
River Road
Port Jervis, N.Y. 12771

Sonic Research
5111 Santa Fe St.
San Diego, Calif. 92109

Subsea Products, Inc.
P.O. Box 9532
San Diego, Calif. 92109

Toshiba Elmo Mfg.
32-10 57 St.
Woodside, N.Y. 11377

Vivitar
Ponder and Best, Inc.
1630 Stewart St.
Santa Monica, Calif. 90404

Zero/Halliburton
Berkey Marketing Co., Inc.
25-20 Brooklyn-Queens Expressway
Woodside, N.Y. 11377

APPENDIX C: Further Reading

Underwater Photography

Church, Jim and Cathy. *Beginning Underwater Photography.* Gilroy, Calif.: Jim and Cathy Church, 1972.

Church, Ron. *Beginner's Guide to Photography Underwater.* La Jolla, Calif.: Ron Church Productions, 1971.

Clark, John. *Basic Underwater Photography.* Los Angeles, Calif.: Petersen Publishing Co., 1973.

Rebikoff, Dimitri, and Paul Cherney. *Underwater Photography.* 2nd Ed. Garden City, N.Y.: Amphoto, 1975.

Strykowski, Joe. *Divers and Cameras.* Northfield, Ill.: Dacor Corp., 1974.

Wallin, Doug. *Basics of Underwater Photography.* Garden City, N.Y.: Amphoto, 1975.

Basic Darkroom

Amphoto Editorial Board. *Developing, Printing, and Enlarging Simplified.* Garden City, N.Y.: Amphoto, 1974.

Carroll, John. *Amphoto Home Darkroom Course: I Elementary Black and White.* Garden City, N.Y.: Amphoto, 1976.

Fineman, Mark. *The Home Darkroom.* 2nd Ed. Garden City, N.Y.: Amphoto, 1976.

Color Darkroom

Coote, Jack. *The Photoguide to Color Printing from Negatives and Slides.* Garden City, N.Y.: Amphoto, 1976.

Current, Ira. *How to Process Color Films at Home.* 2nd Ed. Garden City, N.Y.: Amphoto, 1968.

Engdahl, David A. *Color Printing: Materials, Processes, Controls.* 4th Ed. Garden City, N.Y.: Amphoto, 1976.

Darkroom Special Effects

Litzel, Otto. *Darkroom Magic.* 2nd Ed. Garden City, N.Y.: Amphoto, 1975

Ruggles, Joanne and Philip. *Darkroom Graphics: Creative Techniques for Photographers and Artists.* Garden City, N.Y.: Amphoto, 1975.

Walker, Sandy, and Clarence Rainwater. *Solarization.* Garden City, N.Y.: Amphoto, 1974.

The Nikon System

Amphoto Editorial Board. *Official Nikon-Nikkormat Manual.* 7th Ed. Garden City, N.Y.: Amphoto, 1975.

Cooper, Joseph D. *Nikon-Nikkormat Handbook* (2 Vols.). Garden City, N.Y.: Amphoto, 1974.

Keeping Current (Magazines)

Skin Diver. 8490 Sunset Blvd., Los Angeles, Calif. 90069.

Underwater Photographer. Box 608, Dana Point, Calif. 92629.

Popular Photography. One Park Avenue, New York, N.Y. 10016.

Modern Photography. 130 E. 59 St., New York, N.Y. 10022.

Petersens Photographic Magazine. 8490 Sunset Blvd., Los Angeles, Calif. 90096.

Nikon World. 623 Stewart Ave., Garden City, N.Y. 11530.

INDEX